FREUD

TWENTIETH CENTURY VIEWS

The aim of this series is to present the best in contemporary critical opinion on major authors, providing a twentieth century perspective on their changing status in an era of profound revaluation.

Maynard Mack, *Series Editor*
Yale University

FREUD

A COLLECTION OF CRITICAL ESSAYS

Edited by
Perry Meisel

Prentice-Hall, Inc. *Englewood Cliffs, N.J.*

A SPECTRUM BOOK

Library of Congress Cataloging in Publication Data

Main entry under title:

Freud, a collection of critical essays.

  (A Spectrum Book; S-TC-154)
  Bibliography: p.
  CONTENTS: Meisel, P. Introduction: Freud as
literature.—Woolf, L. Everyday life.—Ransom, J. C.
Freud and literature.—[etc.]
    1. Psychoanalysis and literature—Addresses,
essays, lectures. 2. Freud, Sigmund, 1856-1939—
Addresses, essays, lectures. I. Meisel, Perry.
PN56.P92F7   801'.92   80-25373
ISBN 0-13-331405-7
ISBN 0-13-331397-2 (pbk.)

Editorial/production supervision
by Donald Chanfrau
Cover illustration by Vivian Berger
Manufacturing buyer: Barbara A. Frick

© 1981 by Prentice-Hall, Inc., Englewood Cliffs, New Jersey 07632

A SPECTRUM BOOK

10 9 8 7 6 5 4 3 2 1

Printed in the United States of America

PRENTICE-HALL INTERNATIONAL, INC., *London*
PRENTICE-HALL OF AUSTRALIA PTY. LIMITED, *Sydney*
PRENTICE-HALL OF CANADA, LTD., *Toronto*
PRENTICE-HALL OF INDIA PRIVATE LIMITED, *New Delhi*
PRENTICE-HALL OF JAPAN, INC., *Tokyo*
PRENTICE-HALL OF SOUTHEAST ASIA PTE. LTD., *Singapore*
WHITEHALL BOOKS LIMITED, *Wellington, New Zealand*

Contents

vii

Acknowledgments

Grateful acknowledgment is made to the following for permission to reproduce quotations from the work of Freud:

Sigmund Freud Copyrights Ltd., The Institute of Psycho-Analysis, and the Hogarth Press Ltd., for permission to reproduce quotations from *The Standard Edition of the Complete Psychological Works of Sigmund Freud,* translated and edited by James Strachey; and for permission to reproduce quotations from *The Origins of Psycho-Analysis,* translated by Eric Mosbacher and James Strachey, edited by Marie Bonaparte, Anna Freud, and Ernst Kris.

W. W. Norton and Co., Inc., for permission to reproduce quotations from Freud's *Introductory Lectures* and *Beyond the Pleasure Principle.*

Basic Books, Inc., for permission to reproduce quotations from *The Interpretation of Dreams* by Sigmund Freud, translated and edited by James Strachey, published in the United States by Basic Books, Inc., by arrangement with the Hogarth Press and George Allen & Unwin Ltd., London; from "Fragment of an analysis of a case of hysteria," in Volume III of Freud's *Collected Papers,* edited by Ernest Jones, M.D., published by Basic Books, Inc., by arrangement with the Hogarth Press Ltd., and The Institute of Psycho-Analysis, London; and from *The Origins of Psycho-analysis: Letters to Wilhelm Fliess, Drafts and Notes: 1887-1902,* by Sigmund Freud, edited by Marie Bonaparte, Anna Freud, and Ernst Kris; authorized translation by Eric Mosbacher and James Strachey. Copyright © 1954 Basic Books, Inc., Publishers, New York.

George Allen and Unwin Ltd. for permission to reproduce quotations from *The Interpretation of Dreams.*

FREUD

Introduction:
Freud as Literature

By Perry Meisel

I

The writings of Sigmund Freud have become so decisive a factor in our culture, particularly in America, that it is more difficult than ever to attribute to them the stance of a dispassionate science that simply narrates those unconscious processes of mind discovered by its founder. It is probably more accurate to say that Freud's work has itself become an example of those unconscious determinations that influence us when we least suspect it. Surely the contemporary status of psychoanalytic thinking as ideological reflex or instinct of reason should alert us to the fact that psychoanalysis no longer speaks to us so much as for us, no longer answers or confirms our condition so much as it produces it from the start. Psychoanalysis looks so like the foregone truth about life that it is easy to forget that what truth it has belongs, in the final instance, to the written achievement of Sigmund Freud himself.

Eloquent testimony to Freud's success as a lawgiver in his own right, the unconscious sway of psychoanalysis as an arbiter of modern thought and a staple of therapeutic practice represents the consummate kind of success any mythological system or set of imaginative texts can have. If it is the highest art to conceal art, to make fiction masquerade as a simulacrum of revealed or natural truth, then Freud succeeded more completely than most, more completely, probably, than any writers save Milton and those earlier lawgivers who wrote the Old Testament, and who are, as the late *Moses and Monotheism* attests, the only conceivable rivals so far as Freud himself is concerned.

The burden of the present volume, then, is not to present Freud as a doctrinal figure from the point of view of either science or philosophy, nor is it to present him as a system-maker whose theories can be useful to an applied literary criticism. Rather, it is to situate Freud's achievement as a properly literary one in its own right, and one that casts Freud as both a theoretician of literature and a practitioner of it in exact and specific ways.

As many of our essayists suggest, however, Freud's principal literary speculation is not to be found in the familiar psychosexual reductions that tend to characterize his own overt attempts at the psychoanalysis of art. They lie instead in his notion that the very mechanisms of the mental agencies he describes are themselves the mechanisms of language. Surely the psychoanalysis of Jacques Lacan in France has played a large part in the accommodation of Freud to literary theory from this point of view in recent years, accenting as Lacan does the linguistic complexion of both the analytic session and the Freudian unconscious. It is nonetheless clear as well from the historical record that the linguistic insights ʲattributed to Freud by the French are well anticipated—and far more plainly articulated—in the analysis of Freud by principal American critics such as Kenneth Burke and Lionel Trilling even before World War II.[1]

The essays included here are not only representative of literature's gradual incorporation of Freud into its own ranks from the early days of psychoanalysis to the present, but are themselves the principal building blocks in the process. What follows by way of introduction is a narrative history that clarifies the unfolding of literature's incremental understanding of Freud's work as literary, too, as it moves, step by step, from Thomas Mann's early attempt to systematize Freud's affinities with Romanticism to the contemporary criticism of Jacques Derrida and Harold Bloom. If there is a central preoccupation that organizes this history and gives it a particular shape, it is to be found in literature's increasing understanding of why Freud's characteristic trope or figure, the unconscious, is itself a literary rather than a scientific or philosophical achievement. The movement that begins with Mann's notion of the Freudian unconscious as a reservoir of instinctual energy made available to consciousness through the symbols of myth is corrected and reversed by W.H. Auden, Burke, and Trilling, as they prepare us for the elaborate reading of the Freudian unconscious in Derrida and Bloom that transforms Freud's theory of the psyche into a theory of literary language, and that transforms Freud's own rhetoric into a demonstrably poetic one.

No essay is more direct than Alfred Kazin's "The Language of Pundits" in accounting for the tyranny of Freud's ideas by exclusive reference to

---

[1] Although Lacan's career actually begins in the late 1920s (including a connection with Dada), his major phase is initiated with the 1953 *Discours de Rome* ("The Function and Field of Speech and Language in Psychoanalysis"; see *Ecrits: A Selection,* trans. Alan Sheridan [New York: Norton, 1977], pp. 30-113); his impact, even in France, however, was not widespread until the 1960s. For a history of what has been called "French Freud," see Sherry Turkle, *Psychoanalytic Politics: Freud's French Revolution* (New York: Basic Books, 1978). For accounts of Lacan, see (especially) Louis Althusser, "Freud and Lacan," in *Lenin and Philosophy,* trans. Ben Brewster, rpt. (London: New Left Books, 1977), pp. 181-202; and Anthony Wilden, "Lacan and the Discourse of the Other," in Jacques Lacan, *The Language of the Self: The Function of Language in Psychoanalysis,* trans. Wilden, rpt. (New York: Delta, 1975), pp. 157-311.

Freud's prowess as a writer of visionary prose: "It was, of course, Freud's remarkable literary ability," writes Kazin, "that gave currency to his once difficult and 'bestial' ideas; it was the insight he showed into concrete human problems, the discoveries whose force is revealed to us in a language supple, dramatic, and charged with the excitement of Freud's mission as a 'conquistador' into realms hitherto closed to scientific inquiry, that excited and persuaded so many readers of his books." In the hands of Freud's immediate disciples, however, or as practiced by subsequent generations of intellectuals or by the culture at large, the Freudian method of explanation becomes, as Kazin puts it, sheer punditry. Freud's own writing, by contrast, enlists the devil's party as well as the dogmatist's, and so dramatizes not just a doctrinal clash between consciousness and the unconscious that the pundits simply ventriloquize as though it were fact, but also the struggle within Freud himself between an empirical and an imaginative rationale for the psychoanalytic project as a whole. Certain tendencies in contemporary literature such as the spontaneous aesthetic of the Beats may even be explained, Kazin suggests, as literal or reductive responses to Freud that share with the pundits a failure to distinguish literature from dogma whether in Freud himself or in the tendentious pronouncements of their own work. Virginia Woolf had already identified such a tendency in 1920 among practitioners of what she called "Freudian fiction," writers who treat psychoanalysis as though it were, in Woolf's words, "a patent key that opens every door";[2] who mistake, to borrow Trilling's terms in "Freud and Literature," the instrument of Freud's thought—his language—for its transparent vehicle.

Freud himself offers the best and clearest caution about the status of the scientific language that is, of course, a central feature of his prose. Reflecting in the 1920 *Beyond the Pleasure Principle* on the "bewildering and obscure processes" of instinct invoked by his habitual biological vocabulary,[3] Freud

[2]Virginia Woolf, "Freudian Fiction," in *Contemporary Writers* (London: The Hogarth Press, 1965), p. 154.

[3]Freud's apparent biologism is more evident in English than in the original German or in French, since Freud's *Trieb* is customarily rendered as "instinct" rather than "drive," unlike the French version, *pulsion*, which maintains the oscillation or ambiguity in *Trieb* between natural and cultural determinations. James Strachey, Freud's chief English translator and architect of the *Standard Edition* of Freud's writings, gives his reasons for choosing "instinct" in the "General Preface" to *The Standard Edition of the Complete Psychological Works of Sigmund Freud*, ed. James Strachey (London: The Hogarth Press and the Institute of Psychoanalysis, 1953-74), 1: xxiv-xxvi (all subsequent references and citations from Freud are from the *Standard Edition* and are indicated, as above, by volume and page number alone). On *Trieb* and "instinct," see also Jean Laplanche and J. B. Pontalis, *The Language of Psychoanalysis*, trans. Donald Nicholson-Smith (New York: Norton, 1973), pp. 214-17.

Among Strachey's other notable choices in translating Freudian terms are "cathexis" for *Besetzung* (in French, *investissement*, or "investment," the latter increasingly favored in

meditates overtly on the problem of representation in language, and so
throws the focus of his enterprise away from its apparent objects in nature
and onto the irreducibly literary or figurative medium in which his career
as both practicing analyst and working writer really proceeds. We are
"obliged," says Freud, "to operate with the scientific terms, that is to say with
the figurative language, peculiar to psychology. . . . We could not otherwise
describe the processes in question at all, and indeed we could not have
become aware of them." And though "the deficiencies in our description
would probably vanish," says the empiricist in Freud, "if we were already
in a position to replace the psychological terms by physiological or chemical ones," "it is," concludes the literary Freud, nonetheless "true that they
too are only part of a figurative language."⁴

Indeed, what had transformed Freud in the first place from a creature of
the physiology laboratory into a psychoanalyst whose sole materials were
those of language was his growing realization, in the late summer of 1897,
that his patients' endless stories of infantile seduction at the hands of ser-
vants and relatives were not factually true, but were retrospective fantasies
installed by memory and desire after the fact.⁵ It was at this moment, as
Trilling suggests, that Freud may be said to have crossed the line that
divides empiricism from fiction, at least if by fiction we mean that which
proceeds entirely within language and without regard for the exigencies of
fact. It was, says Trilling, nothing less than a willing suspension of disbelief that finally allowed Freud access to the unconscious mental life of his
patients, and that established the terrain of psychoanalysis as a world of
language and fantasy free, by definition, from the domain of objective
verification.⁶ So when Freud claimed, as he did again and again, that the
poets, not the scientists, had been the real pioneers in the exploration of the

English, too); and "anaclisis" for *Anlehnung,* which Laplanche renders "propping" in *Life
and Death in Psychoanalysis,* trans. Jeffrey Mehlman (Baltimore: John Hopkins University
Press, 1976), pp. 15ff. (see note 36 below). On both terms, see also Laplanche and Pontalis,
p. 65n.; pp. 29-32.

⁴18:60. Here Freud is referring to his early and persistent, but now abandoned, ideal of a
quantitative, physical language for libido, the original goal of his "economic" perspective on
the psyche, one of the three formal angles of vision (the other two are the "dynamic" and the
"topographical") that organize his description of the mind. On the early, empiricist Freud, see
Ernest Jones, *The Life and Work of Sigmund Freud,* 3 vols. (New York: Basic Books, 1953-57),
I, 367ff.; II, 282-83, 290-91.

⁵See Jones, I, 263-67; and Freud's letter to Wilhelm Fliess of September 21, 1897 (*The
Origins of Psychoanalysis: Letters to Wilhelm Fliess, Drafts and Notes, 1887-1902,* trans. Eric
Mosbacher and James Strachey [New York: Basic Books, 1954], pp. 215-18; an extract appears
in the *Standard Edition,* 1: 259-60). See also Laplanche, *Life and Death in Psychoanalysis,*
pp. 31ff.

⁶Lionel Trilling, "Freud: Within and Beyond Culture," in *Beyond Culture: The Works of
Lionel Trilling,* rpt. (New York: Harcourt Brace Jovanovich, 1978), p. 82. "Freud," writes Philip
Rieff, "puts language before body" (*Freud: The Mind of the Moralist,* rpt. [Chicago: Uni-
versity of Chicago Press, 1979]), p. 134.

unconscious, there was not only the presumption of a common shop between psychoanalysis and literature, but also a genuine invitation to treat
psychoanalysis itself as a poetic achievement.

"I consider you the culmination of Austrian literature," wrote the Viennese man of letters Arnold Zweig to Freud in 1934.[7] Indeed, as early as
1896 the reviewer of *Studies on Hysteria* for the Vienna *Neue Freie Presse,*
poet and critic Alfred von Berger, had prophetically concluded that Freud's
work is "nothing but the kind of psychology used by poets."[8] Freud himself had strategically apologized for the extent to which the case histories in
Studies on Hysteria sounded like tales of the imagination—"it strikes me
myself as strange that the case histories I write should read like short stories
and that, as one might say, they lack the serious stamp of science"—even
though it is finally to literature that Freud appeals without embarrassment as the passage concludes: "Local diagnosis and electrical reaction
lead nowhere in the study of hysteria, whereas a detailed description of
mental processes such as we are accustomed to find in the works of imaginative writers enables me, with the use of a few psychological formulas, to
obtain at least some kind of insight into the course of that affection."[9]

But if Freud's literary contemporaries took his suggestion to heart, it
was not always by the benign route of homage. In addition to studied and
almost unbroken public silence—Joyce,[10] for example, or Proust—defensive attacks were often the rule, as Virginia Woolf's judgment attests, and
remind us that Freud early inspired the greatest tribute of all, the tribute
of anxiety on the part of his literary generation's first rank. Even Clive
Bell and Roger Fry lambasted Freud when the opportunities arose, while,
beyond Bloomsbury and as early as 1921, D.H. Lawrence had already as-
sessed Freud's shortcomings in *Psychoanalysis and the Unconscious,* taking his revenge not so much by dismissing Freud as by claiming he had not
gone far enough. By 1931, Gide was declaring Freud simply superfluous,
and for undeniably self-protective reasons: "How embarrassing Freud is.
And how readily we should have discovered his America without him."[11]
Freud himself claims not to have read Nietzsche or Schopenhauer till late

[7]*The Letters of Sigmund Freud and Arnold Zweig,* ed. Ernst L. Freud, rpt. (New York:
Harcourt Brace Jovanovich, 1970), p. 61.

[8]Quoted in Jones, I, 253; for correction of name and date of review, see Frank Sulloway,
Freud: Biologist of the Mind (New York: Basic Books, 1979), p. 522. The playwright Arthur
Schnitzler had even reviewed a paper delivered by Freud on October 14, 1895 (see Henri F.
Ellenberger, *The Discovery of the Unconscious* [New York: Basic Books, 1970], p. 471).

[9]2: 160-61.

[10]"As for psychoanalysis," said Joyce to Djuna Barnes, "It's neither more nor less than black-
mail"; quoted in *Pound/Joyce,* ed. Forrest Read [New York: New Directions, 1967], p. 214; for
the few testy allusions to Freud that appear in Joyce's work, see Frederick J. Hoffman, *Freudianism and the Literary Mind* (Baton Rouge: Louisiana State University Press, 1945), pp. 114ff.

[11]André Gide, *Pretexts,* trans. Justin O'Brien et al. (New York: Meridian, 1959), p. 304.

in life in order to keep from being influenced by their perilously accurate anticipations of psychoanalysis,[12] and surely it is the same kind of anxiety that disturbs Woolf, Lawrence, and Gide as well in their relation to Freud. "Had I not known Dostoevsky or Nietzsche or Freud," says a priority-conscious Gide, "I should have thought just as I did."[13]

"It is shrewd and yet stupid," wrote an overtly scornful T.S. Eliot of Freud's *Future of an Illusion* in 1928, complaining in particular of Freud's "inability to reason."[14] In kindred outrage, Aldous Huxley found the "dangerous and disgusting mythology" of "psychoanalytic theory" so full of "inexact" and "unsupported" claims that reading about the unconscious "is," as he put it, "like reading a fairy story,"[15] and so echoed the sexologist Krafft-Ebing, one of Freud's teachers, who had greeted an early paper by his former student in 1896 with the celebrated remark, "It sounds like a scientific fairy tale."[16]

Literary reaction to psychoanalysis was not, however, always shrill or anxious. As one of Freud's earliest nonmedical champions in England and his future publisher there, Leonard Woolf savored psychoanalysis despite his wife's reservations. Reviewing Freud's *Psychopathology of Everyday Life* in 1914 for *The New English Weekly*, the young journalist found even this largely encyclopedic work "eminently readable," and for a particular reason. Although Freud is "a most difficult and elusive writer and thinker," says Woolf, what saves the day—indeed, what makes it—is that "whether one believes in his theories or not, one is forced to admit that he writes with great subtlety of mind," and, what is more, with "a broad and sweeping imagination more characteristic of the poet than the scientist or the medical practitioner."

For John Crowe Ransom in America ten years later, Freud's work crosses over into poetry by dint of its understanding of the symbolic practices that unify life and fill it with meaning. Knowledge of the "biological," of the "fundamental realities" of the "immitigable passions," as Ransom calls them, is always mediated for Freud by the tokens provided by myth, custom, religion. As a result, psychoanalysis apprehends the way the "passions" make us all alike in the same gesture by which it apprehends the bonds of community itself, and so avoids both a dry sociological determinism and a rampant vitalism even as it accommodates them both to its own generous perspective.

Freud's distinction as a stylist was, of course, officially recognized in 1930 with the award of the annual Goethe Prize by the city of Frankfurt. Freud

[12]See 20: 59-60.
[13]Gide, p. 306.
[14]T.S. Eliot, "Freud's Illusions," *Criterion*, 8:31 (December 1928), 350.
[15]Aldous Huxley, "Our Contemporary Hocus-Pocus," *The Forum*, 73 (1925), 313-20.
[16]Quoted in Jones, I, 263.

called it "the climax of my life as a citizen."[17] It was in fact to Goethe (himself a scientist-poet) that Freud ascribes his decision, fortunate for posterity, to become a doctor rather than a lawyer. "It was hearing Goethe's beautiful essay on Nature read aloud," he writes in his 1925 *Autobiographical Study,* "that decided me to become a medical student."[18] Here Freud reminds us, on the level of an organizing personal conceit, of that resolute strand of literary and otherwise learned allusion that not only furnishes his prose with a conceptual armory assembled at will from Greek tragedy, German Romanticism, or Shakespeare; but that also situates his work from the start within a nexus of overtly literary traditions that rival the scientific ones, and eventually overpower them, in their relative contribution to the texture of his writing.

II

There are, of course, abundant reasons for calling Freud's achievement literary in a strict formal and technical sense. Both Mann's "Freud and the Future" and Trilling's "Freud and Literature" are the crucial texts with which to begin, since they help us to plot the immediate literary resonances that arise from Freud's manifest thematic alliances with Romanticism, chief among them, says Trilling, a shared "devotion to a research into the self." Hence Freud emerges from, and refracts, virtually every principal line of literary history deriving from the tradition of Rousseau and of the *Bildungsroman,* the latter "fathered," says a psychoanalytic Trilling, by *Wilhelm Meister.* Mann is a trifle more exact in locating Freud's especially decisive precursors in Nietzsche, Schopenhauer, and, before them, in the "romantic-biologic fantasies" of Novalis, although the two lines converge in the common links Trilling and Mann alike draw between Freud and Ibsen.

The central tradition of the Romantic quest in both the prose and poetry of the nineteenth and early twentieth centuries is filiated, of course, to the tradition of quest narrative as a whole, and so roots Freud's project equally well in the wider mythic traditions within which Stanley Edgar Hyman places Freud in his reading of *The Interpretation of Dreams* in *The Tangled Bank.* Hyman points to the organizing conceit of the hike or climb through a wooded and "cavernous" landscape as the book's concrete emblem for its own quest for a solution to the legendary enigma of dreaming, and, moreover, as its principal style of imaginative organization. "Planned" as it is, says Hyman, Freud's orchestration of his guiding imagery functions as figurative theme and variation at crucial moments in the text (especially

---

[17]1935 "Postscript" to *An Autobiographical Study,* 20:73.
[18]20:8.

at or near the start of the third, fifth, and seventh chapters) as it proceeds from the thicket of past authorities on dreams through a "narrow defile" that leads Freud to a view of "the finest prospects," prospects that the book as hike or "imaginary walk" will subsequently explore and colonize.

The privileged figure of the journey in *The Interpretation of Dreams* joins the typology of the Romantic quest-poem as we know it in *The Prelude* or in Keats's *Hyperion* fragments to its earlier roots in the mythic quests of classical and Christian tradition. Hyman's reading casts Freud's questing consciousness in the role of "the primeval hero" of myth and so leads him to the myth of Freud himself as the discoverer, the overcomer of his own resistances, the hero of an autobiographical as well as an analytic odyssey. For it is in *The Interpretation of Dreams* that Freud reports his discovery of the Oedipus complex, the result of his own monumental self-analysis that began in the wake of the death of his father, Jakob Freud, in 1896. Here it is Freud himself who is the proper referent of that citation from *The Aeneid* that he belatedly affixed to *The Interpretation of Dreams* ("If I cannot bend the Higher Powers, I will move the Infernal Regions").

The mythical Freud, the Freud of the classic quest, says Hyman, is not only the Sophoclean Freud, the internal hero of *The Interpretation of Dreams* who discovers Oedipus in himself in the tragic agon that functions as the play within Freud's play. He is also the epic Freud, Freud as Odysseus or Virgil, surviving the trials of the underworld or the unconscious and returning home, to consciousness, to narrate them in retrospect. Hence Hyman's reading of Freud's successful quest for the grail-object of unconscious laws suggests psychoanalysis itself to obey the moral shape of epic romance as it rehearses a return to domesticity and culture after trial, after subduing libido. And much as Joyce provides a contemporary version of Homeric epic in *Ulysses,* so Freud, at least in what Hyman hears in the tone of *The Interpretation of Dreams,* provides us with a contemporary version of the successful quester, too, and one which, at least according to Tzvetan Todorov,[19] is the most efficient representative of the typology of the literary quest we have: the detective novel, with Freud the Sherlockian analyst in the role of "the Great Detective."

If Hyman wishes to dramatize a pre-Romantic Freud in *The Interpretation of Dreams,* Steven Marcus's "Freud and Dora" finds a late Romantic or modernist Freud at the helm in Freud's greatest case history, the "Fragment of an Analysis of a Case of Hysteria" (1905), the case of Dora. Here, like Conrad or Borges or Nabokov, Freud is a questing consciousness who keeps coming up against insuperable resistance. In this case, it is his

[19]See "The Typology of Detective Fiction," in *The Poetics of Prose,* trans. Richard Howard (Ithaca: Cornell University Press, 1977), pp. 42-52. For similarities between the classical quest and psychoanalysis, see "The Quest of Narrative," p. 127; see also "The Grammar of Narrative," p. 109.

patient's unwillingness to pursue the analysis far enough to reveal Freud's own conviction that Dora secretly desires—but must repress because of the incestuous identification—that friend of her father's with whose wife her father is himself having an affair. The resistance throws the focus of the project away from its manifest goal and onto the latent one of analytic and narrative procedure themselves. As in *Lord Jim,* the scaffolding of the tale is as much an object of study as the patient at its center. And as in *Lolita,* the quest and the problem of the quest are the same (the detective novel analogy again), with the narrative's desire for the clarity and closure of explanation analogous, at least in structure, with desire as such.

What is most interesting about Marcus's essay, though, is the ease with which it makes clear that Freud's world is a thoroughgoing world of language. Above all, Marcus insists, the analytic scene enacts the same processes as its narration, subject and method becoming virtual doubles since, both as practice and as product, the very element of being in psychoanalysis is language and symbolization. Difficult as it is to achieve coherence amid the fragments of Dora's story that Freud receives at different times and in no particular order (Freud's own *Autobiographical Study* also scrambles such fragments in a Proustian puzzle of subjectivity), coherent narrative is not only a metaphor for mental health or stable selfhood. It is, within Freud's already metaphoric universe, health itself. "Everything," says Marcus, "is transformed into literature, into reading and writing." Freud's notion of the world as a text becomes the tenor rather than the vehicle in both the analytic scenario and its narrative representation. "The patient does not merely provide the text; she also *is* the text, the writing to be read, the language to be interpreted." The psyche itself, then, becomes a texture of language, a grid or honeycomb of representations, chief among them the pathways of memory which it is Freud's task to negotiate and map.[20] Hence Freud's texts insist on their place in modernist fiction by collapsing the distinction (as do Borges, Blanchot, and Barthelme) between fiction and criticism, art and interpretation, taking as the center of their own action the representation of representation, the criticism of criticism, the interpretation of interpretation. The 1909 case history of Freud's Rat Man ("Notes Upon a Case of Obsessional Neurosis") suggests just how definitive the linguistic metaphor is, since the case organizes itself around a precise verbal puzzle—the multiple German pun *"Ratten"*—whose overdeterminations must be unravelled in order for Freud to discover the lines of association by which repressed ideas are joined together. Like *The Interpretation of Dreams,* the case history, too, is, in Hyman's words, "a poem about a poem." The models of Freud's text presented by Hyman and Marcus, then, are

[20]For a reading of the Wolf Man case history that teases out the links between "narrativity" and subjectivity, see Peter Brooks, "Fictions of the Wolfman: Freud and Narrative Understanding," *Diacritics,* 9:1 (Spring 1979), 72-81.

both literary in exact ways, even though they differ in the traditions and assumptions to which they appeal in their attempt to situate Freud's achievement as a writer. For Hyman, it is myth and psychosexuality that characterize Freud's imagination, every present psychoanalytic quest a repetition of earlier romance cycles whose archetypal scenes, especially those mediated by overtly symbolic myth, represent psychoanalysis as a truth about nature seized on the level of instinct or biology. For Marcus, on the other hand, Freud's world is characterized above all by language as such, and by the letter of the law of language, which Freud follows like an exegete or detective as he elucidates the radiating puns of *Ratten* or the uncanny chemical formula in the dream of Irma's injection in *The Interpretation of Dreams*. Here even desire is to be represented as a linguistic conundrum in its unconscious structure, a text rather than a natural fact. So despite the equal literary authority of each mapping of Freud as literature, a symptomatic difference persists between them. It is in fact the very difference that separates Thomas Mann from Derrida and Bloom, and that organizes the history of Freud's accommodation to letters as a movement from libido to language. We can begin to map the process from the moment Mann announces the first "formal encounter" between Freud and literature on the occasion of Freud's eightieth birthday in 1936.

III

Mann's birthday lecture, "Freud and the Future," shows his notion of Freud as Romantic to be more radical than Trilling's later one, since Freud and literature share not only Trilling's notion of a "research into the self," but, in Mann's bolder and apparently more solipsistic pronouncement, they also share a notion that "the mystery of reality" as a whole is "an operation of the psyche." Noting the connections between his own novelistic heroes and Freud's neurotics, Mann finds the sickly young artist Tonio Kröger or the bourgeois neurasthenic Hans Castorp in *The Magic Mountain* to share with Freud's patients a privileged route to the secrets of the unconscious. "Disease," in short, becomes "an instrument of knowledge."

Mann's grandest accents, then, are reserved for that Freud who, following Schopenhauer and Ibsen, asserts "the primacy of the instinct over mind and reason." Duly acknowledging the present political implications in Germany of a "worship of the unconscious" and the "moral devastation" it may imply in the world of action, Mann nonetheless identifies the Freudian unconscious with the "primitive and irrational," with "pure dynamic." The ego, of course, is at the id's mercy, "its situation pathetic."[21]

---

[21] It should be noted that Freud's introduction of the new triad of psychic agencies in 1923— ego, id, and superego—is intended to clarify, indeed to shift, his earlier division of the psyche

Territory won by culture from the "seething excitations" of the id, the ego in Mann's view fears and opposes the superego far less than it fears and resists those resolutely biological forces that make up the id's rugged complexion.

And yet instead of carrying to its solipsistic extreme the notion of the ego as an isolated and besieged entity, Mann swerves from his radical romanticism in order to embrace instead the collective vision that emerges through a mythical reading of Freud's biologism and psychosexuality. Freud's apparently brutal picture of the fiery instinctual depths is in fact "familiar," communal, downright pacifying: "can any line be sharply and unequivocally drawn," asks Mann, "between the typical and the individual?" The truth is "that life is a mingling of the individual elements and the formal stock-in-trade; a mingling in which the individual, as it were, only lifts his head above the formal and impersonal elements. Much that is extra-personal, much unconscious identification, much that is conventional and schematic, is nonetheless decisive for the experience not only of the artist but of the human being in general."

Here the "psychological interest passes over into the mythical," says Mann, since Freud's notion of instinct is, in his reading, not tragic but romantic in the generic sense. It is, says Mann, "a smiling knowledge of the eternal, the ever-being and authentic," since the rhythms of myth, the representative of instinct, of what is abiding in man, inflect and determine life in the present and give the individual, not the vertigo normally associated with a vision of the ego at the mercy of the id, but, rather, a "formula and repetition" that assure that man's "path is marked out for him by those who trod it before." Individual character itself becomes not a nightmare of isolation but "a mythical role which the actor just emerged from the depths to the light plays in the illusion that it is his own and unique, that he, as it were, has invented it all himself." In fact, says Mann, "he creates out of the deeper consciousness in order that something which was once founded and legitimized shall again be represented."

We are, then, the "theatre-manager of our own dreams," not their authors, and the public scripts we are called upon to play as particular actors in our drama are the scripts of myth. These mythical constellations are, of course, not cultural or linguistic at all, but grandly naturalistic, eternal signatures of eternal human rhythms. Although Trilling rightly points out in "Freud and Literature" that Mann here corrects the far more radically irrationalist

---

(dating from the 1895 *Project for a Scientific Psychology*) into the systems of consciousness and the preconscious on the one hand and the unconscious proper on the other. In the later theory, much of the ego itself is seen as unconscious, thus making the earlier identification of ego with consciousness problematic, with consciousness proper becoming less and less decisive a factor as Freud's career progresses. As Harold Bloom points out (see p. 218 below), Freud's use of the term "unconscious" tends to move from noun to adjective as the theory proceeds through its various revisionary stages.

assessment of Freud in his 1929 "Freud's Position in the History of Modern Thought," Mann has in fact simply exchanged the vocabulary of what he calls the night side of life in the earlier essay—the underworld of instinct and biology—for the vocabulary of myth. Myth for Mann is a cultural representative of instinct, but it apparently admits of no historical or linguistic variation in its handling or reception from age to age, and so speaks directly for man's unchanging biological core as though language and the other products of culture were mere windows on a world of nature and truth that culture simply apprehends.

For Mann, then, "mythical identification," that mode of past power in antiquity, can and should be called upon again for a "reanimation of life" in the present late Romantic crisis of modernity. Hence Mann's own career moves from the neurotic inwardness of *Death in Venice* or *The Magic Mountain* to the mythical re-enactments of the *Joseph* novels, doubling the movement of the careers of Joyce and Eliot, for example, in an equal shift from Romantic individualism to classical community. Mann's alignment here with Joyce and Eliot pivots on the category of myth as a resolver of late Romantic solipsism, a way of tying the self's vanities and agonies to the larger rhythms of history and community on the level of a human nature that is static and enduring.

We should bear in mind, however, that Romanticism fashions its own mythology of belatedness by means of an anxious nostalgia for classical antiquity, the locus of a lost golden age, and so a privileged version of the grail-object itself ("O for a beaker full of the warm South," says Keats). The classical, the mythical, the South become the locus, in short, of a wish for the warmth and immediacy of an earliness, a closeness to beginnings, to instinct, that Mann's salutary notion of myth wishes to embody both as an assurance that modernity, too, is in touch with the same original springs of humanity as the Greeks and Hebrews, and, moreover, that the language of myth allows us to bypass the mediation of history by giving us direct access to man's natural core. Like Winckelmann, and like Mann himself, Freud, too, shared the especially acute desire for the South that is the pointed German version of this Romantic mythology (Freud's first trip to Rome in 1901 was the fulfillment of a lifetime wish), although it is Mann who teases out this strand in Freud and allows us to situate it in relation to that classicizing Eliotic modernism that seeks in myth an end to Romantic solipsism, too. For Mann, after all, appeals to myth as an exact representative or static symbol for man's biological center. Mediterranean myth here functions, in other words, as access to the immediacy of the South on the new level of psychoanalytic science, the level of enduring and unchanging instinct that modernity shares with antiquity.

Opposing Mann's claims for instinct and the fashion in which its representative or delegate, myth, shapes things for us, W.H. Auden's "Psychology and Art To-day," published just a year after Mann's lecture, in 1937, insists instead on the difference between the symbolic labor of the neurotic and that of the poet. Although Auden mentions in passing the use by criticism of certain Freudian notions and the use by the Surrealists of an "associational" writing "resembling the procedure in the analyst's consulting-room," he throws up his hands at the possibility of tracing Freud's influence on modern art, and wishes instead to designate Freud simply as "representative of a certain attitude" within modern art itself, an attitude probably best summed up in his terse remark that identifies artist and scientist in terms just the reverse of Mann's: "To understand the mechanism of the trap: The scientist and the artist."

What this "trap" may be remains to some extent unclear (it is rhetorical, though we shall have to wait for Derrida and Bloom to spell it out), since Auden's tone, like Ransom's, dances between a moving appreciation of Freud and a kind of humorous, if largely implicit, parody of the reductive side of Freud's familiar argument about the similarities between the poet, the dreamer, and the madman. By 1937, those similarities have, it appears, already been popularized, and Auden's reservations about the ease with which art and neurosis, poetry and untrammeled spontaneity, have been joined in the public imagination already anticipate Trilling's definitive account of the problem in "Art and Neurosis."[22]

Auden is willing, however, to accept Freud's notion of the artist as someone immersed in fantasy, as his citation from the *Introductory Lectures* attests, although, with Freud, he asserts, too, that what separates the artist from the neurotic is that the artist "finds a way back to reality," thanks, above all, Auden argues, to his "mysterious ability to mould his particular material." Even in dreams, there is already a touch of poetry beyond the simple exercise of wish-fulfillment, since in the dream there is "something which resembles art much more closely": it is "constructive, and, if you like, moral." It is a "picture," says Auden of his sample dream—that of a potential morphine addict whose dreaming suggests a flirtation with addiction rather than a capitulation to it—"of the balance of interest." Insisting as he does, contra Mann, on the "constructive" side of dream and art alike, Auden takes "the automatic element" of fantasy and its link to a notion of poetry as "inspiration" as only part of the process, as what is simply "given." Against it he counterposes both the rhetorical exactitudes of the dream and the conscious technical labor of poetry. "Misappropriated" as Freud has been "by irrationalists eager to escape their conscience"—Lawrence and Gide are his prime examples—Auden insists on the fact that the artist, like the individual, must fashion and transform what is "given"—"instinctive

---

[22]See Lionel Trilling, "Art and Neurosis," in *The Liberal Imagination* (New York: Scribner's, 1950), pp. 160-80.

need" on the level of life, the "racial property" of myth and symbol on the level of artistic "medium." The neurotic, like the poor artist, succumbs to fantasy in a parody of Mann's late Romantic notion of inspiration, while the successful artist, like the healthy man, recognizes his obligation to shape, construct, fashion, with craft and consciousness, what has been bequeathed to him by history and instinct. Reversing Mann's attitude of virtual surrender to primary process, Auden accents the secondary-process prerogatives of craft and reason instead. Much as Mann veers toward Jung, Auden veers toward the ego psychologists in his notion that conscious craftsmanship informs both poetry and personality, and so disavows the dependence of both on inspiration or daemonization. As a corrective to Mann's mythical instinctualism, then, Auden rights the balance in the ongoing interpretation of Freud, and adumbrates in the process the antithetical schismatic traditions to which he and Mann may each be assigned within psychoanalytic tradition proper.

The reaction to Mann is especially clear in Auden's paramount insistence on "words" rather than "symbols" as the poet's fundamental materials, an insistence that translates into an assertion that art and psychoanalysis are not mythical re-enactments of eternal instinctual patterns, but are "particular stories of particular people and experiences." If Mann's notion of psychoanalysis as a discourse about myth aligns him with the classical modernism of Eliot, Pound, or Joyce, Auden's notion of psychoanalysis as a discourse about language and particularity aligns him instead with that strand of modernism in Conrad, Virginia Woolf, and Joyce, too, that celebrates and sanctifies the quotidian.[23] It also aligns Auden with a view of Freud's language exceedingly different from Mann's, although it is a difference that will become manifest only with Kenneth Burke.

IV

Kenneth Burke's 1939 essay on Freud and the analysis of poetry makes clear what is at stake in Mann and Auden, and serves as the conceptual centerpiece in the history of Freud's interpretation by literature. Like Mann and Auden, Burke wishes to consider "the analogous features" in psychoanalysis and aesthetics, and that "margin of overlap" between them: "the acts of the neurotic," says Burke in a summary of earlier opinion, "are symbolic acts." But rather than choose or decide, at least at the start, between the alternative views of the symbolic or imaginative act given by Mann and

[23]See for example, David Thorburn, *Conrad's Romanticism* (New Haven: Yale University Press, 1974); see also Peter Gay, *Freud, Jews and Other Germans: Masters and Victims in Modernist Culture* (New York: Oxford University Press, 1978), especially pp. 24-28.

Auden (and by Hyman and Marcus), he will instead simply situate them in relation to one another.

Noting Freud's work to be "full," as it is, "of páradoxes," Burke goes to the heart of the interpretative rift within Freud himself: "a distinction between...an essentializing mode of interpretation and a mode that stresses proportion of ingredients." At the start of his argument, Burke assigns Freud, as a scientist, to the first of these positions:

> ...if one found a complex of, let us say, seven ingredients in a man's motivation, the Freudian tendency would be to take one of these as the essence of the motivation and to consider the other six as sublimated variants. We could imagine, for instance, manifestations of sexual incompetence accompanying a conflict in one's relations with his familiars and one's relations at the office. The proportional strategy would involve the study of these three as a cluster. The motivation would be synonymous with the interrelationships among them. But the essentializing strategy would, in Freud's case, place the emphasis upon the sexual manifestation, as causal ancestor of the other two.
>
> This essentializing strategy is linked with a normal ideal of science: to "explain the complex in terms of the simple." This ideal almost vows one to select one or another motive from a cluster and interpret the others in terms of it.

And in Freud, says Burke, "the sexual wish, or libido, is the basic category," the motive that psychoanalysis selects from the cluster and endows with exclusive explanatory power. Or does it?

In an impromptu examination of "bodily posture," it becomes clear, says Burke, that the same posture in two individuals, for example, may express two entirely different experiences of "dejection"—"the details of experience behind A's dejection may be vastly different from the details of experience behind B's dejection, yet both A and B may fall into the same bodily posture in expressing their dejection." The same "posture" or symbol, in other words, may have vastly different determinations, hence vastly different meanings, depending on the context in which it emerges. And psychoanalysis, implies Burke, can hardly be immune to this critique.

As it turns out, of course, this is precisely Freud's own argument against symbolism or "absolute content" in the interpretation of dreams, although it coexists uneasily with his use, too, of the symbolic method and its system of fixed meanings.[24] Hence when Burke turns to this crucial interpretative topos in Freud himself, he finds him no longer simply the reductive, essentializing scientist, but a proportionalist, too:

---

[24]See *The Interpretation of Dreams*, 4:105; 5:353. It should be noted, too, that Burke himself clarifies the confusion that may arise from the two distinct senses in which he uses the word "symbolic" (see p. 78 below, n.3).

Freud explicitly resisted the study of motivation by way of symbols. He distinguished his own mode of analysis from the symbolic by laying stress upon free association. That is, he would begin the analysis of a neurosis without any preconceived notion as to the absolute meaning of any image that the patient might reveal in the account of a dream. His procedure involved the breaking-down of the dream into a set of fragments, with the analyst then inducing the patient to improvise associations on each of these fragments in turn. And afterward, by charting recurrent themes, he would arrive at the crux of the patient's conflict.

Others (particularly Stekel), however, proposed a great short cut here. They offered an absolute content for various items of imagery.

Freud himself, Burke concludes, "fluctuates in his search for essence." And to situate this fluctuation in relation to literature (and, implicitly, to countermand Mann far more rigorously than Auden does), Burke shows us exactly why the proportional mode of interpretation—nonscientific and nonmythic as it is—is both crucial to psychoanalysis (recall *Ratten*) and to the exactly distinguishing feature of poetic or literary language as well, especially when it is compared to other modes of language, particularly the language of science:

> The examination of a poetic work's internal organization would bring us nearer to a variant of the typically Freudian free-association method than to the purely symbolic method toward which he subsequently gravitated.
>
> The critic should adopt a variant of the free-association method. One obviously cannot invite an author, especially a dead author, to oblige him by telling what the author thinks of when the critic isolates some detail or other for improvisation. But what he can do is to note the context of imagery and ideas in which an image takes its place. He can also note, by such analysis, the kinds of evaluations surrounding the image of a crossing; for instance, is it an escape from or a return to an evil or a good, etc? Until finally, by noting the ways in which this crossing behaves, what subsidiary imagery accompanies it, what kind of event it grows out of,...one grasps its significance as motivation. And there is no essential motive offered here. The motive of the work is equated with the structure of interrelationships within the work itself.

So it is at the "dream level" that the "Freudian coordinates come closest to the charting of the logic of poetic structure"—not on the rather imprecise level of myth or symbol, nor indeed on the level of what Auden calls "words," but on the exact level of technique, the level of trope. In a startling anticipation of the most prophetic accents of Trilling's "Freud and Literature" (Trilling's essay appeared in its original form only a year after Burke's), Burke finds the rhetoric of mind and poetry to be not just similar but virtually identical in the shared predominance of the two functions in the dreamwork that Freud calls "condensation" and "displacement," functions that are, as Trilling will tell us, no less than the rhetorical tropes metaphor and metonymy:

> Condensation…deals with the respects in which house in a dream may be more than house, or house plus. And displacement deals with the way in which house may be other than house, or house minus. … One can understand the resistance to both of these emphases. It leaves no opportunity for a house to be purely and simply a house—and whatever we may feel about it as regards dreams, it is a very disturbing state of affairs when transferred to the realm of art.

Here, of course, the poem as dream is virtually the same as the poem as chart, since dream and poem alike are plotted within a common network or system—a chart or table of combinations—whose resources are deployed according to Freud's two ruling tropes, and whose structure, both psychic and semantic, is the structure of language itself. Moreover, the linguistic rather than grossly symbolic character of the analogous systems of psyche and text or poem precludes from the start anything but a proportional or variable notion of psychic and poetic meaning: "the Freudian emphasis on the pun," says Burke, "brings it about that something can only be in so far as it is something else." This "something else" is not, of course, a fixed and final end to interpretation, like Mann's essentializing notion of myth as biology, as "the eternal, the ever-being and authentic," as the essentializing or literal language of science and scientific meaning. Rather, it is a notion of motive or cause in terms of a "cluster" of "structural interrelationships," each term gaining its meaning from its relation to other terms in the cluster rather than from its relation to a direct and self-sufficient ground of truth or nature. Between Mann and Burke, in other words, is a wholesale difference in literature's very notion of language, of what and how language, especially literary language, means. It is, moreover, a difference or dispute each side of which may be found in Freud himself, who thereby contains the critical alternatives available to the whole profession of letters. "Even the scientific essay," Burke concludes of Freud, "would have its measure of choreography."

V

If Burke is our conceptual centerpiece, Lionel Trilling is our dramatic one. Like no other writer here save Freud himself, his sympathies are so wide that they can admit both sides of the dispute almost coterminously. Trilling does, however, decide, and in both ways, even though the opposed celebrations of what is opposed in Freud himself are separated by almost fifteen years. It is to Trilling's later essay, the 1955 "Freud: Within

and Beyond Culture," that we should turn first (originally published as a
separate volume under the title *Freud and the Crisis of Our Culture*, and
included in the 1965 collection, *Beyond Culture*), since it stands in the line
of Mann's argument just as surely as the 1940 "Freud and Literature" stands
in the line of Burke's.[25] Moreover, each essay dramatizes within itself the
historical split in the interpretation of Freud that they also represent as an
opposed pair.

Although Trilling parts with Mann, in "Art and Neurosis" especially,
on the question of a link between knowledge and disease, he is at the same
time sympathetic to Mann's fascination with the night side of Freud's
thought, and to the notion that it contains a secret affirmation, even if, as
it turns out, Trilling is preparing an affirmation far more radical than
Mann's own. For Trilling, Freud's biological notion of the id embodies the
Freudian insistence that the Cartesian profile of man that identifies being
with consciousness is a wishful myth. But even though this deepest layer of
Freud's thought sees man or consciousness as the object of forces greater
than himself and outside his control, the fact that Freud imagines these
forces as natural or biological—as outside or beyond culture—is the pathway to the discovery of a genuinely reassuring idea. For the abyss, with all
its horrors, is the site of man's moral salvation even if it also provides the
ground of his suffering. To explain why, Trilling presents what is probably
the most eloquent defense of Freud as Romantic modernist in the English
language: "He needed to believe that there was some point at which it was
possible to stand beyond the reach of culture. ... It is our way of coming
close to the idea of Providence." Reacting in advance to the inevitable
response (especially in the days of Neo-Freudianism and its sociological
reductions of psychosexuality), Trilling adds: "It is so far from being a
reactionary idea that it is actually a liberating idea. It proposes to us that
culture is not all-powerful. It suggests that there is a residue of human
quality beyond the reach of cultural control, and that this residue of human
quality, elemental as it may be, serves to bring culture itself under criticism
and keeps it from being absolute." After all, the primacy of the biological
abyss in Freud's thinking means that man does not belong to culture alone.
If culture represses, denies man his freedom, the biological or instinctual
core of being that it represses still springs forward to speak for man even
when man can no longer speak for himself.

Trilling's Romantic valorization of the abyss, in short, is in the service
of a notion of self or personality that exists apart from culture, that retains

---

[25]The text of "Freud and Literature" included here is the (only slightly) revised version
that appears in the 1950 collection, *The Liberal Imagination* (New York: Scribner's, 1950),
reprinted as a volume in *The Works of Lionel Trilling* (New York: Harcourt Brace Jovanovich,
1978). For the original text of "Freud: Within and Beyond Culture," see *Freud and the Crisis
of Our Culture* (Boston: Beacon, 1955).

an essence of being that culture can never compromise. If "there is a hard, irreducible, stubborn core of biological urgency, and biological necessity, and biological *reason*, that culture cannot reach and that reserves the right, which sooner or later it will exercise, to judge the culture and resist and revise it," then "there is," says Trilling, "a sanction beyond the culture." The great peroration follows: "This intense conviction of the existence of a self apart from culture is, as culture well knows, its noblest and most generous achievement."[26] Trilling gives the game away, however, in that famous sentence. For the notion of a self beyond culture is, alas, itself an achievement of culture, its "noblest" achievement and, therefore, like any cultural product, a trope or fiction.

In the earlier "Freud and Literature," the question, put simply, is whether there is indeed a self, a core of being, beyond culture. Is Freud's theory of the drive a biological theory of instinct, or is it a cultural theory of merely human indoctrination into the order of things? For the Trilling of "Freud and Literature," Mann's assertion of the instinctual basis of psychoanalysis is not only too close to the false popular notion of "art and neurosis," but also one that tries to meld Freud's admittedly double vision into an impossible single perspective. Indeed, Mann's thoroughgoing instinctualism (like Trilling's own saving belief in biology fifteen years later) is in fact to be identified with the "naive" positivism of the early Freud: "of claiming for his theories a perfect correspondence with an external reality." The same position is, after all, implicit in Mann's definition of the instinctual truth embodied in myth as "the external, the ever-being and authentic," for it presumes, as Freud the scientist does, a way out of language and history by an appeal to an unchanging biology viewed through the fixity or essence of symbols. Although Trilling distinguishes between the practical reality the working analyst must discern with "a certain firm crudeness" and a notion of "reality" evolved under conditions of "theoretical refinement," he places both kinds of reality, finally, in the service of what should be called a poetic and social rather than a scientific and universal real. For the reality to which Freud really appeals—even at times despite himself, says Trilling—is "the reality of social life and of value, conceived and maintained by the human mind and will. Love, morality, honor, esteem—these are the components of a created reality. If we are to call art an illusion then we must call most of the activities and satisfactions of the ego illusions; Freud, of course, has no desire to call them that." What has occurred here, of course, is an implicit redefinition of the contents and mechanism of the Freudian unconscious. Although Trilling will, at the close of the essay, attempt a compromise vision in which man is "an inextricable tangle of culture and biology," here, at the start of the essay's

[26] Trilling, "Freud: Within and Beyond Culture," pp. 99, 101, 102.

genuinely radical moments, it is culture alone that is the decisive if silent term.

What follows is a Burkean corrective to the notion of a fixed, symbolically apprehended meaning, on the level of motive, in the psychoanalysis of a work of art like *Hamlet:* "We must rather object to the conclusions of Freud and Dr. Jones on the ground that their proponents do not have an adequate conception of what an artistic meaning is. There is no single meaning to any work of art; this is true not merely because it is better that it should be true, that is, because it makes art a richer thing, but because historical and personal experience show it to be true." Once again rejecting the notion that the truth of psychoanalysis, the truth of the unconscious, resides in an indwelling "reality to which the play," for example, "stands in the relation that a dream stands to the wish that generates it and from which it is separable," Trilling suggests, again along the lines of Burke's argument, that both mind and poem acquire their meanings in some other way. Like the dream in relation to the dreamer, *Hamlet,* says Trilling, "is not merely the product of Shakespeare's thought, it is the very instrument of his thought." This returns us to Trilling's already implicit notion of the unconscious as the repository, not so much of an instinctual payload of raw nature—a "reality" or essence like that which motivates *Hamlet* in Freud's and Jones's celebrated reduction—as of the fictions, the "created reality," of the social order itself. When Trilling makes the famous claim that "of all mental systems, the Freudian psychology is the one which makes poetry indigenous to the very constitution of the mind," makes the mind "a poetry-making organ," he is less concerned with the factor of poetic craft than he is with something else: the identification of both the object of Freudian analysis—the unconscious mind—and the Freudian text with the necessary fiction of language itself. Even science, says Trilling in the later essay, "is organized improbability, or organized fantasy."

It is at this point that Trilling unleashes that boldest and most precise of interpretative announcements, the prophetic words that Bloom celebrates in "Freud and the Poetic Sublime," and that Burke, in his attentiveness to condensation and displacement, has brought us to the brink of just a year before:

> Freud has not merely naturalized poetry; he has discovered its status as a pioneer settler, and he sees it as a method of thought. Often enough he tries to show how, as a method of thought, it is unreliable and ineffective for conquering reality; yet he himself is forced to use it in the very shaping of his own science, as when he speaks of the topography of the mind and tells us with a kind of defiant apology that the metaphors of space relationship which he is using are really most inexact since the mind is not a thing of space at all, but that there is no other way of conceiving the difficult idea except by metaphor. In the eighteenth century Vico spoke of the metaphorical,

imagistic language of the early stages of culture; it was left to Freud to discover how, in a scientific age, we still feel and think in figurative formations,
and to create, what psychoanalysis is, a science of tropes, of metaphor and its
variants, synecdoche and metonymy.

"We still feel and think in figurative formations" because we think and feel
through language and all the figures that culture has provided us in order
to be human at all. It is, ironically but also suitably, a passage in support
of this side of the dispute in "Freud: Within and Beyond Culture" that is
the best gloss for Trilling's argument here. "The unconscious of society,"
writes Trilling, "may be said to have been imagined before the unconscious
of the individual." Freud "made it apparent to us how entirely implicated
in culture we all are...how the culture suffuses the remotest parts of the
individual mind, being taken in almost literally," the argument concludes,
"with the mother's milk."[27]

VI

Despite preconceptions, it is hardly a jump, then, from Trilling's "Freud
and Literature" to the contemporary world of French Freud, premised as
both are on the decisive function of culture and language in the very constitution of subjectivity, and on a notion of the unconscious as a web of
ideological determinations that fashions the self from the ground up.[28]
Jacques Derrida, however, is not to be identified with the work of Lacan,[29]
even though a sympathy for the notion of the Freudian unconscious as a
language (or, to be more exactly Lacanian, to say that the unconscious is
structured "like a language")[30] is surely Derrida's starting point, especially since he wishes to distinguish writing from language at large, and,
in the process, formulate a precise definition of literary language as Freud
himself conceives it, and, indeed, as Freud also practices it.

Derrida summarizes our historical dispute and brings it to a head by
criticizing what, in Burke's vocabulary, we might call an "essentializing"
notion of Freud—a notion of the unconscious in particular as what Burke
himself might call a "God term" or what Ransom refers to as a "gospel
truth." Instead, claims Derrida, Freud's real achievement lies precisely
in the rupture or break his work enacts with all such metaphysical quests

[27] Trilling, "Freud: Within and Beyond Culture," pp. 90, 91.

[28] See Althusser, "Freud and Lacan."

[29] For Derrida's "deconstruction" of Lacan, see "The Purveyor of Truth," trans. Domingo,
Hulbert, et. al., *Yale French Studies,* 49 (1975), 31-113.

[30] At times, however, simile seems to give way to identity: "What the psychoanalytic experience discovers in the unconscious is the whole structure of language" (Lacan, *Ecrits: A Selection,* p. 147).

for essence or natural core. What Freud discovers, says Derrida, is just the reverse of Mann's notion of the unconscious as a plentitude of instinct represented by myth or symbol, and which is directly translatable, as a dream element may seem to be, back into its fixed natural or sexual meaning in a world beyond language. This view of the unconscious and of language as it appears in Mann's notion of myth and symbol is what Derrida calls "logocentrism"—a notion of meaning as a full measure or transcript of a truth in nature or things that language merely apprehends and conveys. Rather, says Derrida, neither language nor the unconscious signify in that way.[31] It is Freud's particular achievement to have made such a discovery and to demonstrate instead the way language and the psyche really work.

To call the unconscious a language is to make a precise but occluded claim, says Derrida. By turning to Freud's earliest attempt at representing mental functioning in the 1895 *Project,* Derrida shows that Freud's linguistic metaphors are not only present in his work from the start and that they will eventually overthrow all naively biologistic, instinctual, even neurological metaphors in his later work. He also suggests that the metaphors Freud draws from language, both here and in *The Interpretation of Dreams* five years later, are drawn not so much from language generally as from one special—or apparently special—subdivision of it: writing, "nonphonetic writing" in particular, such as ideograms or hieroglyphs.

What is especially powerful about writing as a metaphor for representing the unconscious—for representing, if you will, the way it is inscribed by culture—is that it represents Freud's primary process as a writing that is cut off, from the start, from any connection to the kind of language that is customarily associated with the fullness of a natural breath, with the direct expression of immediate feelings that well up in the throat spontaneously, authentically, without art. Here Derrida argues against both Mann's notion of the unconscious as a repository of myths that simply "transcribe" the "living, full speech" of instinct, and Freud's own neurological metaphors that function in the *Project* as his version of an ideal language capable of grasping the "living, full speech" of psychic energy in the mimetic discourse of a positivist science.

Instead, Derrida argues, Freud gives us a notion of the unconscious as a field of memory traces constituted by a kind of psychic writing. In the *Project,* Freud describes the origin or emergence of these memory traces or writings not as tokens of experience that are added to or engraved upon a self-sufficient natural core of unconscious instinct that grows progressively conscious over time. Rather, the origin of the first memory traces

---

[31] For Derrida, the same is also true for spoken speech despite its misleading and only apparently privileged connection with voice and breath. See *Of Grammatology,* trans. Gayatri Chakravorty Spivak (Baltimore: John Hopkins University Press, 1976).

can only be accounted for by the hypothesis of a sudden catastrophic moment or jolt that sets the whole psyche into play at once. ("Life is already threatened by the memory which constitutes it.") The psyche seems to originate, in other words, at the moment it begins to resist stimuli (here Freud's allegory of the birth of the ego in *Beyond the Pleasure Principle* is Derrida's implicit allusion) at which point a difference emerges between such force or stimulation and the organism's resistance to it, thus separating self and world while constituting each in relation to the other. It is this difference alone that opens up what Freud calls, in Bass's translation, a "breaching," a fracturing that lays down paths or traces on the psyche's virgin surface, which comes into being only at the moment it begins the process of resistance.

The *Project*, however, has no satisfactory model with which to go on to represent how the psyche stores these traces or pathways as memory, given the simultaneous fact that the psyche continues to be able to receive new impressions without cease, and to which the mind stays fresh and open. It is at this point that the essay's manifest project comes into focus. Derrida's aim here is to trace Freud's thirty-year search (from the *Project* to the brief but, for Derrida, crucial essay of 1925, the "Note upon the 'Mystic Writing-Pad'") for a model or metaphor that can account for and represent the functioning of the mental apparatus in the two separate but linked registers of unconscious memory and conscious perception. The problem, as the *Project* lays it out, is to find a figure capable of representing both processes in a single stroke: the constant ability of consciousness to receive fresh impressions and the equal and constant ability of the unconscious to store the traces they leave. No single system can do both jobs at once, since a glut or saturation point is inevitable. Hence the search for a metaphor.

The metaphor, however, cannot be found until Freud clarifies his notion of that psychic writing known as memory. Memory is not a thing or a substance, says Derrida, but the very difference between one pathway or "breaching" and another, an apparently simple difference of intensity that distinguishes one trace from another, and so elaborates a field of memory even as it elucidates or differentiates one memory from another. Of course, this vision of memory as a set of differences or traces is precisely what Burke means by a proportional rather than an essentialist view of how both language and the psyche operate—by means of the relations, the differences as well as the similarities, among the elements in a given cluster of language or (what amounts in certain ways to the same thing) of memory proper. Derrida simply draws out the epistemological implications of the proportional view of the "writing" that is the common medium of both literature and the psyche.

And yet one special problem bothers Derrida in addition to Freud's own problem of finding a suitable representation for the double and simultaneous psychic systems of memory and fresh reception. It is the problem of the psyche's origin, of the origin of primary process or unconscious thought that the *Project* can imagine only as having happened in a single moment. The notion of an origin requires, of course, such a notion of a single, originating moment, and yet the origin Freud describes in the *Project* is, as we have seen, a function of the relation "between *two* forces," as Derrida points out. "Resistance itself is possible only if the opposition of forces"—of stimulation and resistance—"lasts and is repeated at the beginning." But how can "the beginning" be a repetition?

This, alas, is a key Derridean paradox, the paradox Derrida calls "originary repetition," a notion that disallows, on Freud's own authority, the primariness of the primary process itself, and so disallows any notion of unconscious functioning as one based in the primacy of nature, whether neurologically or mythically apprehended. "Primariness," says Derrida, becomes for Freud a "theoretical fiction."

As he moves from the *Project* to *The Interpretation of Dreams*, Derrida brings all this to bear on the central problem of dream interpretation, whose significance Burke has already alerted us to. Among Freud's predominant metaphors for the dream-work, of course, are those metaphors of "non-linguistic writing," of "a model of writing irreducible to speech" whose figures include "hieroglyphics, pictographic, ideogrammatic, and phonetic elements." These figures are important, says Derrida, because they distinguish the genuinely Freudian method of interpretation from the merely secondary method borrowed from Stekel that simply decodes dream elements as though they were fixed universal symbols rather than the particular tokens of particular lives. Derrida calls upon Freud himself for the exact specifications of the case: "My procedure," says Freud, "is not so convenient as the popular decoding which translates any given piece of a dream's content by a fixed key. I, on the contrary, am prepared to find that the same piece of content may conceal a different meaning when it occurs in various people or in various contexts." Freud even calls on "Chinese script," says Derrida—ideogrammatic script, which has no bond with the mythology of natural speech that accompanies the spoken word—to illustrate and insure the connection between proportional or contextual interpretation and a notion of writing that is not linked to oral speech: The dream symbols, says Freud, "frequently have more than one or even several meanings, and, as with Chinese script, the correct interpretation can only be arrived at on each occasion from the context." The reason universal symbol-translation will not do, as Burke has already suggested, is that it "presupposes," in Derrida's words, "a text which would be already there, immobile"—a text of truth behind the dream symbols to which they univocally refer, rather than meanings that are apprehended "on each occasion from the context," from their relationships with other elements in it.

Hence by the celebrated route of dream interpretation—the "royal road to the unconscious," as Freud himself describes it in *The Interpretation of Dreams*—Derrida radically criticizes a notion of the unconscious as a cauldron of seething natural energies or even as a locus of impulses that can be apprehended, measured, quantified by science as though they were really there: "There is then no unconscious truth to be discovered by virtue of [its] having been written elsewhere," says Derrida, whether by nature or any other determinable source. "The unconscious text is already a weave of pure traces...a text nowhere present, consisting of archives"—of memory traces—"which are *always already* transcriptions.... Everything begins with reproduction." Here, of course, Derrida alludes to his notion of the origin of the psyche itself as a repetition, although what is crucial in both dream interpretation and any meditation on origins, says Derrida, is that in both cases the object of the interpretative quest is always deferred. For if writing, whether psychic or literary, functions as a proportional system of differences—as a system of comparisons and contrasts among the elements of language that alone sets those elements apart from one another —then writing surely cannot refer to anything more than the phantom objects produced by its own rhetoric. So both the meaning of dreams and the origin of the psyche must be deferred, if by "meaning" and "origin" one means the grasp of an immanent, "eternal" or "authentic" essence in instinct, say, or sexuality, whether in Mann's version or in that of Freud the neurological quantifier.

Derrida's notion of deferral is linked not only to his Saussurean notion of language itself as a system of writing or differences (hence Derrida's neologism, "differance," a compound of "differ" and "defer"),[32] but also to Freud's term *Nachträglichkeit,* usually translated as "deferred action."[33] By "deferred action," Freud himself means what Derrida means by "differance"—that the past or, indeed, any object of memory or language (the two are, of course, intimately associated in any case) comes into being only after the fact, as a function of the place language or memory requires it to hold. And not only is the past or the linguistic object always reconstituted belatedly by the rhetorical operations of memory and reading. The present, too, is always an effect of repetition, since the moment can be grasped, understood as such only in relation to something else as well. Freud's most elaborate discussion of "deferred action" comes in the 1918 case of the Wolf Man ("From the History of an Infantile Neurosis"), who "remembers"

[32]See "Differance," in Jacques Derrida, *Speech and Phenomena, and other essays on Husserl's Theory of Signs,* trans. David B. Allison (Evanston: Northwestern University Press, 1973), pp. 148ff.
[33]See Laplanche and Pontalis, *The Language of Psychoanalysis,* pp. 111-14.

the primal scene in his parents' bedroom, alluded to by his famous dream of wolves in a tree outside his window, only by means of the knowledge about sex that his subsequent experience bestows upon him. Whether the primal scene of parental coitus really took place remains for Freud an open and finally irrelevant question.

Freud's search for a proper way of representing the double system of the psyche, then, is also a search for a proper way of representing reference in language itself. For language, like the psyche, functions on two levels simultaneously—the level of perpetually fresh speech or writing and the level of memory, each one dependent on the other. No wonder, then, that Derrida claims that Freud's search for such a model remains waylaid until he can find one that will not simply use the metaphor of writing, but one that will also be a "writing machine," as Derrida puts it, in its own right— until, that is, Freud can describe his notion of writing in a way that also demonstrates it. The mystic writing-pad is just such a machine, the self-erasing pad with two surfaces that is still a children's toy even today. Here the "contradictory requirement" of the *Project* is at last met: "a double system contained," says Derrida, "in a single differentiated apparatus: a perpetually available innocence and an infinite reserve of traces have at last been reconciled."

Once again, too, the strains of *Beyond the Pleasure Principle* are implicit as Derrida suggests the precision of the writing-pad as a metaphor for the psyche in its full Freudian profile: "There is no writing which does not devise some means of protection, *to protect against itself,* against the writing by which the 'subject' is himself threatened as he lets himself be written: *as he exposes himself."* This is, surely, a description of consciousness (of the Cartesian "subject") in its peculiar relation to the unconscious, the latter always closing up—by definition—not letting itself be known by consciousness, which is an unknowing function of its own hidden or repressed writing, that record of its journey into and through the world that determines what it knows by making its perceptions repetitions of what is already written beneath it.

This is also, of course, a description of writing itself, especially literary language as it distinguishes itself from the language of a positivist science. Here, in fact, Freud requires the supposedly literal language of science to acknowledge, says Derrida, what "we never dreamed of taking seriously": its real status as metaphor, as literary language in its own right. And in order to demonstrate the purely figurative status of the whole field of psychoanalytic inquiry, Freud does not just describe the scene of writing as a phenomenon of the psyche. "Freud's language is *caught up* in it," says Derrida; "Freud performs for us the scene of writing," reduplicates the structure of the psyche in the structure of his own text. Why? Because his writing, like the psychic text it describes, can only try, endlessly and without success, to designate a genuine beginning, an authentic essence or real immediacy—nature, instinct, biology, sexuality—just as the psyche itself is always unable to recover its own beginnings before repression. And yet here Derrida goes even further, as he introduces a late Freudian concept that clears up the problem of "originary repetition" by asserting that, in the beginning, there can only have been repression itself, even before the emergence of the drive. This Freud calls "primal repression,"[34] and for Derrida it is the only concept that can account for the birth of writing itself, whether psychic or literary. For we can only presume or deduce, without verification, a first barrage of stimuli from the outside world as the event that sets repression or protection from stimuli into motion in the first place, and that, in the difference between them, begins the process of pathbreaking known alternately as memory and writing. What we do know for certain, however, by dint of the logical requirements of rhetoric itself, is that there can't be one without the other—no force without resistance, no stimuli without repression—since each term requires the other in order to be coherent, each notion coming into being, rhetorically at any rate, by means of its difference from the other. It is only repression that can, in the final analysis, account for drive or even stimuli, since the tokens of repression are the only (and ironic) evidence we have for what is unconscious.

Repression, then, comes first, before drive or instinct, much as the Wolf Man's later knowledge of sex actually precedes his earlier knowledge of parental coitus. So for Derrida, what Freud the apparent scientist dramatizes is not something that is also literary, but something that is literary from the start and that dramatizes Freud's very notion of literary language: "A becoming-literary of the literal." Freud's once-literal attempts to break through to a natural truth of libido through the quantifications of chemistry and neurology give way, says Derrida, to an elaborate and reflexive notion of the language of science and psyche themselves as literary languages, too.

VII

As we move from Derrida to Harold Bloom's "Freud and the Poetic Sublime," the definition of Freud as literary in his own right grows to an exact focus, especially if, as Derrida claims, Freud's language is itself im-

---

[34]Although the term first appears in the 1911 Schreber case ("Psychoanalytic Notes on an Autobiographical Account of a Case of Paranoia," 12: 67-68), it is in the 1915 metapsychological essays "Repression" and "The Unconscious" that the notion's conceptual necessity and far-reaching implications are made particularly apparent (see 14: 148-49, 180-81). Although much of *Beyond the Pleasure Principle* may be seen as a gloss on it, the term itself does not appear there. In the 1926 *Inhibitions, Symptoms and Anxiety*, primal repression and the argument of *Beyond the Pleasure Principle* are joined together (20:94). As with many of Freud's later concepts, primal repression is already abumbrated in the *Project* under the name "primary defense" (1:370-71), and for reasons of theoretical coherence like those that require primal repression itself in the later phase.

plicated in the kind of psychic writing it describes. Despite the "antithetical modes" of science and poetry, says Bloom (Trilling's "Freud and Literature," he adds, is still the classic demonstration of the problem), Freud is, finally, a poet regardless of his scientific intentions, since "he cannot invoke the trope of the Unconscious"—for the unconscious is, as Freud himself never fails to remind us, a hypothesis, a fiction, a trope—"as though he were doing more (or less) than the poet or critic does by invoking the trope of the Imagination, or than the theologian does by invoking the trope of the Divine." And for Freud, the "most vital trope or fiction in his theory of the mind" is "the primary process," the original seat of the unconscious which, in Freud's later terminology, will be called the id.

But "to quarry" the poetic Freud for "theories-of-creativity," says Bloom, we need to study him, not in his reductive profile as psychoanalyst of art in the sense Trilling deplores, but "where he himself is most imaginative." For Bloom, this is principally the late phase of Freud's career that begins with *Beyond the Pleasure Principle,* moves to the 1925 essay "Negation" and the 1926 *Inhibitions, Symptoms and Anxiety,* and whose "climax," as Bloom puts it, is "Analysis Terminable and Interminable" in 1937.

The centrality of *Beyond the Pleasure Principle* (whose significance Derrida's essay has only hinted at)[35] lies in its formulation, decisive for this entire late phase of Freud's career, of "the priority," says Bloom, "of anxiety over stimuli." The notion of repetition-compulsion that Freud interrogates at the start of the book stymies him because it is a factor in dreams, fantasy, and neurotic symptoms that does not accord with the wish-fulfillment theory that otherwise explains all three phenomena. Why one repeats a painful or fearful event troubles Freud. His principal example here is the portrait of his grandson playing a game with a spool, which he makes disappear behind his bed only to make it reappear again by pulling it out. This, says Freud, is a repetition in fantasy of the daily comings and goings of the child's mother. Her departures can only be disturbing to the child, and yet it is these moments of loss which the child, despite his distinct lack of pleasure, willfully repeats in his symbolic play. Trilling points out in "Freud and Literature" that the episode represents a deliberate attempt to promote "fear" so as to gain "active mastery" over it. Bloom takes it further still by remarking that such behavior, especially on the part of children, is an attempt "to master a stimulus retroactively by first developing the anxiety." What is shocking here, but also illuminating, is that this is *the creation of anxiety,* and so cannot be considered a sublimation of any kind." This intentional development of fear or anxiety, in other words,

[35]For Derrida on *Beyond the Pleasure Principle,* see "Coming into One's Own," trans. James Hulbert, in *Psychoanalysis and the Question of the Text: Selected Papers from the English Institute, 1976-77,* ed. Geoffrey Hartman (Baltimore: Johns Hopkins University Press, 1978), pp. 114-48; and "Speculations—on Freud," trans. Ian McLeod, *Oxford Literary Review,* 3:2 (1978), 78-97.

is not a reaction or resistance to an actual threat (in the case of Freud's grandson, the game proceeds even when the mother is at home, when the real threat of departure is absent), but an anxiety that precedes all threats. In the biological allegory of the birth of the ego that follows Freud's portrait of the child, this original anxiety motivates what Freud has already named "primal repression," the "theoretical fiction" that sets the primary process in motion from the start.

What the portraits of Freud's grandson and the hypothetical birth of the ego share, then, is the exercise of repression—a primal repression—before there is anything to repress. If original anxiety creates primal repression, primal repression, as Derrida has already suggested, creates in turn the force that any repression requires so as to be what it is, a resistance to force. For Bloom, this force is the drive itself, which anxiety and primal repression install retroactively, belatedly (Bloom's way of translating *Nachträglichkeit*), as a scenario of origins by which consciousness can imagine its beginnings as jolt or catastrophe, as the moment at which drive surprised it. The drive, that is, is "propped," as Jean Laplanche puts it,[36] upon or against the repression that brings it into being after the fact, the fiction the psyche invents in order to account for and represent its own birth or origin. Or, to put it in the terms of Freud's "Negation," it is by means of its negation that drive as such emerges, as the resistance to its erasure that the notion of resistance itself requires in order to be what it is. Bloom calls this rhetoric of the psyche a rhetoric of "contamination" or "crossing-over" in a later essay,[37] a graphic suggestion of the way drive and repression, drive and negation, each come into being by means of crossing or contaminating one another.

There is, then, ample reason for Bloom to assent to Trilling's contention—and Lacan's—that psychoanalysis is a "science of tropes," and that the rhetoric it studies is the rhetoric of the defense mechanisms by which the ego establishes and sustains itself. Indeed, in Bloom's reading, the rhetoric of psychic defense is a rhetoric precisely because, in its attempt to turn away from stimuli or influence—to "trope" them, for among the root meanings of "trope" is the meaning "turn"—the psyche in fact fashions the very thing it turns away from, acknowledging, in fact creating, the law of drive, for example, by fleeing from it as though it were there. For Bloom, then, "drives *are* fictions," fictions on the level of both the psyche Freud describes and the level of the Freudian rhetoric that describes it. Just as the drives are the psyche's originating fictions, they are also, says Bloom, Freud's own "enabling fictions" as a writer. Hence the first of a series of formulations of the literary status of Freud's text to emerge from Bloom's

---

[36] See Laplanche, *Life and Death in Psychoanalysis*, pp. 15ff.
[37] Harold Bloom, "Freud's Concepts of Defense and the Poetic Will," in *The Literary Freud: Mechanisms of Defense and the Poetic Will* (*Psychiatry and the Humanities*, vol. 4), ed. Joseph H. Smith (New Haven: Yale University Press, 1980), pp. 1-28.

argument: the structure of the psyche and the structure of Freud's language match one another exactly. They are in fact one and the same, for Freud's description of the psyche is really a description of his own text. Like the belated and inferred emergence of the drive in the rhetoric—the defensive "troping"—of psychic action proper, what Freud calls "the unconscious" also emerges as a deferred effect on the level of his own rhetoric, "a purely inferred division of the psyche," as Bloom reminds us, "an inference necessarily based only upon the supposed effects the unconscious has upon the way we think and act that can be *known,* and that are available to consciousness." Primal repression, then, is Freud's most literary trope, says Bloom, since it is the model, as Derrida has already implied, for the structure of literary reference itself: the retroactive installation of a referent, which languages situates, through rhetoric, outside of language, much as the defense or trope known as primal repression installs the drive, retroactively, as a catastrophic beginning to the individual's life.

If the psychic text and the literary text are, for Freud, one and the same, then the psyche as Freud represents it should also provide us with some account of what Bloom calls the will-to-creativity in poetry. Hence a second literary mapping of the late Freud. If, in *Beyond the Pleasure Principle,* the purpose of the repetition-compulsion is "to master a stimulus retroactively by first developing the anxiety," the will-to-creativity in poetry, says Bloom, is also conditioned by the threat of what he calls "anteriority," an earlier force that looms as a rearguard catastrophe for the poet just as the drive does on the level of psyche itself. Bloom links this psychic structure in Freud to the literary notion of the Sublime, which Bloom defines as follows:

> As a literary idea, the Sublime originally meant a style of "loftiness," that is, of verbal power, of greatness or strength conceived agonistically, which is to say against all possible competition. But in the European Enlightenment, this literary idea was strangely transformed into a vision of the terror that could be perceived both in nature and in art, a terror uneasily allied with pleasurable sensations of augmented power, and even of narcissistic freedom, freedom in the shape of that wildness Freud dubbed "the omnipotence of thought," the greatest of all narcissistic illusions.

Hence "the creative or Sublime 'moment,'" at least in post-Enlightenment poetry, "is a negative moment," and it "tends to rise out of an encounter with someone else's prior moment of negation, which in turn goes back to an anterior moment, and so on."

But how does Bloom manage to equate the catastrophic emergence of drive on the level of the psyche with the fear of a literary precursor on the level of Freud's own writing? By identifying the notion of drive itself as Freud's own earlier achievement, an achievement that rises behind him now as a threat (especially if we inflect *Trieb* as "instinct"), a threat Freud must defend against by revising his whole theory of the drives. Here the structure of Freud's mechanisms of mind match the structure of his own texts in another, more elaborate way. If, in *Beyond the Pleasure Principle,* the force of drive threatens the very emergence of the psyche at its origin, then drive itself must be associated with death. And yet how is such a situation possible if drive is also Eros, the drive in its customary, pleasure-seeking role of instinct or libido? In order to explain this impasse, Freud invents the death drive, that realm of mental functioning "beyond the pleasure principle." The sudden result is the alliance of Eros with repression itself in a common struggle against the death instincts. The sexuality that culture represses is, of course, bound to culture and repression for its very existence, since drive itself is only the effect of its contamination or crossing-over by a repression that presumes its force.

Bloom is therefore led to make two crucial identifications: the death instinct equals literal meaning and the life instinct equals figurative meaning. Why? Because the bond of Eros and repression that signifies their complicity in producing one another in a single rhetorical gesture represents the mature Freud's "Sublime" moment of self-conscious achievement as a poet who knows unabashedly that his drives are fictions, rhetorical products of his own knowingly figurative language. Eros, then, stands for the notion of drive as fiction, as figure, bound to culture because it is a literary invention. The earlier Freud, by contrast—and in Freud's own reading of himself—understands drive in a literal sense, in the sense that it is a real biological energy that science can hope to measure. Thanatos or the death drive, then, stands in turn for Freud's notion of drive as a literally available store of libidinal energy or biological essence, the ideal of the early empiricist Freud that the later, poetic Freud wants to "wound," as Bloom puts it, "un-name" or disavow. He does so, says Bloom, by making his own earlier notion of drive as instinct "uncanny" or unfamiliar to himself, and so enters the Sublime in Bloom's precise, and "negative," sense that explains the "terror" that overtakes the tradition in post-Enlightenment culture: "that mode in which the poet, while expressing a previously repressed thought, desire, or emotion, is able to continue to defend himself against his own created image by disowning it."

If the later Freud revises the early Freud by exchanging a notion of drive as quantifiable libido for a notion of drive as immeasurable fiction or trope, the process also includes a theory of literary language as distinct from the language of science, and one that justifies and sustains Freud's status as poet of the Sublime. This is the third focus to emerge in Bloom's essay, and it centers on the revision of the "economic" metaphor for psychic functioning that in the early Freud stands for that very attempt to measure or quantify libido that the late Freud rejects. Indeed, the late Freud, says Bloom, explicitly modifies his notion of the "economic" functioning of the psyche from one that presumes an energy available in nature that can actually be measured or fixed, to one that presumes no more than a set of relationships among forces that can be measured only proportionally, only in the relation of force to force.[38] If Freud's late notion of economy is what Burke means by the proportional, Freud's early notion of economy is what Burke means by the "essentializing" mode of inquiry already labelled scientific. Thus the late Freud becomes an overt poet by criticizing, as Derrida has already suggested, his earlier assumptions about language as a scientist. By abandoning the literal or essentializing language of empiricism — or, as Bloom suggests, by "wounding" it by calling instinct death — Freud embraces instead the proportional or figurative language of literature, a style of language that presumes no stable referent in nature by which its figures may be verified.

This new notion of the economic, says Bloom, allies Freud once again with the Sublime, this time through an exact link with Milton, Freud's favorite poet:

> To estimate the magnitude of such excitation is to ask the classical, agonistic question that *is* the Sublime, because the Sublime is always a comparison of two forces or beings, in which the agon turns on the answer to three queries: more? equal to? or less than? Satan confronting hell, the abyss, the new world, is still seeking to answer the questions that he set for himself in heaven, all of which turn upon comparing God's force and his own.

Thus, *Paradise Lost* is "the most Freudian text ever written," says Bloom, not only because in it "temporality fully becomes identified with anxiety," but also because Freud's language shares with Milton's the same "economic" mechanism of signification, a purely relational one that relies only on the contrasts and comparisons among the elements of its own language to specify a world. For, as Stanley Fish has pointed out,[39] Milton's poem measures *only* by proportion, never by recourse to fixed "symbolic" codes that can translate the size, for example, of Satan's spear. The reasons, of course, are the same for Milton as they are for Freud: not only must prehistory, whether instinctual or creationist, be narrated by the fallen language of consciousness or of history proper; what is being described are, in both cases, also "enabling fictions" to begin with, things, quite literally, out of this world.

[38]See "The Unconscious" (1915), 14:181.

[39]See Stanley Fish, *Surprised by Sin: The Reader in 'Paradise Lost,'* rpt. (Berkeley and Los Angeles: University of California Press, 1971).

The late Freud summarizes the movement of our essays, then, by taking it upon himself to derive the literary status of his work. The cost is the denial of his early phase as naively literal or empirical, a denial more defensive than accurate, more literary than scientific (*The Interpretation of Dreams,* after all, is already a battleground between literal and figurative meaning in its dual interpretative schema), although an aspect of Freud's imagination clear enough from the lifelong revisions of theory that crest in the 1890s, in 1914-15, and in the 1920s. Its only justification is strategic, since Freud takes himself as his own precursor only in order to misread his early work as literal or scientific; in order to appear, in the contrast so initiated, poetic or figurative by comparison. Freud wins poetry by misreading science.

Psychic defense and the creation of literature are in fact the same, converging as they do in the very figure of trope or rhetoric itself, the turning away that is also a figure or structure of language. Freud's late notion of economy describes rhetoric as a defense and defense as a rhetoric by showing how the very trope of defense produces what it defends against by presuming it, just as repression turns away from the drive and so presumes it, too. Economy is in this sense the master figure of Freud's combined theory of language and the psyche, since it is both the structure of literary language (at least as our essayists understand it) at the same time that it is the structure of power, of forces in contention, of the psychoanalytic agon revisited in rhetorical rather than instinctual terms.

Freud's particular power lies in his ability to persuade us of the pressure of the unconscious at the very horizon of life as we know it, and so reminds us that the center of his rhetoric lies in its efforts to produce the unconscious or the id as an intractable jungle that consciousness can struggle against. Here, too, Freud devalues consciousness as a category in order to make the unconscious loom even more powerfully against it, just as the fiction of a lack of conscious precedent for psychoanalysis assures Freud the role of hero and discoverer.

The daunting overdeterminations that threaten the originality of Freud's achievement from the point of view of external literary influence are well documented in our essays, much as Frank Sulloway's biography of Freud documents an equal external influence from the point of view of the history of science.[40] Freud defends himself against this double vortex of literary and scientific precedent in economic terms, too, since the radically double characteristics that make his language literary and scientific at once are

---

[40]See Frank Sulloway, *Freud: Biologist of the Mind* (New York: Basic Books, 1979).

also the ones that free him in turn from the determinations of both traditions. Though Freud's language swerves, often wildly, from the regularities
of literary and scientific discourse alike, each swerve is nonetheless lawful
from the point of view of the other—what is literary is precisely that which
cannot be vouchsafed in the name of science, and vice versa. After all, the
trope of biology, for example, in a late visionary work like *Beyond the
Pleasure Principle*, stands out as a poetic figure only at the moment it
transgresses what biology as a science is privileged to say, that among the
instincts there is one that wishes for death. The boundaries of poetry and
science, in other words, are in each case an effect of the violation of one by
the other. Freud's double language of science and vision, then, is an apparatus or machine, to use Derrida's vocabulary, that allows Freud to employ the rhetoric of each tradition even as it simultaneously frees him from
the obligation to stay bound by either one. Freud's language, then, is
rhetoric and defense at once, a language that situates itself simultaneously
within the contexts of science and poetry, and that in the same gesture in-
sures its independence from both traditions alike. Nor should we forget
that the same literary economy also sustains the early Freud as he invokes
the traditions of dream interpretation, for example, only to deny them,
placing himself among the authorities even as he frees himself from them.
Nor should we forget either that Freud's early masterpiece, like the work
of his late phase, also brings the unconscious into being as an effect of
resistance to it, for example in the staged repression that Freud exercises
over his dream-associations when he hesitates, overtly, strategically, for
fear of revealing too much.

Whether in relation to his own discoveries, then, or in relation to tradition, Freud establishes his priority as a writer by situating both his texts
and the objects of his science in a realm of imagination that benefits from a
wealth of influences while paying taxes to none. The imaginative priority
to be had through economy is perhaps best represented by the mystic
writing-pad, that compensatory machine whose surface remains fresh and
original because it constantly erases influence or stimulation even as it
absorbs and represses it as a series of traces inscribed on the layer beneath.
Like the fiction of consciousness, the original poet like Freud shields himself from influence by admitting and forgetting it, and so becomes a locus
of influences which his genius manages to erase despite the impossibility
of doing so. Just as Shakespeare uses traditions at will in a mingled discourse that appeals to countless regimens while submitting, in the end, to
none in particular, so Freud contaminates science with literature, literature
with science, to produce a prose-poetry whose only real boundaries are
those of his own imagination. And just as Milton chooses the most authoritative of anterior myths in a gamble to assert his priority over the past, so
Freud chooses for his equivalent purposes the most authoritative of anterior

nineteenth-century myths, the myth of science. Like Milton, too, Freud is poised between belief in his enabling myth and belief in himself; between the acknowledgment of his citizenship in a historical community and his desire to stand apart from it; between an inevitable belatedness and an achieved earliness; between, finally, the epic of certainty and the lyric of anxiety.

Everyday Life

By Leonard Woolf

Dr. Brill,[1] who has already translated Freud's greatest and most difficult work, *Die Traumdeutung (The Interpretation of Dreams)*, now makes available for the English reader the far easier and more popular *Zur Psychopathologie des Alltagsleben[s]*. *The Psychopathology of Everyday Life* is a book which naturally would have a wider appeal than Freud's other writings. In the first place, for the serious student of psychology and of the strange application of that science to the art of medicine through psychoanalysis, this book will serve as the best "introduction" to Freud's peculiar theories. To such students one word of warning is necessary. Freud is a most difficult and elusive writer and thinker. One is tempted to say that he suffers from all the most brilliant defects of genius. Whether one believes in his theories or not, one is forced to admit that he writes with great subtlety of mind, a broad and sweeping imagination more characteristic of the poet than the scientist or the medical practitioner. This wide imaginative power accounts for his power of grasping in the midst of intricate analysis of details the bearing of those details upon a much wider and quite other field of details. The result is that he rarely gives, as one of his American disciples has said, a "complete or systematic exposition" of any subject: his works are often a series of brilliant and suggestive hints. And yet, from another point of view, this series of hints is subtly knit together into a whole in such a way that the full meaning of a passage in one book is often only to be obtained by reference to some passage in another book. No one is really competent to give a final judgment upon even *The Psychopathology of Everyday Life* who has not studied *The Interpretation of Dreams,* and Freud's more distinctly pathological writings.

---

[1]A. A. Brill (1874-1948), American physician and psychoanalyst, and Freud's first English-language translator. [Ed.]

But even to that curious product of civilisation, "the ordinary reader," *The Psychopathology of Everyday Life* should be full of interest. It is an eminently readable book. It deals with subjects which to most people are peculiarly fascinating; in the first place, one's self, the working of one's own mind as one goes about the occupations of one's everyday life, lighting a pipe, writing a letter, forgetting a name, or misquoting a line of poetry. Then, as with most of Freud's works, it deals particularly with the more mysterious workings of the human mind, those "recesses" of our own hearts in which the darkness of our ignorance seems to be greater than almost anywhere else. There are few persons who have not felt the fascination of speculating upon the mysteries of the memories of childhood, the curious way in which the door of forgetfulness seems to have closed for us upon so many important happenings, only to open momentarily in a vivid picture of some utterly trivial scene in those dim and earliest years. Or, again, that disturbing and ghostly feeling, as one walks into a strange room, that one has been here before precisely in these circumstances, that everything is happening, things done and words spoken, precisely as everything happened in that mysterious "before," a time and an event, which though it is so insistently real to us, yet seems to belong to a life lived previously or to some forgotten dream.

Many of these subjects the reader will find touched upon in Freud's characteristic way in this book, imaginatively, often humorously, always briefly and suggestively. The ordinary reader will almost certainly pronounce the verdict: "Very interesting but too far-fetched." To discuss the justice of that verdict would require a volume of many pages instead of the one or two columns allowed the reviewer. But this may be said categorically and confidently, that there can be no doubt that there is a substantial amount of truth in the main thesis of Freud's book, and that truth is of great value. The thesis is briefly that a large number of the mental acts of our everyday life which we ordinarily believe to be determined by chance, such as forgetting a name or an intention, making a *lapsus linguae*, or a mistake in writing, are really strictly determined by unconscious and often repressed motives of our own minds. Probably everyone would admit the simplest instances of the unconscious working of motives within us; for instance, everyone is aware of how much more frequently we forget to carry out an unpleasant than a pleasant intention. But Freud's real originality consists in his subtle analysis of many other ordinary mental processes, his peculiar methods of interpretation by which he seeks to bring to the light of consciousness the thoughts and motives which otherwise remain buried in the darkness of our unconsciousness. Here it is that *The Psychopathology of Everyday Life* is linked up with his theories of dreams and his theories of insanity, for his methods of interpretation are very often precisely similar to those used in his interpretation of dreams. It is his aim to show that it is the "dark half" of the mind which in the perfectly normal waking man produces all kinds of trivial errors and slips and forgettings and rememberings, and which under other conditions will, following the same laws, produce the absurd fantasies of sleep or the terrible fantasies of madness.

Freud and Literature

By John Crowe Ransom

As for psycho-analysis, it is quite becoming that the doctors should still disagree about it; but the poets—and under that title must be included all the "makers" who in their laboratories fashion and dissect the souls of men —find much less difficulty in accepting it as gospel truth.

The legends, the mythologies, the demonologies, and the fairy tales of all the races bear witness to the truth of Doctor Freud's startling yet not quite novel theses. To be the complete psycho-analyst implies not only that you are possessed of the historic sense, but that you are also possessed of the prehistoric or biological sense, which believes beyond other senses in the continuity of the life-forms.

For what are our aberrant behaviours but the ways of ghosts that haunt within us, grotesque, antiquated, and forlorn, but still exuberating a little out of their eternal energies?

A man, in the Freudian concept, is not on the one hand one of those bifurcated radishes, with a locomotor arrangement, and a dome at the top which seethes with chemical reactions of considerable intricacy; nor on the other hand is he an adult angel constructed out of light, who knows what he does and does what he intends to do. The Freudian man is multiple rather than simple, many men bound up loosely in one man. He is in fact a pack of demons, going under the name of John Doe for his legal functions, all of them held under the rod in subjection to a mannerly sort of arch-demon, who persuades himself and the world that he is the real John Doe, the one and only.

The other demons are quiet now, as we contemplate Doe in his beautiful integrity, but they will emerge under pressure. And then John Doe will make motions scandalous and mystifying to his society—clearly diabolical, yet if understood possibly wistful or even splendid.

Marvellous is the presumption of that dogmatic modernist Doe—ignorant that he is a cave within whom the fabulous civil war may at any moment go to raging—who thinks that he will take unto himself a little wife, and buy a little home on terms, and devote his eight laborious hours to business, and accomplish a stout and dreamless happiness. Marvellous, though sometimes his egotism seems to be justified by the event; for nothing happens, and he dies, the same little man of the clock at seventy that he was at twenty, and is buried; and perchance if rumor be true he will be raised up in all his simplicity to live again. But that is the most uninteresting case; or rather, that is the outside of his case, but the inside we can only hypothecate.

Naive literature is full of psycho-analysis; its demoniac possessions are half symbolic, and half literal truth; for there is no length to which the poetic imagination will not go. Now it was hardly through literature that Doctor Freud approached his discoveries; nor is it profitable to ask whether the fantastic seizures which he saw overtaking his contemporaries, co-heirs of an age of reason, and which he labored so nobly to alleviate, evoked from him the wry smile to which the irony of the situation entitled him from the literary point of view. But at any rate literature is bound to make an enormous accession of evidence for Freudianism when it is studied for that purpose. And for that matter, the Freudian psychology, if it keeps that name, will be far more than one man's work before it is completed. It will be like a mediaeval Gothic cathedral, for whole generations of scholars will have helped to put it together; and we could delimit offhand a dozen or so separate fields of labor, such as ethnology, biology, comparative religions, primitivisms, language, the "lost knowledge" of symbols, the biography of genius, and poetry. And when the grand edifice is completed, the result will be a complexity and yet a unification of doctrine, perhaps as imposing a structure as the world has seen.

In what sense a unification? In Freudian doctrine the psyche, for all its demons, has much fewer parts than in the old psychology. The old school, whenever it put its finger on a new behaviour, hypostatized a new instinct, a new "faculty." When it encountered one that was unusually irregular, it always wanted to throw up its hands and say, "Madness." But the way of our intellect demands a reduction of these parts, right down to the irreducible. On the Continent a group of thinkers, less tolerant of the heterogenies than the thinkers in our longitude, had already made a great deal of play with sex as a centralizing concept, explaining as forms of that impulse the romances, the idealisms, the labors of genius, and the art-works of man; and this principle they held to without resorting to much actual demonstration. It was Freud's role to reduce to the sex-principle in more scientific fashion; but he is perfectly willing for you to substitute for sex another term, like love, or affectional tendencies, or centrifugal tendencies, if his term is too limited for you by connotations that are specific. Around this center he makes a multitude of otherwise scattering manifestations of behaviour gravitate. It is a simplification of revolutionary proportions; though it will still be true that this basic force of Freud's attaches itself to a variety of objects and gives rise to very mixed personalities, which permit themselves to be conceived (at least by literary people) as demons inhabiting the psyche; some of them atavistic, and continuing an existence of a previous incarnation, and some of them dating back merely into infant or early adult life.

But sex, though much, is not all; and what Freud would now attempt, as he says in a late work, is no less than a meta-psychology, which would write on its broadest lines the fundamental economy of the psyche, with a minimum of improvised and penultimate or antepenultimate terms.

And if this simplification is fully accomplished, and accepted, the world will wonder how it put up so long with the psychological monstrosity, the fantasticum, that our books said must pass for a man. Nothing in the whole realm of knowledge is changing so fast nor so radically as psychology, and the rate of the change is the rate at which we throw off an inherited accumulation of terms (but not a synthesis) which made a man, the total, a crazy apparatus. Copernicus overthrew the Ptolemaic astronomy by virtue of inventing a principle that accounted economically for the celestial motions without recourse to such vagaries as the eccentrics and epicycles with which the Ptolemaists had to patch their system together. Just such a revolution, it seems to a member of the laity, is in process with respect to the theory of man and his behaviour; and Doctor Freud himself has admitted with charming candor that his psychology offers the best economy in sight.

Already a new literature has sprung up to welcome the new learning. Sherwood Anderson here, and Lawrence and Miss West and Miss Sinclair and the author [David Garnett] of the brilliant (but too facile) *Lady into Fox* in England, to call a few names. Their exhibit is of something deeper and richer that we find in their old-style contemporaries, precisely as one of Doctor Freud's technical studies seems to be less desiccated and to hold a better converse with fundamental realities than the formulas of the eclectics. And yet in this literature generally, it must be admitted, there is an accent which is repulsive to the reading public; it deals too frankly with aberrations of sex, in the specific sense of the term.

In this sense sex is still taboo in literature; it is obscene just as in the Greek tragedy certain parts of the fable were obscene and must take place off the stage. The literary adaptators of psycho-analysis have very boldly and with a rather crude art translated the most sensational features of the science bodily into literature, where they are calculated to become accessible to the general public. This procedure need not be considered fatal to the new art. It is probable that the artists can, as they have usually been required to do, find artistic ways of handling a dangerous material, and that they can also try material no less rich in ultimate interest which is not so immediately spectacular. At any rate it is evident that the world is far from ready to allow these artists, on the plea of their new learning, to alter suddenly the whole technique of literature.

For if we are not mistaken, the fundamental character of literature is to become a public property as soon as it is uttered; and any instance is by so much the less a piece of literature as it has lost sight of this function. It must offer a value readily both to the many and to the few. It may be that we should be too exacting of literature if we required that it should never intimidate the people by its difficulty, but certainly we are in our rights in requiring that it must never affront them with an attack upon their morality. And so the fable, the obvious meaning of literature, lies on the surface to be easily appropriated by the people; but the initiated, according to their several degrees of advancement in the mysteries, can find further meanings suitable to their need, and these become more and more esoteric. Literature emulates the Apostle in attempting to be all things to all men, nor are men ever too humble to be the proper objects of its interest. And since the humblest must have their access as well as the greatest, literature becomes a study in indirection: its highest meaning, which is generally unsuitable for popular use, is discoverable but not manifest, and nowhere by its unconventionality does it flout what the orator terms "the moral sensibilities of decent men."

Our literary giants hitherto, who have obeyed so well this last maxim, have not on the other hand been so conspicuously lacking in the depth of their psychology—that is, in their power to psycho-analyse—as the new school might wish to believe. This phenomenon is easily possible by reason of the fact that psycho-analysis is not at all points a new technique, but rather the systematic or scientific application of a technique that poets and artists have generally been aware of. Any good novelist, for example, tends to derive the behaviour of his characters from the deepest sources that he knows, and shows a considerable power in factoring the multiples which are his characters. Henry James was interested in the study of race—and place—types in their most perfect bloom, or where they were furthest from their roots, and hardest to derive; but he goes conscientiously backwards into origins all the same; and differs eternally from the best-seller writer in this, that he had a perfect sense of the toughness of the strains that compose an individual life, and never works the fiat of the omnipotent author who by a stroke of his pen will make his characters conform to the fable which he has, with an eye to the fruits of his hire, after all predetermined. It was Conrad's habit also to deal in fundamental cores of character which never evaporated even in the unlikeliest milieu. And Galsworthy is extremely sensitive to the conditions of continuance and decay of inherited type-tendencies.

We do not impeach the truthfulness or the profundity of these writers when we say that with access to psycho-analysis proper they might have found truth and depth even readier to their hands and teeming with vaster multitudes of significant life-forms. This we say because we have been convinced in our own experience of how much light psycho-analysis can throw upon the baffling relations of life—and of how much more epic and fascinating it shows the daily business of being human to be.

And another kind of evidence will show us to what a poor pass an inadequate psychology, even in the hands of able writers, can bring a literature. The Main Street school of fiction constitutes this exhibit. Very banal, mean-spirited, and provincial is this pure Americanism which distinguishes the present literary period in America. Writers in this field, for all the smartness of their realism, and of course with more than a tithe of exceptional passages in which they are nobler than their program, are as schoolmasters and schoolma'ams going forth to make a "survey" of some selected section of the American community; preferably a section of rustics; or village-dwellers. The aim of this survey is to ascertain the state of "culture" extant among the specimens; the method is to compile the details of spoken idiom, of interior decoration, of religious ceremonies, of public amusements, of etiquette, of the ritual of sewing societies and luncheon clubs—in all of which the surveyed fall far short of a certain standard. Of course the total effect is devastating. Now it is too true that we have never had in this country a noble literature of the soil, as England has had it; but would not even we miss something from our reading if we can imagine what would happen to the literature of the soil in England (or in Scandinavia or in Russia) if it were systematically rewritten from the Main Street school's point of view? The two performances would differ *toto caelo*. As the case stands, it is unlikely that there has been mourning in Heaven over one sinner of Mr. Hardy's for smacking his lips over his Wessex mead or taking peasant's license with Queen Victoria's English. The dignity of a man does not depend upon his equipment in the negotiable goods of culture, nor could a profound psychologist be deluded into thinking that in such equipment lie the solid satisfactions of a man's life; that is the thinking of pedants and spinsters who do not themselves know life, and, failing that, are not even versed in a thorough-going psychology, like psycho-analysis. But when *Winesburg, Ohio* appeared, it almost seemed as if for the first time in our history American humble folk were depicted in the possession of their inalienable human rights, by virtue of exercising frankly those radical and immitigable passions which are the most that human beings can possess; they were not again being set down in that ignominy to which our literary pedants had usually consigned them.

Demonology is always poetic, and so have been the implications of Doctor Freud's studies in psycho-analysis. But nothing of his has ever so teased the poetic imagination as the vast and brilliant speculations in his last two small volumes.

Incidentally, he has hazarded these speculations with more than his habitual caution, and the modesty with which he propounds his opinions ought to be an example to the embittered anti-Freudians.

In *Beyond the Pleasure Principle,* his thesis is briefly as follows. The instincts generally—though he is unable to say always—seem to have the character of repetition-compulsions. They repeat the reactions that served life in a previous incarnation when it was organically more simple. But one by one these repetitions have to be discarded as inadequate to the new complications of existence; actually, as is very well known, the embryo vainly goes through the successive forms of lower life, and is permitted to stop on none of them. The persistence of these useless repetitions indicates then the resentment which the individual feels towards the pain of his eternal process of adaptations. And therefore it may be said that the instincts express the individual's natural preference for quietude and death rather than life. His evolution into an intricate organism, which in the collective mass with others makes what we call civilization, is an achievement not of his own wish, but due to the stimuli impinging incessantly and inescapably upon him. "In the last resort it must have been the evolution of our earth, and its relation to the sun, that has left its imprint on the development of organisms."

The philosophy shadowed by this remarkable hypothesis has obvious affiliations with Schopenhauer, though the latter's equipment was evidently in intuition rather than science. Schopenhauer's pessimistic consequence is very properly taboo in the moral or practical world, but should at any rate receive from the English-speaking races its due as philosophy.

Without committing themselves at the present time, literary scholars might at least do this service for Freud's latest thesis, since it would in any case constitute a disinterested service to truth in general: they might marshal some of the enormous mass of testimony to be found in English poetry, under its camouflage, for the Will to Die. It is quite likely that the English poets have celebrated one thing more than immortality, and that is mortality. With a veil over their obscenity they gloat on death, to whom even beauty and love are prey. Human life may be surveyed at this stage in that spirit which may turn out to be the last and most rational of all the modes of mind—the spirit of tragic irony. To be a tragic ironist is to be aware sharply and grimly, but not too painfully, of the constant involvement of life with death. In that spirit Homer sang, and the makers of the ballads, and Shakespeare the maker of sonnets and plays—

> To-morrow, and to-morrow, and to-morrow,
> Creeps in this petty pace from day to day,
> To the last syllable of recorded time;
> And all our yesterdays have lighted fools
> The way to dusty death.

Freud and the Future

By Thomas Mann

We are gathered here to do honour to a great scientist. And the question may very properly be raised: what justifies a man of letters in assuming the role of spokesman on such an occasion? Or, passing on the responsibility to the members of the learned society which chose him, why should they not have selected one of their own kind, a man of science, rather than an author, to celebrate in words the birthday of their master? For an author, my friends, is a man essentially not bent upon science, upon knowing, distinguishing, and analysing; he stands for simple creation, for doing and making, and thus may be the object of useful cognition, without, by his very nature, having any competence in it as subject. But is it, perhaps, that the author in his character as artist, and artist in the field of the intellect, is especially called to the celebration of feasts of the mind; that he is by nature more a man of feast-days than the scientist and man of knowledge? It is not for me to dispute such a view. It is true, the poet has understanding of the feasts of life, understanding even of life as a feast — and here I am just touching, very lightly for the moment, upon a theme that may become a main motif in the chorus of homage which we are to perform this evening. But it is more likely that the sponsors of this evening had something else in mind in their choice: that is to say, the solemn and novel confrontation of object and subject, the object of knowledge with the knower — a saturnalia, as it were, in which the knower and seer of dreams himself becomes, by our act of homage, the object of dreamlike penetration. And to such a position I could not object, either; particularly because it strikes a chord capable in the future of great symphonic development. It will recur, more clearly accented and fully instrumented. For, unless I am greatly mistaken, it is just this confrontation of object and subject, their mingling and identification, the resultant insight into the mysterious unity of ego and actuality, destiny and character, doing and happening, and thus into the mystery of reality as an operation of the psyche—it is just this confrontation that is the alpha and omega of all psychoanalytical knowledge.

Be that as it may, the choice of an artist as the encomiast of a great scientist is a comment upon both. In the first place, one deduces from it a connection between the man of genius we now honour and the world of creative literature; in the second place, it displays the peculiar relations between the writer and the field of science whose declared and acknowledged master and creator the other is. Now, the unique and remarkable thing about this mutual close relation is that it remained for so long unconscious—that is, in that region of the soul which we have learned to call the unconscious, a realm whose discovery and investigation, whose conquest for humanity, are precisely the task and mission of the wise genius whose fame we celebrate. The close relation between literature and psychoanalysis has been known for a long time to both sides. But the solemn significance of this hour lies, at least in my eyes and as a matter of personal feeling, in that on this evening there is taking place the first official meeting between the two spheres, in the acknowledgment and demonstration of their relationship.

I repeat that the profound sympathy between the two spheres had existed for a long time unperceived. Actually we know that Sigmund Freud, that mighty spirit in whose honour we are gathered together, founder of psychoanalysis as a general method of research and as a therapeutic technique, trod the steep path alone and independently, as physician and natural scientist, without knowing that reinforcement and encouragement lay to his hand in literature. He did not know Nietzsche, scattered throughout whose pages one finds premonitory flashes of truly Freudian insight; he did not know Novalis, whose romantic-biologic fantasies so often approach astonishingly close to analytic conceptions; he did not know Kierkegaard, whom he must have found profoundly sympathetic and encouraging for the Christian zeal which urged him on to psychological extremes; and, finally, he did not know Schopenhauer, the melancholy symphonist of a philosophy of the instinct, groping for change and redemption. Probably it must be so. By his unaided effort, without knowledge of any previous intuitive achievement, he had methodically to follow out the line of his own researches; the driving force of his activity was probably increased by this very freedom from special advantage. And we think of him as solitary—the attitude is inseparable from our earliest picture of the man. Solitary in the sense of the word used by Nietzsche in that ravishing essay "What is the Meaning of Ascetic Ideals?" when he characterizes Schopenhauer as "a genuine philosopher, a self-poised mind, a man and gallant knight, stern-eyed, with the courage of his own strength, who knows how to stand alone and not wait on the beck and nod of superior officers." In this guise of man and gallant knight, a knight between Death and the Devil, I have been used to picture to myself our psychologist of the unconscious, ever since his figure first swam into my mental ken.

That happened late—much later than one might have expected, considering the connection between this science and the poetic and creative impulse in general and mine in particular. The connection, the bond between them, is twofold: it consists first in a love of truth, in a sense of truth, a sensitiveness and receptivity for truth's sweet and bitter, which largely expresses itself in a psychological excitation, a clarity of vision, to such an extent that the conception of truth actually almost coincides with that of psychological perception and recognition. And secondly it consists in an understanding of disease, a certain affinity with it, outweighed by fundamental health, and an understanding of its productive significance.

As for the love of truth: the suffering, morally conditioned love of truth *as psychology*—that has its origin in Nietzsche's lofty school, where in fact the coincidence of "truth" and "psychological truth," of the knower with the psychologist, is striking indeed. His proud truthfulness, his very conception of intellectual honesty, his conscious and melancholy fearlessness in its service, his self-knowledge, self-crucifixion—all this has psychological intention and bearing. Never shall I forget the deepening, strengthening, formative effect upon my own powers produced by my acquaintance with Nietzsche's psychological agony. In *Tonio Kröger* the artist speaks of being "sick of knowledge." That is true Nietzsche language; and the youth's melancholy has reference to the Hamlet-like in Nietzsche's nature, in which his own mirrored itself: a nature called to knowledge without being genuinely born to it. These are the pangs and anguishes of youth, destined to be lightened and tranquillized as years flowed by and brought ripeness with them. But there has remained with me the desire for a psychological interpretation of knowledge and truth; I still equate them with psychology and feel the psychological will to truth as a desire for truth in general; still interpret psychology as truth in the most actual and courageous sense of the word. One would call the tendency a naturalistic one, I suppose, and ascribe it to a training in literary naturalism; it forms a precondition of receptivity for the natural science of the psyche—in other words, for what is known as psychoanalysis.

I spoke of a second bond between that science and the creative impulse: the understanding of disease, or, more precisely, of disease as an instrument of knowledge. That, too, one may derive from Nietzsche. He well knew what he owed to his morbid state, and on every page he seems to instruct us that there is no deeper knowledge without experience of disease, and that all heightened healthiness must be achieved by the route of illness. This attitude too may be referred to his experience; but it is bound up with the nature of the intellectual man in general, of the creative artist in particular, yes, with the nature of humanity and the human being, of which last of course the creative artist is an extreme expression. *"L 'humanité,"* says Victor Hugo, *"s'affirme par l'infirmité."* A saying which frankly and proudly admits the delicate constitution of all higher humanity and culture and their connoisseurship in the realm of disease. Man has been called *"das kranke Tier"* because of the burden of strain and explicit difficulties laid upon him by his position between nature and spirit, between angel and brute. What wonder, then, that by the approach through abnormality we have succeeded in penetrating most deeply into the darkness of human nature; that the study of disease—that is to say, neurosis—has revealed itself as a first-class technique of anthropological research?

The literary artist should be the last person to be surprised at the fact. Sooner might he be surprised that he, considering his strong general and individual tendency, should have so late become aware of the close sympathetic relations which connected his own existence with psychoanalytic research and the life-work of Sigmund Freud. I realized this connection only at a time when his achievement was no longer thought of as merely a therapeutic method, whether recognized or disputed; when it had long since outgrown his purely medical implications and become a world movement which penetrated into every field of science and every domain of the intellect: literature, the history of art, religion and prehistory; mythology, folklore, pedagogy, and what not— thanks to the practical and constructive zeal of experts who erected a structure of more general investigation round the psychiatric and medical core. Indeed, it would be too much to say that I came to psychoanalysis. It came to me. Through the friendly interest that some younger workers in the field had shown in my work, from *Little Herr Friedemann* to *Death in Venice, The Magic Mountain,* and the *Joseph* novels, it gave me to understand that in my way I "belonged"; it made me aware, as probably behoved it, of my own latent, preconscious sympathies; and when I began to occupy myself with the literature of psychoanalysis I recognized, arrayed in the ideas and the language of scientific exactitude, much that had long been familiar to me through my youthful mental experiences.

Perhaps you will kindly permit me to continue for a while in this autobiographical strain, and not take it amiss if instead of speaking of Freud I speak of myself. And indeed I scarcely trust myself to speak *about* him. What new thing could I hope to say? But I shall also, quite explicitly, be speaking in his honour in speaking of myself, in telling you how profoundly and peculiarly certain experiences decisive for my development prepared me for the Freudian experience. More than once, and in many places, I have confessed to the profound, even shattering impression made upon me as a young man by contact with the philosophy of Arthur Schopenhauer, to which then a monument was erected in the pages of *Budden-*

brooks. Here first, in the pessimism of a metaphysics already very strongly equipped on the natural-science side, I encountered the dauntless zeal for truth that stands for the moral aspect of the psychology of the unconscious. This metaphysics, in obscure revolt against centuries-old beliefs, preached the primacy of the instinct over mind and reason; it recognized the will as the core and the essential foundation of the world, in man as in all other created beings; and the intellect as secondary and accidental, servant of the will and its pale illuminant. This it preached not in malice, not in the anti-human spirit of the mind-hostile doctrines of today, but in the stern love of truth characteristic of the century which combated idealism out of love for the ideal. It was so sincere, that nineteenth century, that—through the mouth of Ibsen—it pronounced the lie, the lies of life, to be indispensable. Clearly there is a vast difference whether one assents to a lie out of sheer hatred of truth and the spirit or for the sake of that spirit, in bitter irony and anguished pessimism! Yet the distinction is not clear to everybody today.

Now, Freud, the psychologist of the unconscious, is a true son of the century of Schopenhauer and Ibsen—he was born in the middle of it. How closely related is his revolution to Schopenhauer's, not only in its content, but also in its moral attitude! His discovery of the great role played by the unconscious, the id, in the soul-life of man challenged and challenges classical psychology, to which the consciousness and the psyche are one and the same, as offensively as once Schopenhauer's doctrine of the will challenged philosophical belief in reason and the intellect. Certainly the early devotee of *The World as Will and Idea* is at home in the admirable essay that is included in Freud's *New Introductory Essays in Psychoanalysis* under the title "The Anatomy of the Mental Personality." It describes the soul-world of the unconscious, the id, in language as strong, and at the same time in as coolly intellectual, objective, and professional a tone, as Schopenhauer might have used to describe his sinister kingdom of the will. "The domain of the id," he says, "is the dark, inaccessible part of our personality; the little that we know of it we have learned through the study of dreams and of the formation of neurotic symptoms." He depicts it as a chaos, a melting-pot of seething excitations. The id, he thinks, is, so to speak, open towards the somatic, and receives thence into itself compulsions which there find psychic expression—in what substratum is unknown. From these impulses it receives its energy; but it is not organized, produces no collective will, merely the striving to achieve satisfaction for the impulsive needs operating under the pleasure principle. In it no laws of thought are valid, and certainly not the law of opposites. "Contradictory stimuli exist alongside each other without cancelling each other out or even detracting from each other; at most they unite in compromise forms under the compulsion of the controlling economy for the release of energy." You perceive that this is a situation which, in the historical experience of our own day, can take the upper hand with the ego, with a whole mass-ego, thanks to a moral devastation which is produced by worship of the unconscious, the glorification of its dynamic as the only life-promoting force, the systematic glorification of the primitive and irrational. For the unconscious, the id, is primitive and irrational, is pure dynamic. It knows no values, no good or evil, no morality. It even knows no time, no temporal flow, nor any effect of time upon its psychic process. "Wish stimuli," says Freud, "which have never overpassed the id, and impressions which have been repressed into its depths, are virtually indestructible, they survive decade after decade as though they had just happened. They can only be recognized as belonging to the past, devalued and robbed of their charge of energy, by becoming conscious through the analytic procedure." And he adds that therein lies pre-eminently the healing effect of analytic treatment. We perceive accordingly how antipathetic deep analysis must be to an ego that is intoxicated by a worship of the unconscious to the point of being in a condition of subterranean dynamic. It is only too clear and understandable that such an ego is deaf to analysis and that the name of Freud must not be mentioned in its hearing.

As for the ego itself, its situation is pathetic, well-nigh alarming. It is an alert, prominent, and enlightened little part of the id—much as Europe is a small and lively province of the greater Asia. The ego is that part of the id which became modified by contact with the outer world; equipped for the reception and preservation of stimuli; comparable to the integument with which any piece of living matter surrounds itself. A very perspicuous biological picture. Freud writes indeed a very perspicuous prose, he is an artist of thought, like Schopenhauer, and like him a writer of European rank. The relation with the outer world is, he says, decisive for the ego, it is the ego's task to represent the world to the id—for its good! For without regard for the superior power of the outer world the id, in its blind striving towards the satisfaction of its instincts, would not escape destruction. The ego takes cognizance of the outer world, it is mindful, it honourably tries to distinguish the objectively real from whatever is an accretion from its inward sources of stimulation. It is entrusted by the id with the lever of action; but between the impulse and the action it has interposed the delay of the thought-process, during which it summons experience to its aid and thus possesses a certain regulative superiority over the pleasure principle which rules supreme in the unconscious, correcting it by means of the principle of reality. But even so, how feeble it is! Hemmed in between the unconscious, the outer world, and what Freud calls the super-ego, it leads a pretty nervous and anguished existence. Its own dynamic is rather weak. It derives its energy from the id and in general has to carry out the latter's behests. It is fain to regard itself as the rider and the unconscious as the horse. But many a time it is ridden by the unconscious; and I take leave to add what Freud's rational morality prevents him from saying, that under some circumstances it makes more progress by this illegitimate means.

But Freud's description of the id and the ego—is it not to a hair Schopenhauer's description of the Will and the Intellect, a translation of the latter's metaphysics into psychology? So he who had been initiated into the metaphysics of Schopenhauer and in Nietzsche tasted the painful pleasure of psychology—he must needs have been filled with a sense of recognition and familiarity when first, encouraged thereto by its denizens, he entered the realms of psychoanalysis and looked about him.

He found too that his new knowledge had a strange and strong retroactive effect upon the old. After a sojourn in the world of Freud, how differently, in the light of one's new knowledge, does one reread the reflections of Schopenhauer, for instance his great essay "Transcendent Speculations on Apparent Design in the Fate of the Individual"! And here I am about to touch upon the most profound and mysterious point of contact between Freud's natural-scientific world and Schopenhauer's philosophic one. For the essay I have named, a marvel of profundity and penetration, constitutes this point of contact. The pregnant and mysterious idea there developed by Schopenhauer is briefly this: that precisely as in a dream it is our own will that unconsciously appears as inexorable objective destiny, everything in it proceeding out of ourselves and each of us being the secret theatre-manager of our own dreams, so also in reality the great dream that a single essence, the will itself, dreams with us all, our fate, may be the product of our inmost selves, of our wills, and we are actually ourselves bringing about what seems to be happening to us. I have only briefly indicated here the content of the essay, for these representations are winged with the strongest and most sweeping powers of suggestion. But not only does the dream psychology which Schopenhauer calls to his aid bear an explicitly psychoanalytic character, even to the presence of the sexual argument and paradigm; but the whole complexus of thought is a philosophical anticipation of analytical conceptions, to a quite astonishing extent. For, to repeat what I said in the beginning, I see in the mystery of the unity of the ego and the world, of being and happening, in the perception of the apparently objective and accidental as a matter of the soul's own contriving, the innermost core of psychoanalytic theory.

And here there occurs to me a phrase from the pen of C. G. Jung, an able but somewhat ungrateful scion of the Freudian school, in his significant introduction to the Tibetan *Book of the Dead*. "It is so much more direct, striking, impressive, and thus convincing," he says, "to see how it happens to me than to see how I do it." A bold, even an extravagant statement, plainly betraying the calmness with which in a certain school of psychology certain things are regarded which even Schopenhauer con-

sidered prodigiously daring speculation. Would this unmasking of the
"happening" as in reality "doing" be conceivable without Freud? Never!
It owes him everything. It is weighted down with assumptions, it could not
be understood, it could never have been written, without all that analysis
has brought to light about slips of tongue and pen, the whole field of human
error, the retreat into illness, the psychology of accidents, the self-punish-
ment compulsion—in short, all the wizardry of the unconscious. Just as
little, moreover, would that close-packed sentence of Jung's, including its
psychological premises, have been possible without Schopenhauer's ad-
venturous pioneering speculation. Perhaps this is the moment, my friends,
to indulge on this festive occasion in a little polemic against Freud himself. He does not esteem philosophy very highly. His scientific exactitude
does not permit him to regard it as a science. He reproaches it with imagining that it can present a continuous and consistent picture of the world;
with overestimating the objective value of logical operations; with believing
in intuitions as a source of knowledge and with indulging in positively
animistic tendencies, in that it believes in the magic of words and the influence of thought upon reality. But would philosophy really be thinking too
highly of itself on these assumptions? Has the world ever been changed by
anything save by thought and its magic vehicle the Word? I believe that in
actual fact philosophy ranks before and above the natural sciences and that
all method and exactness serve its intuitions and its intellectual and historical will. In the last analysis it is always a matter of the *quod erat demon-
strandum*. Scientific freedom from assumptions is or should be a moral
fact. But intellectually it is, as Freud points out, probably an illusion. One
might strain the point and say that science has never made a discovery
without being authorized and encouraged thereto by philosophy.

All this by the way. But it is in line with my general intention to pause
a little longer at the sentence that I quoted from Jung. In this essay and also
as a general method which he uses by preference, Jung applies analytical
evidence to form a bridge between Occidental thought and Oriental esoteric.
Nobody has focused so sharply as he the Schopenhauer-Freud perception
that "the giver of all given conditions resides in ourselves—a truth which
despite all evidence in the greatest as well as in the smallest things *never*
becomes conscious, though it is only too often necessary, even indispensable, that it should be." A great and costly change, he thinks, is needed
before we understand how the world is "given" by the nature of the soul;
for man's animal nature strives against seeing himself as the maker of his
own conditions. It is true that the East has always shown itself stronger than
the West in the conquest of our animal nature, and we need not be surprised
to hear that in its wisdom it conceives even the gods among the "given conditions" originating from the soul and one with her, light and reflection
of the human soul. This knowledge, which, according to the *Book of the*

Dead, one gives to the deceased to accompany him on his way, is a paradox to the Occidental mind, conflicting with its sense of logic, which distinguishes between subject and object and refuses to have them coincide or make one proceed from the other. True, European mysticism has been aware of such attitudes, and Angelus Silesius said:

> I know that without me God cannot live a moment;
> If I am destroyed He must give up the ghost.

But on the whole a psychological conception of God, an idea of the godhead which is not pure condition, absolute reality, but one with the soul and bound up with it, must be intolerable to Occidental religious sense—it would be equivalent to abandoning the idea of God.

Yet religion—perhaps even etymologically—essentially implies a bond. In Genesis we have talk of the bond (covenant) between God and man, the psychological basis of which I have attempted to give in the mythological novel *Joseph and His Brothers.* Perhaps my hearers will be indulgent if I speak a little about my own work; there may be some justification for introducing it here in this hour of formal encounter between creative literature and the psychoanalytic. It is strange—and perhaps strange not only to me—that in this work there obtains precisely that psychological theology which the scholar ascribes to Oriental esoteric. This Abram is in a sense the father of God. He perceived and brought Him forth; His mighty qualities, ascribed to Him by Abram, were probably His original possession, Abram was not their inventor, yet in a sense he was, by virtue of his recognizing them and therewith, by taking thought, making them real. God's mighty qualities—and thus God Himself—are indeed something objective, exterior to Abram; but at the same time they are in him and of him as well; the power of his own soul is at moments scarcely to be distinguished from them, it consciously interpenetrates and fuses with them—and such is the origin of the bond which then the Lord strikes with Abram, as the explicit confirmation of an inward fact. The bond, it is stated, is made in the interest of both, to the end of their common sanctification. Need human and need divine here entwine until it is hard to say whether it was the human or the divine that took the initiative. In any case the arrangement shows that the holiness of man and the holiness of God constituted a twofold process, one part being most intimately bound up with the other. Wherefore else, one asks, should there be a bond at all?

The soul as "giver of the given"—yes, my friends, I am well aware that in the novel this conception reaches an ironic pitch which is not authorized either in Oriental wisdom or in psychological perception. But there is something thrilling about the unconscious and only later discovered harmony. Shall I call it the power of suggestion? But sympathy would be a better word: a kind of intellectual affinity, of which naturally psychoanaly-

sis was earlier aware than was I, and which proceeded out of those literary
appreciations which I owed to it at an earlier stage. The latest of these was
an offprint of an article that appeared in *Imago,* written by a Viennese
scholar of the Freudian school, under the title "On the Psychology of the
Older School of Biography." The rather dry title gives no indication of the
remarkable contents. The writer shows how the older and simpler type of
biography and in particular the written lives of artists, nourished and conditioned by popular legend and tradition, assimilate, as it were, the life of
the subject to the conventionalized stock-in-trade of biography in general,
thus imparting a sort of sanction to their own performance and establishing
its genuineness; making it authentic in the sense of "as it always was" and
"as it has been written." For man sets store by recognition, he likes to find
the old in the new, the typical in the individual. From that recognition he
draws a sense of the familiar in life, whereas if it painted itself as entirely
new, singular in time and space, without any possibility of resting upon
the known, it could only bewilder and alarm. The question, then, which is
raised by the essay, is this: can any line be sharply and unequivocally
drawn between the formal stock-in-trade of legendary biography and the
characteristics of the single personality—in other words, between the
typical and the individual? A question negatived by its very statement. For
the truth is that life is a mingling of the individual elements and the formal
stock-in-trade; a mingling in which the individual, as it were, only lifts his
head above the formal and impersonal elements. Much that is extra-personal, much unconscious identification, much that is conventional and
schematic, is none the less decisive for the experience not only of the artist
but of the human being in general. "Many of us," says the writer of the article, "'live' today a biographical type, the destiny of a class or rank or
calling. The freedom in the shaping of the human being's life is obviously
connected with that bond which we term 'lived *vita.*'" And then, to my delight, but scarcely to my surprise, he begins to cite from *Joseph,* the fundamental motif of which he says is precisely this idea of the "lived life," life
as succession, as a moving in others' steps, as identification—such as Joseph's
teacher, Eliezer, practises with droll solemnity. For in him time is can-
celled and all the Eliezers of the past gather to shape the Eliezer of the
present, so that he speaks in the first person of that Eliezer who was Abram's
servant, though he was far from being the same man.

I must admit that I find the train of thought extraordinarily convincing.
The essay indicates the precise point at which the psychological interest
passes over into the mythical. It makes it clear that the typical is actually
the mythical, and that one may as well say "lived myth" as "lived life."
But the mythus as lived is the epic idea embodied in my novel; and it is
plain to me that when as a novelist I took the step in my subject-matter
from the bourgeois and individual to the mythical and typical my personal

connection with the analytic field passed into its acute stage. The mythical interest is as native to psychoanalysis as the psychological interest is to all creative writing. Its penetration into the childhood of the individual soul is at the same time a penetration into the childhood of mankind, into the primitive and mythical. Freud has told us that for him all natural science, medicine, and psychotherapy were a lifelong journey round and back to the early passion of his youth for the history of mankind, for the origins of religion and morality—an interest which at the height of his career broke out to such magnificent effect in *Totem and Taboo*. The word *Tiefenpsychologie* ("deep" psychology) has a temporal significance; the primitive foundations of the human soul are likewise primitive time, they are those profound time-sources where the myth has its home and shapes the primeval norms and forms of life. For the myth is the foundation of life; it is the timeless schema, the pious formula into which life flows when it reproduces its traits out of the unconscious. Certainly when a writer has acquired the habit of regarding life as mythical and typical there comes a curious heightening of his artist temper, a new refreshment to his perceiving and shaping powers, which otherwise occurs much later in life; for while in the life of the human race the mythical is an early and primitive stage, in the life of the individual it is a late and mature one. What is gained is an insight into the higher truth depicted in the actual; a smiling knowledge of the eternal, the ever-being and authentic; a knowledge of the schema in which and according to which the supposed individual lives, unaware, in his naive belief in himself as unique in space and time, of the extent to which his life is but formula and repetition and his path marked out for him by those who trod it before him. His character is a mythical role which the actor just emerged from the depths to the light plays in the illusion that it is his own and unique, that he, as it were, has invented it all himself, with a dignity and security of which his supposed unique individuality in time and space is not the source, but rather which he creates out of his deeper consciousness in order that something which was once founded and legitimized shall again be represented and once more for good or ill, whether nobly or basely, in any case after its own kind conduct itself according to pattern. Actually, if his existence consisted merely in the unique and the present, he would not know how to conduct himself at all; he would be confused, helpless, unstable in his own self-regard, would not know which foot to put foremost or what sort of face to put on. His dignity and security lie all unconsciously in the fact that with him something timeless has once more emerged into the light and become present; it is a mythical value added to the otherwise poor and valueless single character; it is native worth, because its origin lies in the unconscious.

Such is the gaze which the mythically oriented artist bends upon the phenomena about him—an ironic and superior gaze, as you can see, for the mythical knowledge resides in the gazer and not in that at which he gazes. But let us suppose that the mythical point of view could become subjective; that it could pass over into the active ego and become conscious there, proudly and darkly yet joyously, of its recurrence and its typicality, could celebrate its role and realize its own value exclusively in the knowledge that it was a fresh incarnation of the traditional upon earth. One might say that such a phenomenon alone could be the "lived-myth"; nor should we think that it is anything novel or unknown. The life in the myth, life as a sacred repetition, is a historical form of life, for the man of ancient times lived thus. An instance is the figure of the Egyptian Cleopatra, which is Ishtar, Astarte, Aphrodite in person. Bachofen, in his description of the cult of Bacchus, the Dionysiac religion, regards the Egyptian queen as the consummate picture of a Dionysiac *stimula;* and according to Plutarch it was far more her erotic intellectual culture than her physical charms that entitled her to represent the female as developed into the earthly embodiment of Aphrodite. But her Aphrodite nature, her role of Hathor-Isis, is not only objective, not only a treatment of her by Plutarch or Bachofen; it was the content of her subjective existence as well, she lived the part. This we can see by the manner of her death: she is supposed to have killed herself by laying an asp upon her bosom. But the snake was the familiar of Ishtar, the Egyptian Isis, who is represented clad in a garment of scales; also there exists a statuette of Ishtar holding a snake to her bosom. So that if Cleopatra's death was as the legend represents, the manner of it was a manifestation of her mythical ego. Moreover, did she not adopt the falcon hood of the goddess Isis and adorn herself with the insignia of Hathor, the cow's horns with the crescent moon between? And name her two children by Mark Antony Helios and Selene? No doubt she was a very significant figure indeed—significant in the antique sense, that she was well aware who she was and in whose footsteps she trod!

The ego of antiquity and its consciousness of itself were different from our own, less exclusive, less sharply defined. It was, as it were, open behind; it received much from the past and by repeating it gave it presentness again. The Spanish scholar Ortega y Gasset puts it that the man of antiquity, before he did anything, took a step backwards, like the bull-fighter who leaps back to deliver the mortal thrust. He searched the past for a pattern into which he might slip as into a diving-bell, and being thus at once disguised and protected might rush upon his present problem. Thus his life was in a sense a reanimation, an archaizing attitude. But it is just this life as reanimation that is the life as myth. Alexander walked in the footsteps of Miltiades; the ancient biographers of Caesar were convinced, rightly or wrongly, that he took Alexander as his prototype. But such "imitation" meant far more than we mean by the word today. It was a mythical identification, peculiarly familiar to antiquity; but it is operative far into modern times, and at all times is psychically possible. How often have we not been told that the figure of Napoleon was cast in the antique mould! He regretted that the mentality of the time forbade him to give himself out for the son of Jupiter Ammon, in imitation of Alexander. But we need not doubt that—at least at the period of his Eastern exploits—he mythically confounded himself with Alexander; while after he turned his face westwards he is said to have declared: "I am Charlemagne." Note that: not "I am like Charlemagne" or "My situation is like Charlemagne's," but quite simply: "I am he." That is the formulation of the myth. Life, then—at any rate, significant life—was in ancient times the reconstitution of the myth in flesh and blood; it referred to and appealed to the myth; only through it, through reference to the past, could it approve itself as genuine and significant. The myth is the legitimization of life; only through and in it does life find self-awareness, sanction, consecration. Cleopatra fulfilled her Aphrodite character even unto death—and can one live and die more significantly or worthily than in the celebration of the myth? We have only to think of Jesus and His life, which was lived in order that that which was written might be fulfilled. It is not easy to distinguish between His own consciousness and the conventionalizations of the Evangelists. But His word on the Cross, about the ninth hour, that *"Eli, Eli, lama sabachthani?"* was evidently not in the least an outburst of despair and disillusionment; but on the contrary a lofty messianic sense of self. For the phrase is not original, not a spontaneous outcry. It stands at the beginning of the Twenty-second Psalm, which from one end to the other is an announcement of the Messiah. Jesus was quoting, and the quotation meant: "Yes, it is I!" Precisely thus did Cleopatra quote when she took the asp to her breast to die; and again the quotation meant: "Yes, it is I!"

Let us consider for a moment the word "celebration" which I used in this connection. It is a pardonable, even a proper usage. For life in the myth, life, so to speak, in quotation, is a kind of celebration, in that it is a making present of the past, it becomes a religious act, the performance by a celebrant of a prescribed procedure; it becomes a feast. For a feast is an anniversary, a renewal of the past in the present. Every Christmas the world-saving Babe is born again on earth, to suffer, to die, and to arise. The feast is the abrogation of time, an event, a solemn narrative being played out conformably to an immemorial pattern; the events in it take place not for the first time, but ceremonially according to the prototype. It achieves presentness as feasts do, recurring in time with their phases and hours following on each other in time as they did in the original occurrence. In antiquity each feast was essentially a dramatic performance, a mask; it was the scenic reproduction, with priests as actors, of stories about the gods—as for instance the life and sufferings of Osiris. The Christian Middle Ages had their mystery play, with heaven, earth, and the torments of hell—just as we have it later in Goethe's *Faust;* they had their carnival farce, their folk-mime. The artist eye has a mythical slant upon life, which makes it look like a farce, like a theatrical performance of a prescribed feast, like a Punch and Judy epic, wherein mythical character puppets reel off a plot abiding from past time and now again present in a jest. It only lacks that this mythical slant pass over and become subjective in the performers themselves, become a festival and mythical consciousness of part and play, for an epic to be produced such as that in the first volume of the *Joseph and His Brothers* series, particularly in the chapter "The Great Hoaxing." There a mythical recurrent farce is tragicomically played by personages all of whom well know in whose steps they tread: Isaac, Esau, and Jacob; and who act out the cruel and grotesque tale of how Esau the Red is led by the nose and cheated of his birthright to the huge delight of all the bystanders. Joseph too is another such celebrant of life; with charming mythological hocus-pocus he enacts in his own person the Tammuz-Osiris myth, "bringing to pass" anew the story of the mangled, buried, and arisen god, playing his festival game with that which mysteriously and secretly shapes life out of its own depths—the unconscious. The mystery of the metaphysician and psychologist, that the soul is the giver of all given conditions, becomes in Joseph easy, playful, blithe—like a consummately artistic performance by a fencer or juggler. It reveals his *infantile* nature—and the word I have used betrays how closely, though seeming to wander so far afield, we have kept to the subject of our evening's homage.

Infantilism—in other words, regression to childhood—what a role this genuinely psychoanalytic element plays in all our lives! What a large share it has in shaping the life of a human being; operating, indeed, in just the way I have described: as mythical identification, as survival, as a treading in footprints already made! The bond with the father, the imitation of the father, the game of being the father, and the transference to father-substitute pictures of a higher and more developed type—how these infantile traits work upon the life of the individual to mark and shape it! I use the word "shape," for to me in all seriousness the happiest, most pleasurable element of what we call education *(Bildung),* the shaping of the human being, is just this powerful influence of admiration and love, this childish identification with a father-image elected out of profound affinity. The artist in particular, a passionately childlike and play-possessed being, can tell us of the mysterious yet after all obvious effect of such infantile imitation upon his own life, his productive conduct of a career which after all is often nothing but a reanimation of the hero under very different temporal and personal conditions and with very different, shall we say childish means. The *imitatio* Goethe, with its Werther and Wilhelm Meister stages, its old-age period of *Faust* and *Diwan,* can still shape and mythically mould the life of an artist—rising out of his unconscious, yet playing over—as is the artist way—into a smiling, childlike, and profound awareness.

The Joseph of the novel is an artist, playing with his *imitatio dei* upon the unconscious string; and I know not how to express the feelings which possess me—something like a joyful sense of divination of the future—when I indulge in this encouragement of the unconscious to play, to make itself fruitful in a serious product, in a narrational meeting of psychology and myth, which is at the same time a celebration of the meeting between poetry and analysis.

And now this word "future": I have used it in the title of my address, because it is this idea, the idea of the future, that I involuntarily like best to connect with the name of Freud. But even as I have been speaking I have been asking myself whether I have not been guilty of a cause of confusion; whether—from what I have said up to now—a better title might not have been something like "Freud and the Myth." And yet I rather cling to the combination of name and word and I should like to justify and make clear its relation to what I have so far said. I make bold to believe that in that novel so kin to the Freudian world, making as it does the light of psychology play upon the myth, there lie hidden seeds and elements of a new and coming sense of our humanity. And no less firmly do I hold that we shall one day recognize in Freud's life-work the cornerstone for the building of a new anthropology and therewith of a new structure, to which many stones are being brought up today, which shall be the future dwelling of a wiser and freer humanity. This physicianly psychologist will, I make no doubt at all, be honoured as the path-finder towards a humanism of the future, which we dimly divine and which will have experienced much that the earlier humanism knew not of. It will be a humanism standing in a different relation to the powers of the lower world, the unconscious, the id: a relation bolder, freer, blither, productive of a riper art than any possible in our neurotic, fear-ridden, hate-ridden world. Freud is of the opinion that the significance of psychoanalysis as a science of the unconscious will in the future far outrank its value as a therapeutic method. But even as a science of the unconscious it is a therapeutic method, in the grand style, a method overarching the individual case. Call this, if you choose, a poet's utopia; but the thought is after all not unthinkable that the resolution of our great fear and our great hate, their conversion into a different relation to the unconscious which shall be more the artist's, more ironic and yet not necessarily irreverent, may one day be due to the healing effect of this very science.

The analytic revelation is a revolutionary force. With it a blithe scepticism has come into the world, a mistrust that unmasks all the schemes and subterfuges of our own souls. Once roused and on the alert, it cannot be put to sleep again. It infiltrates life, undermines its raw naïveté, takes from it the strain of its own ignorance, de-emotionalizes it, as it were, inculcates the taste for understatement, as the English call it—for the deflated rather than for the inflated word, for the cult which exerts its influence by moderation, by modesty. Modesty—what a beautiful word! In the German *(Bescheidenheit)* it originally had to do with knowing and only later got its present meaning; while the Latin word from which the English comes means a way of doing—in short, both together give us almost the sense of the French *savoir faire*—to know how to do. May we hope that this may be the fundamental temper of that more blithely objective and peaceful world which the science of the unconscious may be called to usher in?

Its mingling of the pioneer with the physicianly spirit justifies such a hope. Freud once called his theory of dreams "a bit of scientific new-found land won from superstition and mysticism." The word "won" expresses the colonizing spirit and significance of his work. "Where id was, shall be ego," he epigrammatically says. And he calls analysis a cultural labour comparable to the draining of the Zuider Zee. Almost in the end the traits of the venerable man merge into the lineaments of the grey-haired Faust, whose spirit urges him

> to shut the imperious sea from the shore away,
> Set narrower bounds to the broad water's waste.
>
> Then open I to many millions space
> Where they may live, not safe-secure, but free
> And active. And such a busy swarming I would see
> Standing amid free folk on a free soil.

The free folk are the people of a future freed from fear and hate, and ripe for peace.

Psychology and Art To-Day

By W. H. Auden

> Neither in my youth nor later was I able to detect in myself any
> particular fondness for the position or work of a doctor. I was,
> rather, spurred on by a sort of itch for knowledge which con-
> cerned human relationships far more than the data of natural
> science.
>
> FREUD
>
> Mutual forgiveness of each vice
> Such are the gates of paradise.
>
> BLAKE

To trace, in the manner of the textual critic, the influence of Freud
upon modern art, as one might trace the influence of Plutarch upon
Shakespeare, would not only demand an erudition which few, if any,
possess, but would be of very doubtful utility. Certain writers, notably
Thomas Mann and D. H. Lawrence, have actually written about Freud,
certain critics, Robert Graves in *Poetic Unreason* and Herbert Read in
Form in Modern Poetry, for example, have made use of Freudian terminology, surrealism has adopted a technique resembling the procedure in
the analyst's consulting-room;[1] but the importance of Freud to art is
greater than his language, technique or the truth of theoretical details. He
is the most typical but not the only representative of a certain attitude to
life and living relationships, and to define that attitude and its importance
to creative art must be the purpose of this essay.

"Psychology and Art To-day," by W. H. Auden. From *The English Auden: Poems, Essays,
and Dramatic Writings, 1927-39* by W. H. Auden, edited by Edward Mendelson (New York:
Random House, 1977), pp. 332-42. Copyright © 1977 by Edward Mendelson, William Meredith,
and Monroe K. Spears, Executors of the Estate of W. H. Auden. Reprinted by permission of
Random House, Inc., and Faber and Faber, Ltd. The essay originally appeared in *The Arts
To-day* (1935), ed. Geoffrey Grigson.

[1]But not the first. The Elizabethans used madness, not as a subject for clinical description but
as opportunity for a particular kind of associational writing (e.g., *Lear* or *The Duchess of Malfi*).
Something of the kind occurs even earlier in the nonsense passages in the mummer's play.

The Artist in History

Of the earliest artists, the palaeolithic rock-drawers, we can of course know nothing for certain, but it is generally agreed that their aim was a practical one, to gain power over objects by representing them; and it has been suggested that they were probably bachelors, i.e., those who, isolated from the social group, had leisure to objectify the phantasies of their group, and were tolerated for their power to do so. Be that as it may, the popular idea of the artist as socially ill adapted has been a constant one, and not unjustified. Homer may have been blind, Milton certainly was, Beethoven deaf, Villon a crook, Dante very difficult, Pope deformed, Swift impotent, Proust asthmatic, Van Gogh mental, and so on. Yet parallel with this has gone a belief in their social value. From the chiefs who kept a bard, down to the Shell-Mex exhibition, patronage, however undiscriminating, has never been wanting as a sign that art provides society with something for which it is worth paying. On both these beliefs, in the artist as neurotic, and in the social value of art, psychology has thrown a good deal of light.

The Artist as Neurotic

There is a famous passage in Freud's introductory lectures which has infuriated artists, not altogether unjustly:

> Before you leave to-day I should like to direct your attention for a moment to a side of phantasy-life of very general interest. There is, in fact, a path from phantasy back again to reality, and that is—art. The artist has also an introverted disposition and has not far to go to become neurotic. He is one who is urged on by instinctive needs which are too clamorous; he longs to attain to honour, power, riches, fame, and the love of women; but he lacks the means of achieving these gratifications. So, like any other with an unsatisfied longing, he turns away from reality and transfers all his interest, and all his Libido, too, on to the creation of his wishes in life. There must be many factors in combination to prevent this becoming the whole outcome of his development; it is well known how often artists in particular suffer from partial inhibition of their capacities through neurosis. Probably their constitution is endowed with a powerful capacity for sublimation and with a certain flexibility in the repressions determining the conflict. But the way back to reality is found by the artist thus: He is not the only one who has a life of phantasy; the intermediate world of phantasy is sanctioned by general human consent, and every hungry soul looks to it for comfort and consolation. But to those who are not artists the gratification that can be drawn from the springs of phantasy is very limited; their inexorable repressions prevent the enjoyment

of all but the meagre daydreams which can become conscious. A true artist has more at his disposal. First of all he understands how to elaborate his day-dreams, so that they lose that personal note which grates upon strange ears and become enjoyable to others; he knows too how to modify them sufficiently so that their origin in prohibited sources is not easily detected. Further, he possesses the mysterious ability to mould his particular material until it expresses the idea of his phantasy faithfully; and then he knows how to attach to this reflection of his phantasy-life so strong a stream of pleasure that, for a time at least, the repressions are out-balanced and dispelled by it. When he can do all this, he opens out to others the way back to the comfort and consolation of their own unconscious sources of pleasure, and so reaps their gratitude and admiration; then he has won—through his phantasy—what before he could only win in phantasy: honour, power, and the love of women.

Misleading though this may be, it draws attention to two facts, firstly that no artist, however "pure", is disinterested: he expects certain rewards from his activity, however much his opinion of their nature may change as he develops; and he starts from the same point as the neurotic and the day-dreamer, from emotional frustration in early childhood.

The artist like every other kind of "highbrow" is self-conscious, i.e., he is all of the time what everyone is some of the time, a man who is active rather than passive to his experience. A man struggling for life in the water, a schoolboy evading an imposition, or a cook getting her mistress out of the house is in the widest sense a highbrow. We only think when we are prevented from feeling or acting as we should like. Perfect satisfaction would be complete unconsciousness. Most people, however, fit into society too neatly for the stimulus to arise except in a crisis such as falling in love or losing their money.[2] The possible family situations which may produce the artist or intellectual are of course innumerable, but those in which one of the parents, usually the mother, seeks a conscious spiritual, in a sense, adult relationship with the child are probably the commonest. E.g.,

(1) When the parents are not physically in love with each other. There are several varieties of this: the complete fiasco; the brother-sister relationship on a basis of common mental interests; the invalid-nurse relationship when one parent is a child to be maternally cared for; and the unpassionate relation of old parents.

(2) The only child. This alone is most likely to produce early life confidence which on meeting dissappointment, turns like the unwanted child, to illness and anti-social behaviour to secure attention.

[2] E.g., the sale of popular text-books on economics since 1929.

(3)   The youngest child. Not only are the parents old but the whole family field is one of mental stimulation.[3]

Early mental stimulation can interfere with physical development and intensify the conflict. It is a true intuition that makes the caricaturist provide the highbrow with a pair of spectacles. Myopia, deafness, delayed puberty, asthma—breathing is the first independent act of the child— are some of the attempts of the mentally awakened child to resist the demands of life.

To a situation of danger and difficulty there are five solutions:

(1)   To sham dead: The idiot.

(2)   To retire into a life of phantasy: The schizophrene.

(3)   To panic, i.e., to wreak one's grudge upon society: The criminal.

(4)   To excite pity, to become ill: The invalid.

(5)   To understand the mechanism of the trap: The scientist and the artist.

Art and Phantasy

In the passage of Freud quoted above, no distinction was drawn between art and phantasy, between—as Mr. Roger Fry once pointed out—*Madame Bovary* and a *Daily Mirror* serial about earls and housemaids. The distinction is one which may perhaps be best illustrated by the difference between two kinds of dream. "A child has in the afternoon passed the window of a sweetshop, and would have liked to buy some chocolate it saw there, but its parents have refused the gift—so the child dreams of chocolate"—here is a simple wish fulfillment dream of the *Daily Mirror* kind, and all art, as the juvenile work of artists, starts from this level. But it does not remain there. For the following dream and its analysis I am indebted to Dr. Maurice Nicoll's *Dream Psychology:*

A young man who had begun to take morphia, but was not an addict, had the following dream:

"I was hanging by a rope a short way down a precipice. Above me on the top of the cliff was a small boy who held the rope. I was not alarmed because I knew I had only to tell the boy to pull and I would get to the top safely." The patient could give no associations.

The dream shows that the morphinist has gone a certain way from the top of the cliff—the position of normal safety—down the side of the precipice, but he is still in contact with that which remains on the top. That

[3]The success of the youngest son in folk tales is instructive. He is generally his mother's favourite as physically weaker and less assertive than his brothers. If he is often called stupid, his stupidity is physical. He is clumsy and lazy rather than dull. (Clumsiness being due to the interference of fancies with sense data.) He succeeds partly out of good nature and partly because confronted with a problem he overcomes it by understanding rather than with force.

which remains on the top is now relatively small, but is not inanimate like a fort, but alive: it is a force operating from the level of normal safety. This force is holding the dreamer back from the gulf, but that is all. It is for the dreamer himself to say the word if he wants to be pulled up (i.e., the morphinist is *deliberately* a morphinist).

When the common phrase is used that a man's will is weakening as he goes along some path of self-indulgence, it implies that something is strengthening. What is strengthening is the attractive power of vice. But in the dream, the attractive power of morphia is represented by the force of gravitation, and the force of gravitation is constant.

But there are certain variable elements in the dream. The position of the figure over the cliff can vary and with it the length of the rope. The size of the figure at the top of the cliff might also vary without in any way violating the spirit of the dream. If then, we examine the length of the rope and the size of the figure on the cliff top in the light of relatively variable factors, the explanation of the *smallness* of the figure on the cliff top may be found to lie in the length of the rope, as if the rope drew itself out of the figure, and so caused it to shrink.

Now the figure at the top of the cliff is on firm ground and may there symbolise the forces of some habit and custom that exist in the morphinist and from which he has departed over the edge of the cliff, but which still hold him back from disaster although they are now shrunken. The attractive power of the morphia is not increasing, but *the interest the morphinist takes in morphia* is increasing.

A picture of the balance of interest in the morphinist is thus given, and the dream shows that the part of interest situated in the cliff top is now being drawn increasingly over the precipice.

In this dream, we have something which resembles art much more closely. Not only has the censor transformed the latent content of the dream into symbols but the dream itself is no longer a simple wish fulfilment, it has become constructive, and, if you like, moral. "A picture of the balance of interest"—that is a good description of a work of art. To use a phrase of Blake's, "It's like a lawyer serving a writ."

Craftsmanship

There have always been two views of the poetic process, as an inspiration and as a craft, of the poet as the Possessed and as the Maker, e.g.,

> All good poets, epic as well as lyric, compose their beautiful poems not by art, but because they are inspired and possessed.
>
> SOCRATES

> That talk of inspiration is sheer nonsense: there is no
> such thing; it is a matter of craftsmanship.
>
> WILLIAM MORRIS

And corresponding to this, two theories of imagination:

> Natural objects always weaken, deaden, and obliterate
> imagination in me.
>
> BLAKE

> Time and education beget experience: experience
> begets memory; memory begets judgment and fancy.
> ...Imagination is nothing else but sense decaying or
> weakened by the absence of the object.
>
> HOBBES

The public, fond of marvels and envious of success without trouble, has
favoured the first (see any film of artists at work); but the poets themselves,
painfully aware of the labour involved, on the whole have inclined towards
the second. Psycho-analysis, naturally enough, first turned its attention to
those works where the workings of the unconscious were easiest to follow —
Romantic literature like *Peer Gynt,* "queer" plays like *Hamlet,* or fairy
tales like *Alice in Wonderland.* I should doubt if Pope's name occurs in any
text-book. The poet is inclined to retort that a great deal of literature is not
of this kind, that even in a short lyric, let alone a sustained work, the
material immediately "given" to consciousness, the automatic element, is
very small, that, in his own experience, what he is most aware of are technical problems, the management of consonants and vowels, the counterpoint-
ing of scenes, or how to get the husband off the stage before the lover's
arrival, and that psychology concentrating on the symbols, ignores words;
in his treatment of symbols and facts he fails to explain why of two works
dealing with the same unconscious material, one is aesthetically good and
the other bad; indeed that few psycho-analysts in their published work
show any signs of knowing that aesthetic standards exist.

Psycho-analysis, he would agree, has increased the artist's interest in
dreams, mnemonic fragments, child art and graffiti, etc., but that the interest is a *conscious* one. Even the most surrealistic writing or Mr. James
Joyce's latest prose shows every sign of being non-automatic and extremely
carefully worked over.

The Conscious Element

Creation, like psycho-analysis, is a process of re-living in a new situation.
There are three chief elements:

(1) The artist himself, a certain person at a certain time with his own limited conflicts, phantasies and interests.

(2) The data from the outer world which his senses bring him, and which, under the influence of his instincts, he selects, stores, enlarges upon, and by which he sets value and significance.

(3) The artistic medium, the new situation, which because it is not a personal, but a racial property (and psychological research into the universality of certain symbols confirms this), makes communication possible, and art more than an autobiographical record. Just as modern physics teaches that every physical object is the centre of a field of force which radiating outwards occupies all space and time, so psychology states that every word through fainter and fainter associations is ultimately a sign for the universe. The associations are always greater than those of an individual. A medium complicates and distorts the creative impulse behind it. It is, in fact, largely the medium, and thorough familiarity with the medium, with its unexpected results, that enables the artist to develop from elementary uncontrolled phantasy, to deliberate phantasy directed towards understanding.

What Would Be a Freudian Literature

Freudianism cannot be considered apart from other features of the contemporary environment, apart from modern physics with its conception of transformable energy, modern technics, and modern politics. The chart here given makes no attempt to be complete, or accurate; it ignores the perpetual overlap of one historical period with another, and highly important transition periods, like the Renaissance. It is only meant to be suggestive, dividing the Christian era into three periods, the first ending with the fifteenth century, the second with the nineteenth, and the third just beginning; including what would seem the typical characteristics of such periods.

	1st Period.	*2nd Period.*	*3rd Period.*
First Cause:	God immanent and transcendent.	Official: God transcendent. The universal mechanic. Opposition: God immanent. Pantheism. Romantic.	Energy appearing in many measurable forms, fundamental nature unknown.
World View:	The visible world as symbol of the eternal.	Official: The material world as a mechanism. Opposition: The spiritual world as a private concern.	The interdependence of observed and observer.

	1st Period. (cont.)	*2nd Period.* (cont.)	*3rd Period.* (cont.)
The End of Life:	The City of God.	Official: Power over material. Opposition: Personal salvation.	The good life on earth.
Means of Realisation:	Faith and work. The rules of the Church.	Official: Works without moral values. Opposition: Faith.	Self-understanding.
Personal Driving Forces:	Love of God. Submission of private will to will of God.	Official: Conscious will. Rationalised. Mechanised. Opposition: Emotion. Irrational.	The unconscious directed by reason.
The Sign of Success:	The mystical union.	Wealth and power.	Joy.
The Worst Sinner:	The heretic.	The idle poor (Opposition view— the respectable bourgeois).	The deliberate irrationalist.
Scientific Method:	Reasoning without experiment.	Experiment and reason: the experimenter considered impartial. Pure truth. Specialisation.	Experiment directed by conscious human needs.
Sources of Power:	Animal. Wind. Water.	Water. Steam.	Electricity.
Technical Materials:	Wood. Stone.	Iron. Steel.	Light alloys.
Way of Living:	Agricultural and trading. Small towns. Balance of town and country.	Valley towns. Industrialism. Balance of town and country upset.	Dispersed units connected by electrical wires. Restored balance of town and country.
Economic System:	Regional units. Production for use. Usury discouraged.	Laissez-faire Capitalism. Scramble for markets.	Planned socialism.
Political System:	Feudal hierarchy.	National democracy. Power in hands of capitalists.	International Democracy. Government by an Order.

Freud belongs to the third of these phases, which in the sphere of psychology may be said to have begun with Nietzsche (though the whole of Freud's teaching may be found in *The Marriage of Heaven and Hell*). Such psychology is historically derived from the Romantic reaction, in particular from Rousseau, and this connection has obscured in the minds of the general public, and others, its essential nature. To the man in the street, "Freudian" literature would embody the following beliefs:

(1) Sexual pleasure is the only real satisfaction. All other activities are an inadequate and remote substitute.

(2) All reasoning is rationalisation.

(3) All men are equal before instincts. It is my parents' fault in the way they brought me up if I am not a Napoleon or a Shakespeare.

(4) The good life is to do as you like.

(5) The cure for all ills is *(a)* indiscriminate sexual intercourse; *(b)* autobiography.

The Implications of Freud

I do not intend to take writers one by one and examine the influence of Freud upon them. I wish merely to show what the essence of Freud's teaching is, that the reader may judge for himself. I shall enumerate the chief points as briefly as possible:

(1) The driving force in all forms of life is instinctive; a libido which of itself is undifferentiated and unmoral, the "seed of every virtue and of every act which deserves punishment."

(2) Its first forms of creative activity are in the ordinary sense of the word physical. It binds cells together and separates them. The first bond observable between individuals is a sexual bond.

(3) With the growth in importance of the central nervous system with central rather than peripheral control, the number of modes of satisfaction to which the libido can adapt itself become universally increased.

(4) Man differs from the rest of the organic world in that his development is unfinished.

(5) The introduction of self-consciousness was a complete break in development, and all that we recognise as evil or sin is its consequence. Freud differs both from Rousseau who denied the Fall, attributing evil to purely local conditions ("Rousseau thought all men good by nature. He found them evil and made no friend"), and also from the theological doctrine which makes the Fall the result of a deliberate choice, man being therefore morally responsible.

(6)   The result of this Fall was a divided consciousness in place of the single animal consciousness, consisting of at least three parts: a conscious mind governed by ideas and ideals; the impersonal unconscious from which all its power of the living creature is derived but to which it was largely denied access; and a personal unconscious, all that morality or society demanded should be forgotten and unexpressed.[4]

(7)   The nineteenth century doctrine of evolutionary progress, of man working out the beast and letting the ape and tiger die, is largely false. Man's phylogenetic ancestors were meek and sociable, and cruelty, violence, war, all the so-called primitive instincts, do not appear until civilisation has reached a high level. A golden age, comparatively speaking (and anthropological research tends to confirm this), is an historical fact.

(8)   What we call evil was once good, but has been outgrown, and refused development by the conscious mind with its moral ideas. This is the point in Freud which D. H. Lawrence seized and to which he devoted his life:

> Man is immoral because he has got a mind
> And can't get used to the fact.

The danger of Lawrence's writing is the ease with which his teaching about the unconscious, by which he means the impersonal unconscious, may be read as meaning, "let your personal unconscious have its fling," i.e., the *acte gratuit* of André Gide. In personal relations this itself may have a liberating effect for the individual. "If the fool would persist in his folly he would become wise." But folly is folly all the same and a piece of advice like "Anger is just. Justice is never just," which in private life is a plea for emotional honesty, is rotten political advice, where it means "beat up those who disagree with you." Also Lawrence's concentration on the fact that if you want to know what a man is, you must look at his sexual life, is apt to lead many to believe that pursuit of a sexual goal is the only necessary activity.

(9)   Not only what we recognise as sin or crime, but all illness, is purposive. It is an attempt at cure.

(10)   All change, either progressive or regressive, is caused by frustration or tension. Had sexual satisfaction been completely adequate human development could never have occurred. Illness and intellectual activity are both reactions to the same thing, but not of equal value.

(11)   The nature of our moral ideas depends on the nature of our relations with our parents.

(12)   At the root of all disease and sin is a sense of guilt.

(13)   Cure consists in taking away the guilt feeling, in the forgiveness of sins, by confession, the re-living of the experience, and by absolution, understanding its significance.

---

[4]The difference between the two unconscious minds is expressed symbolically in dreams, e.g., motor-cars and manufactured things express the personal unconscious, horses, etc., the impersonal.

(14) The task of psychology, or art for that matter, is not to tell people how to behave, but by drawing their attention to what the impersonal unconscious is trying to tell them, and by increasing their knowledge of good and evil, to render them better able to choose, to become increasingly morally responsible for their destiny.

(15) For this reason psychology is opposed to all generalisations; force people to hold a generalisation and there will come a time when a situation will arise to which it does not apply. Either they will force the generalisation, the situation, the repression, when it will haunt them, or they will embrace its opposite. The value of advice depends entirely upon the context. You cannot tell people what to do, you can only tell them parables; and that is what art really is, particular stories of particular people and experiences, from which each according to his immediate and peculiar needs may draw his own conclusions.

(16) Both Marx and Freud start from the failures of civilisation, one from the poor, one from the ill. Both see human behaviour determined, not consciously, but by instinctive needs, hunger and love. Both desire a world where rational choice and self-determination are possible. The difference between them is the inevitable difference between the man who studies crowds in the street, and the man who sees the patient, or at most the family, in the consulting-room. Marx sees the direction of the relations between outer and inner world from without inwards, Freud vice versa. Both are therefore suspicious of each other. The socialist accuses the psychologist of caving in to the status quo, trying to adapt the neurotic to the system, thus depriving him of a potential revolutionary: the psychologist retorts that the socialist is trying to lift himself by his own boot tags, that he fails to understand himself, or the fact that lust for money is only one form of the lust for power; and so that after he has won his power by revolution he will recreate the same conditions. Both are right. As long as civilisation remains as it is, the number of patients the psychologist can cure are very few, and as soon as socialism attains power, it must learn to direct its own interior energy and will need the psychologist.

Conclusion

Freud has had certain obvious technical influences on literature, particularly in its treatment of space and time, and the use of words in associational rather than logical sequence. He has directed the attention of the writer to material such as dreams and nervous tics hitherto disregarded; to relations as hitherto unconsidered as the relations between people playing tennis; he has revised hero-worship.

He has been misappropriated by irrationalists eager to escape their conscience. But with these we have not, in this essay, been concerned. We have tried to show what light Freud has thrown on the genesis of the artist and his place and function in society, and what demands he would make upon the serious writer. There must always be two kinds of art, escape-art, for man needs escape as he needs food and deep sleep, and parable-art, that art which shall teach man to unlearn hatred and learn love, which can enable Freud to say with greater conviction:

> We may insist as often as we please that the human intellect is powerless when compared with the impulses of man, and we may be right in what we say. All the same there is something peculiar about this weakness. The voice of the intellect is soft and low, but it is persistent and continues until it has secured a hearing. After what may be countless repetitions, it does get a hearing. This is one of the few facts which may help to make us rather more hopeful about the future of mankind.

Freud—and the Analysis of Poetry

By Kenneth Burke

The reading of Freud I find suggestive almost to the point of bewilderment. Accordingly, what I should like most to do would be simply to take representative excerpts from his work, copy them out, and write glosses upon them. Very often these glosses would be straight extensions of his own thinking. At other times they would be attempts to characterize his strategy of presentation with reference to interpretative method in general. And, finally, the Freudian perspective was developed primarily to chart a psychiatric field rather than an aesthetic one; but since we are here considering the analogous features of these two fields rather than their important differences, there would be glosses attempting to suggest how far the literary critic should go along with Freud and what extra-Freudian material he would have to add. Such a desire to write an article on Freud in the margins of his books, must for practical reasons here remain a frustrated desire. An article such as this must condense by generalization, which requires me to slight the most stimulating factor of all—the detailed articulacy in which he embodies his extraordinary frankness.

Freud's frankness is no less remarkable by reason of the fact that he had perfected a method for being frank. He could say humble, even humiliating, things about himself and us because he had changed the rules somewhat and could make capital of observations that others, with vested interests of a different sort, would feel called upon to suppress by dictatorial decree. Or we might say that what for him could fall within the benign category of observation could for them fall only within its malign counterpart, spying.

Yet though honesty is, in Freud, methodologically made easier, it is by no means honesty made easy. And Freud's own accounts of his own dreams show how poignantly he felt at times the "disgrace" of his occupation. There are doubtless many thinkers whose strange device might be *ecclesia super cloacam.* What more fitting place to erect one's church than above a sewer! One might even say that sewers are what churches are for. But usually this is done by laying all the stress upon the ecclesia and its beauty. So that, even when the man's work fails to be completed for him as a social act, by the approval of his group, he has the conviction of its intrinsic beauty to give him courage and solace.

But to think of Freud, during the formative years of his doctrines, confronting something like repugnance among his colleagues, and even, as his dreams show, in his own eyes, is to think of such heroism as Unamuno found in Don Quixote; and if Don Quixote risked the social judgment of ridicule, he still had the consolatory thought that his imaginings were beautiful, stressing the ecclesia aspect, whereas Freud's theories bound him to a more drastic self-ostracizing act—the charting of the relations between ecclesia and cloaca that forced him to analyze the cloaca itself. Hence, his work was with the confessional as cathartic, as purgative; this haruspicy required an inspection of the entrails; it was, bluntly, an interpretative sculpting of excrement, with beauty replaced by a science of the grotesque.

Confronting this, Freud does nonetheless advance to erect a structure which, if it lacks beauty, has astounding ingeniousness and fancy. It is full of paradoxes, of leaps across gaps, of vistas—much more so than the work of many a modern poet who sought for nothing else but these and had no search for accuracy to motivate his work. These qualities alone would make it unlikely that readers literarily inclined could fail to be attracted, even while repelled. Nor can one miss in it the profound charitableness that is missing in so many modern writers who, likewise concerned with the cloaca, become efficiently concerned with nothing else, and make of their work pure indictment, pure oath, pure striking-down, pure spitting-upon, pure kill. True, this man, who taught us so much about father-rejection and who ironically became himself so frequently the rejected father in the works of his schismatic disciples, does finally descend to quarrelsomeness, despite himself, when recounting the history of the psychoanalytic movement. But, over the great course of his work, it is the matter of human rescue that he is concerned with—not the matter of vengeance. On a few occasions, let us say, he is surprised into vengefulness. But the very essence of his studies, even at their most forbidding moments (in fact, precisely at those moments), is its charitableness, its concern with salvation. To borrow an excellent meaningful pun from Trigant Burrow, this salvation is approached not in terms of religious hospitality but rather in terms of secular hospitalization. Yet it is the spirit of Freud; it is what Freud's courage is for.

Perhaps, therefore, the most fitting thing for a writer to do, particularly in view of the fact that Freud is now among the highly honored class—the exiles from Nazi Germany (how accurate those fellows are! how they seem, with almost 100 per cent efficiency, to have weeded out their greatest citizens!)—perhaps the most fitting thing to do would be simply to attempt an article of the "homage to Freud" sort and call it a day.

However, my job here cannot be confined to that. I have been commissioned to consider the bearing of Freud's theories upon literary criticism. And these theories were not designed primarily for literary criticism at all but were rather a perspective that, developed for the charting of a nonaesthetic field, was able (by reason of its scope) to migrate into the aesthetic field. The margin of overlap was this: The acts of the neurotic are symbolic acts. Hence in so far as both the neurotic act and the poetic act share this property in common, they may share a terminological chart in common. But in so far as they deviate, terminology likewise must deviate. And this deviation is a fact that literary criticism must explicitly consider.

As for the glosses on the interpretative strategy in general, they would be of this sort: For one thing, they would concern a distinction between what I should call an essentializing mode of interpretation and a mode that stresses proportion of ingredients. The tendency in Freud is toward the first of these. That is, if one found a complex of, let us say, seven ingredients in a man's motivation, the Freudian tendency would be to take one of these as the essence of the motivation and to consider the other six as sublimated variants. We could imagine, for instance, manifestations of sexual impotence accompanying a conflict's in one's relations with his familiars and one's relations at the office. The proportional strategy would involve the study of these three as a cluster. The motivation would be synonymous with the interrelationships among them. But the essentializing strategy would, in Freud's case, place the emphasis upon the sexual manifestation, as causal ancestor of the other two.

This essentializing strategy is linked with a normal ideal of science: to "explain the complex in terms of the simple." This ideal almost vows one to select one or another motive from a cluster and interpret the others in terms of it. The naive proponent of economic determinism, for instance, would select the quarrel at the office as the essential motive, and would treat the quarrel with familiars and the sexual impotence as mere results of this. Now, I don't see how you can possibly explain the complex in terms of the simple without having your very success used as a charge against you. When you get through, all that your opponent need say is: "But you have explained the complex in terms of the simple—and the simple is precisely what the complex is not."

Perhaps the faith philosophers, as against the reason philosophers, did not have to encounter a paradox at this point. Not that they avoided paradoxes, for I think they must always cheat when trying to explain how evil can exist in a world created by an all-powerful and wholly good Creator. But at least they did not have to confront the complexity-simplicity difficulty, since their theological reductions referred to a ground in God, who was simultaneously the ultimately complex and the ultimately simple. Naturalistic strategies lack this convenient "out"—hence their explanations are simplifications, and every simplification is an over-simplification.[1]

It is possible that the literary critic, taking communication as his basic category, may avoid this particular paradox (communication thereby being a kind of attenuated God term). You can reduce everything to communication—yet communication is extremely complex. But, in any case, communication is by no means the basic category of Freud. The sexual wish, or libido, is the basic category; and the complex forms of communication that we see in a highly alembicated philosophy would be mere sublimations of this.

A writer deprived of Freud's clinical experience would be a fool to question the value of his category as a way of analyzing the motives of the class of neurotics Freud encountered. There is a pronouncedly individualistic element in any technique of salvation (my toothache being alas! my private property), and even those beset by a pandemic of sin or microbes will enter heaven or get discharged from the hospital one by one; and the especially elaborate process of diagnosis involved in Freudian analysis even to this day makes it more available to those suffering from the ills of preoccupation and leisure than to those suffering from the ills of occupation and unemployment (with people generally tending to be only as mentally sick as they can afford to be). This state of affairs makes it all the more likely that the typical psychoanalytic patient would have primarily private sexual motivations behind his difficulties. (Did not Henry James say that sex is something about which we think a great deal when we are not thinking about anything else?)[2] Furthermore, I believe that studies of artistic imagery, outside the strict pale of psychoanalytic emphasis, will bear out Freud's

---

[1]The essentializing strategy has its function when dealing with classes of items; the proportional one is for dealing with an item in its uniqueness. By isolating the matter of voluntarism, we put Freud in a line or class with Augustine. By isolating the matter of his concern with a distinction between unconscious and conscious, we may put him in a line with Leibniz's distinction between perception and apperception. Or we could link him with the Spinozistic *conatus* and the Schopenhauerian will. Or, as a rationalist, he falls into the bin with Aquinas (who is himself most conveniently isolated as a rationalist if you employ the essentializing as against the proportional strategy, stressing what he added rather than what he retained). Many arguments seem to hinge about the fact that there is an unverbalized disagreement as to the choice between these strategies. The same man, for instance, who might employ the essentializing strategy in proclaiming Aquinas as a rationalist, taking as the significant factor in Aquinas' philosophy his additions to rationalism rather than considering this as an ingredient in a faith philosophy, might object to the bracketing of Aquinas and Freud (here shifting to the proportional strategy, as he pointed out the totally different materials with which Aquinas surrounded his rational principle).

[2]We may distinguish between a public and universal motive. In so far as one acts in a certain way because of his connection with a business or party, he would act from a public motive. His need of response to a new glandular stimulation at adolescence, on the other hand, would arise

brilliant speculations as to the sexual puns, the *double-entendres,* lurking behind the most unlikely facades. If a man acquires a method of thinking about everything else, for instance, during the sexual deprivations and rigors of adolescence, this cure may well take on the qualities of the disease; and in so far as he continues with this same method in adult years, though his life has since become sexually less exacting, such modes as incipient homosexuality or masturbation may very well be informatively interwoven in the strands of his thought and be discoverable by inspection of the underlying imagery or patterns in this thought.

Indeed, there are only a few fundamental bodily idioms—and why should it not be likely that an attitude, no matter how complex its ideational expression, could only be completed by a channelization within its corresponding gestures? That is, the details of experience behind A's dejection may be vastly different from the details of experience behind B's dejection, yet both A and B may fall into the same bodily posture in expressing their dejection. And in an era like ours, coming at the end of a long individualistic emphasis, where we frequently find expressed an attitude of complete independence, of total, uncompromising self-reliance, this expression would not reach its fulfillment in choreography except in the act of "practical narcissism" (that is, the only wholly independent person would be the one who practiced self-abuse and really meant it).

But it may be noticed that we have here tended to consider mind-body relations from an interactive point of view rather than a materialistic one (which would take the body as the essence of the act and the mentation as the sublimation).

Freud himself, interestingly enough, was originally nearer to this view (necessary, as I hope to show later, for specifically literary purposes) than he later became. Freud explicitly resisted the study of motivation by way of symbols. He distinguished his own mode of analysis from the symbolic by laying the stress upon free association. That is, he would begin the analysis of a neurosis without any preconceived notion as to the absolute meaning of any image that the patient might reveal in the account of a dream. His procedure involved the breaking-down of the dream into a set of fragments, with the analyst then inducing the patient to improvise associations on each of these fragments in turn. And afterward, by charting recurrent themes, he would arrive at the crux of the patient's conflict.

Others (particularly Stekel), however, proposed a great short cut here. They offered an absolute content for various items of imagery. For instance, in Stekel's dictionary of symbols, which has the absoluteness of an old-

---

regardless of social values, and in that sense would be at once private and universal. The particular forms in which he expressed this need would, of course, be channelized in accordance with public or social factors.

fashioned dreambook, the right-hand path equals the road to righteousness, the left-hand path equals the road to crime, in anybody's dreams (in Lenin's presumably, as well as the Pope's). Sisters are breasts and brothers are buttocks. "The luggage of a traveller is the burden of sin by which one is oppressed," etc. Freud criticizes these on the basis of his own clinical experiences—and whereas he had reservations against specific equations, and rightly treats the method as antithetical to his own contribution, he decides that a high percentage of Stekel's purely intuitive hunches were corroborated. And after warning that such a gift as Stekel's is often evidence of paranoia, he decides that normal persons may also occasionally be capable of it.

Its lure as efficiency is understandable. And, indeed, if we revert to the matter of luggage, for instance, does it not immediately give us insight into a remark of André Gide, who is a specialist in the portrayal of scrupulous criminals, who has developed a stylistic trick for calling to seduction in the accents of evangelism, and who advises that one should learn to "travel light"?

But the trouble with short cuts is that they deny us a chance to take longer routes. With them, the essentializing strategy takes a momentous step forward. You have next but to essentialize your short cuts in turn (a short cut atop a short cut), and you get the sexual emphasis of Freud, the all-embracing ego compensation of Adler, or Rank's master-emphasis upon the birth trauma, etc.

Freud himself fluctuates in his search for essence. At some places you find him proclaiming the all-importance of the sexual, at other places you find him indignantly denying that his psychology is a pansexual one at all, and at still other places you get something halfway between the two, via the concept of the libido, which embraces a spectrum from phallus to philanthropy.

The important matter for our purposes is to suggest that the examination of a poetic work's internal organization would bring us nearer to a variant of the typically Freudian free-association method than to the purely symbolic method toward which he subsequently gravitated.[3]

The critic should adopt a variant of the free-association method. One obviously cannot invite an author, especially a dead author, to oblige him by telling what the author thinks of when the critic isolates some detail or

[3]Perhaps, to avoid confusion, I should call attention to the fact that symbolic in this context is being used differently by me from its use in the expression "symbolic action." If a man crosses a street, it is a practical act. If he writes a book about crossings—crossing streets, bridges, oceans, etc.—that is a symbolic act. Symbolic, as used in the restricted sense (in contrast with free association), would refer to the imputation of an absolute meaning to a crossing, a meaning that I might impute even before reading the book in question. Against this, I should maintain: One can never know what a crossing means, in a specific book, until he has studied its tie-up with other imagery in that particular book.

other for improvisation. But what he can do is to note the context of imagery and ideas in which an image takes its place. He can also note, by such analysis, the kinds of evaluations surrounding the image of a crossing; for instance, is it an escape from or a return to an evil or a good, etc.? Until finally, by noting the ways in which this crossing behaves, what subsidiary imagery accompanies it, what kind of event it grows out of, what kind of event grows out of it, what altered rhythmic and tonal effects characterize it, etc., one grasps its significance as motivation. And there is no essential motive offered here. The motive of the work is equated with the structure of interrelationships within the work itself.

"But there is more to a work of art than that." I hear this objection being raised. And I agree with it. And I wonder whether we could properly consider the matter in this wise:

For convenience using the word "poem" to cover any complete made artistic product, let us divide this artifact (the invention, creation, formation, poetic construct) in accordance with three modes of analysis: dream, prayer, chart.

The psychoanalysis of Freud and of the schools stemming from Freud has brought forward an astoundingly fertile range of observations that give us insight into the poem as dream. There is opened up before us a sometimes almost terrifying glimpse into the ways in which we may, while overtly doing one thing, be covertly doing another. Yet, there is nothing mystical or even unusual about this. I may, for instance, consciously place my elbow upon the table. Yet at the same time I am clearly unconscious of the exact distance between my elbow and my nose. Or, if that analogy seems like cheating, let us try another: I may be unconscious of the way in which a painter-friend, observant of my postures, would find the particular position of my arm characteristic of me.

Or let us similarly try to take the terror out of infantile regression. In so far as I speak the same language that I learned as a child, every time I speak there is, within my speech, an ingredient of regression to the infantile level. Regression, we might say, is a function of progression. Where the progression has been a development by evolution or continuity of growth (as were one to have learned to speak and think in English as a child, and still spoke and thought in English) rather than by revolution or discontinuity of growth (as were one to have learned German in childhood, to have moved elsewhere at an early age, and since become so at home in English that he could not even understand a mature conversation in the language of his childhood), the archaic and the now would be identical. You could say, indifferently, either that the speech is regression or that it is not regression. But were the man who had forgot the language of his childhood, to begin speaking nothing but this early language (under a sudden agitation or as the result of some steady pressure), we should have the kind of regression that goes formally by this name in psychoanalytic nomenclature.

The ideal growth, I suppose—the growth without elements of alienation, discontinuity, homelessness—is that wherein regression is natural. We might sloganize it as "the adult a child matured." Growth has here been simply a successive adding of cells—the growth of the chambered nautilus. But there is also the growth of the adult who, "when he became a man, put away childish things." This is the growth of the crab, that grows by abandoning one room and taking on another. It produces moments of crisis. It makes for philosophies of emancipation and enlightenment, where one gets a jolt and is "awakened from the sleep of dogma" (and alas! in leaving his profound "Asiatic slumber," he risks getting in exchange more than mere wakefulness, more than the eternal vigilance that is the price of liberty—he may get wakefulness plus, i.e., insomnia).

There are, in short, critical points (or, in the Hegel-Marx vocabulary, changes of quantity leading to changes of quality) where the process of growth or change converts a previous circle of protection into a circle of confinement. The first such revolution may well be, for the human individual, a purely biological one—the change at birth when the fetus, heretofore enjoying a larval existence in the womb, being fed on manna from the placenta, so outgrows this circle of protection that the benign protection becomes a malign circle of confinement, whereat it must burst forth into a different kind of world—a world of locomotion, aggression, competition, hunt. The mother, it is true, may have already been living in such a world; but the fetus was in a world within this world—in a monastery—a world such as is lived in by "coupon clippers," who get their dividends as the result of sharp economic combat but who may, so long as the payments are regular, devote themselves to thoughts and diseases far "above" these harsh material operations.

In the private life of the individual there may be many subsequent jolts of a less purely biological nature, as with the death of some one person who had become pivotal to this individual's mental economy. But whatever these unique variants may be, there is again a universal variant at adolescence, when radical changes in the glandular structure of the body make this body a correspondingly altered environment for the mind, requiring a corresponding change in our perspective, our structure of interpretations, meanings, values, purposes, and inhibitions, if we are to take it properly into account.

In the informative period of childhood our experiences are strongly personalized. Our attitudes take shape with respect to distinct people who have roles, even animals and objects being vessels of character. Increasingly, however, we begin to glimpse a world of abstract relationships, of functions understood solely through the medium of symbols in books. Even such real things as Tibet and Eskimos and Napoleon are for us, who have not been to Tibet, or lived with Eskimos, or fought under Napoleon, but a structure of signs. In a sense, it could be said that we learn these signs flat. We must start from scratch. There is no tradition in them; they are pure present. For though they have been handed down by tradition, we can read meaning into them only in so far as we can project or extend them out of our own experience. We may, through being burned a little, understand the signs for being burned a lot—it is in this sense that the coaching of interpretation could be called traditional. But we cannot understand the signs for being burned a lot until we have in our own flat experience, here and now, been burned a little.

Out of what can these extensions possibly be drawn? Only out of the informative years of childhood. Psychoanalysis talks of purposive forgetting. Yet purposive forgetting is the only way of remembering. One learns the meaning of "table," "book," "father," "mother," "mustn't," by forgetting the contexts in which these words were used. The Darwinian ancestry (locating the individual in his feudal line of descent from the ape) is matched in Freud by a still more striking causal ancestry that we might sloganize as "the child is father to the man."[4]

As we grow up new meanings must either be engrafted upon old meanings (being to that extent *double-entendres)* or they must be new starts (hence, involving problems of dissociation).

It is in the study of the poem as dream that we find revealed the ways in which the poetic organization takes shape under these necessities. Revise Freud's terms, if you will. But nothing is done by simply trying to refute them or to tie them into knots. One may complain at this procedure, for instance: Freud characterizes the dream as the fulfillment of a wish; an opponent shows him a dream of frustration, and he answers: "But the dreamer wishes to be frustrated." You may demur at that, pointing out that

---

[4]Maybe the kind of forgetting that is revealed by psychoanalysis could, within this frame, be better characterized as an incomplete forgetting. That is, whereas table, for instance, acquires an absolute and emotionally neutral meaning, as a name merely for a class of objects, by a merging of all the contexts involving the presence of a table, a table becomes symbolic, or a *double-entendre,* or more than table, when some particular informative context is more important than the others. That is, when table, as used by the poet, has overtones of, let us say, *one* table at which his mother worked when he was a child. In this way the table, its food, and the cloth may become surrogates for the mother, her breasts, and her apron. And incest awe may become merged with "mustn't touch" injunctions, stemming from attempts to keep the child from meddling with the objects on the table. In a dream play by Edmund Wilson, *The Crime in the Whistler Room,* there are two worlds of plot, with the characters belonging in the one world looking upon those in the other as dead, and the hero of this living world taking a dream shape as werewolf. The worlds switch back and forth, depending upon the presence or removal of a gate-leg table. In this instance I think we should not be far wrong in attributing some such content as the above to the table when considering it as a fulcrum upon which the structure of the plot is swung.

Freud has developed a "heads I win, tails you lose" mode of discourse here. But I maintain that, in doing so, you have contributed nothing. For there are people whose values are askew, for whom frustration itself is a kind of grotesque ambition. If you would, accordingly, propose to chart this field by offering better terms, by all means do so. But better terms are the only kind of refutation here that is worth the trouble. Similarly, one may be unhappy with the concept of ambivalence, which allows pretty much of an open season on explanations (though the specific filling-out may provide a better case for the explanation than appears in this key term itself). But, again, nothing but an alternative explanation is worth the effort of discussion here. Freud's terminology is a dictionary, a lexicon for charting a vastly complex and hitherto largely uncharted field. You can't refute a dictionary. The only profitable answer to a dictionary is another one.

A profitable answer to Freud's treatment of the Oedipus complex, for instance, was Malinowski's study of its variants in a matriarchal society.[5] Here we get at once a corroboration and a refutation of the Freudian doctrine. It is corroborated in that the same general patterns of enmity are revealed; it is refuted in that these patterns are shown not to be innate but to take shape with relation to the difference in family structure itself, with corresponding difference in roles.

Freud's overemphasis upon the patriarchal pattern (an assumption of its absoluteness that is responsible for the Freudian tendency to underrate greatly the economic factors influencing the relationships of persons or roles) is a prejudicial factor that must be discounted, in Freud, even when treating the poem as dream. Though totemistic religion, for instance, flourished with matriarchal patterns, Freud treats even this in patriarchal terms. And I submit that this emphasis will conceal from us, to a large degree, what is going on in art (still confining ourselves to the dream level —the level at which Freudian coordinates come closest to the charting of the logic of poetic structure).

In the literature of transitional eras, for instance, we find an especial profusion of rebirth rituals, where the poet is making the symbolic passes that will endow him with a new identity. Now, imagine him trying to do a very thorough job of this reidentification. To be completely reborn, he

[5]It is wrong, I think, to consider Freud's general picture as that of an individual psychology. Adler's start from the concept of ego compensation fits this description par excellence. But Freud's is a family psychology. He has offered a critique of the family, though it is the family of a neo-patriarch. It is interesting to watch Freud, in his *Group Psychology and the Analysis of the Ego,* frankly shifting between the primacy of group psychology and the primacy of individual psychology, changing his mind as he debates with himself in public and leaves in his pages the record of his fluctuations, frankly stated as such. Finally, he compromises by leaving both, drawing individual psychology from the role of the monopolistic father, and group psychology from the roles of the sons, deprived of sexual gratification by the monopolistic father, and banded together for their mutual benefit. But note that the whole picture is that of a family albeit of a family in which the woman is a mere passive object of male wealth.

would have to change his very lineage itself. He would have to revise not only his present but also his past. (Ancestry and cause are forever becoming intermingled—the thing is that from which it came—cause is *Ur-sache*, etc.) And could a personalized past be properly confined to a descent through the father, when it is the *mater* that is *semper certa?* Totemism, when not interpreted with Freud's patriarchal bias, may possibly provide us with the necessary cue here. Totemism, as Freud himself reminds us, was a magical device whereby the members of a group were identified with one another by the sharing of the same substance (a process often completed by the ritualistic eating of this substance, though it might, for this very reason, be prohibited on less festive occasions). And it is to the mother that the basic informative experiences of eating are related.

So, all told, even in strongly patriarchal societies (and much more so in a society like ours, where theories of sexual equality, with a corresponding confusion in sexual differentiation along occupational lines, have radically broken the symmetry of pure patriarchalism), would there not be a tendency for rebirth rituals to be completed by symbolizations of matricide and without derivation from competitive, monopolistic ingredients at all?[6]

To consider explicitly a bit of political dreaming, is not Hitler's doctrine of Aryanism something analogous to the adoption of a new totemic line? Has he not voted himself a new identity and, in keeping with a bastardized variant of the strategy of materialistic science, rounded this out by laying claim to a distinct blood stream? What the Pope is saying, benignly, in proclaiming the Hebrew prophets as the spiritual ancestors of Catholicism, Hitler is saying malignly in proclaiming for himself a lineage totally distinct.

Freud, working within the patriarchal perspective, has explained how such thinking becomes tied up with persecution. The paranoid, he says, assigns his imagined persecutor the role of rejected father. This persecutor is all-powerful, as the father seems to the child. He is responsible for every

---

[6]Or you might put it this way: Rebirth would require a killing of the old self. Such symbolic suicide, to be complete, would require a snapping of the total ancestral line (as being an integral aspect of one's identity). Hence, a tendency for the emancipatory crime to become sexually ambivalent. Freud's patriarchal emphasis leads to an overstress upon father-rejection as a basic cause rather than as a by-product of conversion (the Kierkegaard earthquake, that was accompanied by a changed attitude toward his father). Suicide, to be thorough, would have to go farther, and the phenomena of identity revealed in totemism might require the introduction of matricidal ingredients also. Freud himself, toward the end of *Totem and Taboo*, gives us an opening wedge by stating frankly, "In this evolution I am at a loss to indicate the place of the great maternal deities who perhaps everywhere preceded the paternal deities...." This same patriarchal emphasis also reinforces the Freudian tendency to treat social love as a mere sublimation of balked male sexual appetite, whereas a more matriarchal concern, with the Madonna and Child relationship, would suggest a place for affection as a primary biological motivation. Not even a naturalistic account of motivation would necessarily require reinforcement from the debunking strategy (in accordance with which the real motives would be incipient perversions, and social motives as we know them would be but their appearances, or censored disguise).

imagined machination (as the Jews, in Hitler's scheme, become the universal devil-function, the leading brains behind every "plot"). Advancing from this brilliant insight, it is not hard to understand why, once Hitler's fantasies are implemented by the vast resources of a nation, the "persecutor" becomes the persecuted.

The point I am trying to bring out is that this assigning of a new lineage to one's self (as would be necessary, in assigning one's self a new identity) could not be complete were it confined to symbolic patricide. There must also be ingredients of symbolic matricide intermingled here (with the phenomena of totemism giving cause to believe that the ritualistic slaying of the maternal relationship may draw upon an even deeper level than the ritualistic slaying of the paternal relationship). Lineage itself is charted after the metaphor of the family tree, which is, to be sure, patriarchalized in Western heraldry, though we get a different quality in the tree of life. MacLeish, in his period of aesthetic negativism, likens the sound of good verse to the ring of the ax in the tree, and if I may mention an early story of my own, *In Quest of Olympus,* a rebirth fantasy, it begins by the felling of a tree, followed by the quick change from child to adult, or, within the conventions of the fiction, the change from tiny "Treep" to gigantic "Arjk"; and though, for a long time, under the influence of the Freudian patriarchal emphasis, I tended to consider such trees as fathers, I later felt compelled to make them ambiguously parents. The symbolic structure of Peter Blume's painting, "The Eternal City," almost forces me to assign the tree, in that instance, to a purely maternal category, since the rejected father is pictured in the repellent phallus-like figure of Mussolini, leaving only the feminine role for the luxuriant tree that, by my interpretation of the picture, rounds out the lineage (with the dishonored Christ and the beggarwoman as vessels of the past lineage, and the lewd Mussolini and the impersonal tree as vessels of the new lineage, which I should interpret on the nonpolitical level as saying that sexuality is welcomed, but as a problem, while home is relegated to the world of the impersonal, abstract, observed).

From another point of view we may consider the sacrifice of gods, or of kings, as stylistic modes for dignifying human concerns (a kind of neo-euhemerism). In his stimulating study of the ritual drama, *The Hero,* Lord Raglan overstresses, it seems to me, the notion that these dramas appealed purely as spectacles. Would it not be more likely that the fate of the sacrificial king was also the fate of the audience, in stylized form, dignified, "writ large"? Thus, their engrossment in the drama would not be merely that of watching a parade, or the utilitarian belief that the ritual would insure rainfall, crops, fertility, a good year, etc.; but, also, the stages of the hero's journey would chart the stages of their journey (as an Elizabethan play about royalty was not merely an opportunity for the pit to get a glimpse of high life, a living newspaper on the doings of society, but a dignification or memorializing of their own concerns, translated into the idiom then currently accepted as the proper language of magnification).[7]

But though we may want to introduce minor revisions in the Freudian perspective here, I submit that we should take Freud's key terms, "condensation" and "displacement," as the over-all categories for the analysis of the poem as dream. The terms are really two different approaches to the same phenomenon. Condensation, we might say, deals with the respects in which house in a dream may be more than house, or house plus. And displacement deals with the way in which house may be other than house, or house minus. (Perhaps we should say, more accurately, minus house.)

One can understand the resistance to both of these emphases. It leaves no opportunity for a house to be purely and simply a house—and whatever we may feel about it as regards dreams, it is a very disturbing state of affairs when transferred to the realm of art. We must acknowledge, however, that the house in a poem is, when judged purely and simply as a house, a very flimsy structure for protection against wind and rain. So there seems to be some justice in retaining the Freudian terms when trying to decide what is going on in poetry. As Freud fills them out, the justification becomes stronger. The ways in which grammatical rules are violated, for instance; the dream's ways of enacting conjunctions, of solving arguments by club offers of mutually contradictory assertions; the importance of both concomitances and discontinuities for interpretative purposes (the phenomena of either association or dissociation, as you prefer, revealed with greatest clarity in the *lapsus linguae*); the conversion of an expression into its corresponding act (as were one, at a time when "over the fence is out" was an expression in vogue, to apply this comment upon some act by following the dream of this act by a dreamed incident of a ball going over a fence); and, above all, the notion that the optative is in dreams, as often in poetry and essay, presented in the indicative (a Freudian observation fertile to the neopositivists' critique of language)—the pliancy and ingenuity of Freud's researches here make entrancing reading, and continually provide insights that can be carried over, *mutatis mutandis,* to the operations of poetry. Perhaps we might sloganize the point thus: In so far as art contains a surrealist ingredient (and all art contains some of this ingredient), psychoanalytic coordinates are required to explain the logic of its structure.

Perhaps we might take some of the pain from the notions of condensation and displacement (with the tendency of one event to become the synecdochic

[7]Might not the sacrificial figure (as parent, king, or god) also at times derive from no resistance or vindictiveness whatsoever, but be the recipient of the burden simply through "having stronger shoulders, better able to bear it"? And might the choice of guilty scapegoats (such as a bad father) be but a secondary development for accommodating this socialization of a loss to the patterns of legality?

representative of some other event in the same cluster) by imagining a hypothetical case of authorship. A novelist, let us say, is trying to build up for us a sense of secrecy. He is picturing a conspiracy, yet he was never himself quite this kind of conspirator. Might not this novelist draw upon whatever kinds of conspiracy he himself had experientially known (as for instance were he to draft for this purpose memories of his participation in some childhood *Bund)?* If this were so, an objective breakdown of the imagery with which he surrounded the conspiratorial events in his novel would reveal this contributory ingredient. You would not have to read your interpretation into it. It would be objectively, structurally, there, and could be pointed to by scissor work. For instance, the novelist might explicitly state that, when joining the conspiracy, the hero recalled some incident of his childhood. Or the adult conspirators would, at strategic points, be explicitly likened by the novelist to children, etc. A statement about the ingredients of the work's motivation would thus be identical with a statement about the work's structure—a statement as to what goes with what in the work itself. Thus, in Coleridge's "The Eolian Harp," you do not have to interpret the poet's communion with the universe as an affront to his wife; the poet himself explicitly apologizes to her for it. Also, it is an objectively citable fact that imagery of noon goes with this apology. If, then, we look at other poems by Coleridge, noting the part played by the Sun at noon in the punishments of the guilt-laden Ancient Mariner, along with the fact that the situation of the narrator's confession involves the detention of a wedding guest from the marriage feast, plus the fact that a preference for church as against marriage is explicitly stated at the end of the poem, we begin to see a motivational cluster emerging. It is obvious that such structural interrelationships cannot be wholly conscious, since they are generalizations about acts that can only be made inductively and statistically after the acts have been accumulated. (This applies as much to the acts of a single poem as to the acts of many poems. We may find a theme emerging in one work that attains fruition in that same work—the ambiguities of its implications where it first emerges attaining explication in the same integer. Or its full character may not be developed until a later work. In its ambiguous emergent form it is a synecdochic representative of the form it later assumes when it comes to fruition in either the same work or in another one.)

However, though the synecdochic process (whereby something does service for the other members of its same cluster or as the foreshadowing of itself in a later development) cannot be wholly conscious, the dream is not all dream. We might say, in fact, that the Freudian analysis of art was handicapped by the aesthetic of the period—an aesthetic shared even by those who would have considered themselves greatly at odds with Freud and who were, in contrast with his delving into the unbeautiful, concerned with beauty only. This was the aesthetic that placed the emphasis wholly upon the function of self-expression. The artist had a number—some unique character or identity—and his art was the externalizing of this inwardness. The general Schopenhauerian trend contributed to this. Von Hartmann's *Philosophy of the Unconscious* has reinforced the same pattern. This version of voluntaristic processes, as connected with current theories of emancipation, resulted in a picture of the dark, unconscious drive calling for the artist to "out with it." The necessary function of the Freudian secular confessional, as a preparatory step to redemption, gave further strength to the same picture. Add the "complex in terms of the simple" strategy (with its variants—higher in terms of lower, normal as a mere attenuation of the abnormal, civilized as the primitive sublimated); add the war of the generations (which was considered as a kind of absolute rather than as a by-product of other factors, as those who hated the idea of class war took in its stead either the war of the generations or the war of the sexes)—and you get a picture that almost automatically places the emphasis upon art as utterance, as the naming of one's number, as a blurting-out, as catharsis by secretion.

I suggested two other broad categories for the analysis of poetic organization: prayer and chart.

Prayer would enter the Freudian picture in so far as it concerns the optative. But prayer does not stop at that. Prayer is also an act of communion. Hence, the concept of prayer, as extended to cover also secular forms of petition, moves us into the corresponding area of communication in general. We might say that, whereas the expressionistic emphasis reveals the ways in which the poet, with an attitude, embodies it in appropriate gesture, communication deals with the choice of gesture for the inducement of corresponding attitudes. Sensory imagery has this same communicative function, inviting the reader, within the limits of the fiction at least, to make himself over in the image of the imagery.

Considering the poem from this point of view, we begin with the incantatory elements in art, the ways of leading in or leading on the hypothetical audience X to which the poem, as a medium, is addressed (though this hypothetical audience X be nothing more concrete, as regards social relations, than a critical aspect of the poet's own personality). Even Freud's dream had a censor; but the poet's censor is still more exacting, as his shapings and revisions are made for the purpose of forestalling resistances (be those an essay reader's resistances to arguments and evidence or the novel reader's resistance to developments of narrative or character). We move here into the sphere of rhetoric (reader-writer relationships, an aspect of art that Freud explicitly impinges upon only to a degree in his analysis of wit), with the notion of address being most evident in oration and letter, less so in drama, and least in the lyric. Roughly, I should say that the slightest presence of revision is per se indication of a poet's feeling that his work is addressed (if only, as Mead might say, the address of an "I" to its "me").

Here would enter consideration of formal devices, ways of pointing up and fulfilling expectations, of living up to a contract with the reader (as Wordsworth and Coleridge might put it), of easing by transition or sharpening by ellipsis; in short, all that falls within the sphere of incantation, imprecation, exhortation, inducement, weaving and releasing of spells; matters of style and form, of meter and rhythm, as contributing to these results; and thence to the conventions and social values that the poet draws upon in forming the appropriate recipes for the roles of protagonist and antagonist, into which the total agon is analytically broken down, with subsidiary roles polarized about one or the other of the two agonists tapering off to form a region of overlap between the two principles—the ground of the agon. Here, as the reverse of prayer, would come also invective, indictment, oath. And the gestures might well be tracked down eventually to choices far closer to bodily pantomime than is revealed on the level of social evaluation alone (as were a poet, seeking the gestures appropriate for the conveying of a social negativeness, to draw finally upon imagery of disgust, and perhaps even, at felicitous moments, to select his speech by playing up the very consonants that come nearest to the enacting of repulsion).

As to the poem as chart: the Freudian emphasis upon the pun brings it about that something can only be in so far as it is something else. But, aside from these ambiguities, there is also a statement's value as being exactly what it is. Perhaps we could best indicate what we mean by speaking of the poem as chart if we called it the poet's contribution to an informal dictionary. As with proverbs, he finds some experience or relationship typical, or recurrent, or significant enough for him to need a word for it. Except that his way of defining the word is not to use purely conceptual terms, as in a formal dictionary, but to show how his vision behaves, with appropriate attitudes. In this, again, it is like the proverb that does not merely name but names vindictively, or plaintively, or promisingly, or consolingly, etc. His namings need not be new ones. Often they are but memorializings of an experience long recognized.

But, essentially, they are enactments, with every form of expression being capable of treatment as the efficient extension of one aspect or another of ritual drama (so that even the scientific essay would have its measure of choreography, its pedestrian pace itself being analyzed as gesture or incantation, its polysyllables being as style the mimetics of a distinct monasticism, etc.). And this observation, whereby we have willy-nilly slipped back into the former subject, the symbolic act as prayer, leads us to observe that the three aspects of the poem, here proposed, are not elements that can be isolated in the poem itself, with one line revealing the "dream," another the "prayer," and a third the "chart." They merely suggest three convenient modes in which to approach the task of analysis.[8]

The primary category, for the explicit purposes of literary criticism, would thus seem to me to be that of communication rather than that of wish, with its disguises, frustrations, and fulfillments. Wishes themselves, in fact, become from this point of view analyzable as purposes that get their shape from the poet's perspective in general (while this perspective is in turn shaped by the collective medium of communication). The choice of communication also has the advantage, from the sociological point of view, that it resists the Freudian tendency to overplay the psychological factor (as the total medium of communication is not merely that of words, colors, forms, etc., or of the values and conventions with which these are endowed, but also the productive materials, cooperative resources, property rights, authorities, and their various bottlenecks, which figure in the total act of human conversation).

Hence, to sum up: I should say that, for the explicit purposes of literary criticism, we should require more emphasis than the Freudian structure gives, (1) to the proportional strategy as against the essentializing one, (2) to matriarchal symbolizations as against the Freudian patriarchal bias, (3) to poem as prayer and chart, as against simply the poem as dream.

But I fully recognize that, once the ingenious and complex structure has been erected, nearly anyone can turn up with proposals that it be given a little more of this, a little less of that, a pinch of so-and-so, etc. And I recognize that, above all, we owe an enormous debt of gratitude to the man who, by his insight, his energy, and his remarkably keen powers of articulation, made such tinkering possible. It is almost fabulous to think that, after so many centuries of the family, it is only now that this central factor in our social organization has attained its counterpart in an organized critique of the family and of the ways in which the informative experience with familiar roles may be carried over, or "metaphored," into the experience with extra-familiar roles, giving these latter, in so far as they are, or are felt to be, analogous with the former, a structure of interpretations and attitudes borrowed from the former. And in so far as poets, like everyone else, are regularly involved in such informative familiar relationships, long before any but a few rudimentary bodily gestures are available for communicative use (with their first use unquestionably being the purely self-expressive one), the child is indeed the adult poet's father, as he is the father of us all

---

[8]Dream has its opposite, nightmare; prayer has its opposite, oath. Charts merely vary—in scope and relevance. In "Kubla Khan," automatically composed during an opium dream, the dream ingredient is uppermost. In "The Ancient Mariner," the prayer ingredient is uppermost. In "Dejection" and "The Pains of Sleep," the chart ingredient is uppermost: here Coleridge is explicitly discussing his situation.

(if not so in essence, then at least as regards an important predisposing factor "to look out for"). Thence we get to "like father like son." And thence we get to Freud's brilliant documentation of this ancestry, as it affects the maintenance of a continuity in the growing personality.

Only if we eliminate biography entirely as a relevant fact about poetic organization can we eliminate the importance of the psychoanalyst's search for universal patterns of biography (as revealed in the search for basic myths which recur in new guises as a theme with variations); and we can eliminate biography as a relevant fact about poetic organization only if we consider the work of art as if it were written neither by people nor for people, involving neither inducements nor resistances.[9] Such can be done, but the cost is tremendous in so far as the critic considers it his task to disclose the poem's eventfulness.

However, this is decidedly not the same thing as saying that "we cannot appreciate the poem without knowing about its relation to the poet's life as an individual." Rather, it is equivalent to saying: "We cannot understand a poem's structure without understanding the function of that structure. And to understand its function we must understand its purpose." To be sure, there are respects in which the poem, as purpose, is doing things for

[9]Those who stress form of this sort, as against content, usually feel that they are concerned with judgments of excellence as against judgments of the merely representative. Yet, just as a content category such as the Oedipus complex is neutral, i.e., includes both good and bad examples of its kind, so does a form category, such as sonnet or iambic pentameter, include both good and bad examples of its kind. In fact, though categories or classifications may be employed for evaluative purposes, they should be of themselves nonevaluative. Apples is a neutral, nonevaluative class, including firm apples and rotten ones. Categories that are in themselves evaluative are merely circular arguments—disguised ways of saying "this is good because it is good." The orthodox strategy of disguise is to break the statement into two parts, such as: "This is good because it has form; and form is good." The lure behind the feeling that the miracle of evaluation can be replaced by a codified scientific routine of evaluation seems to get its backing from the hope that a concept of quality can be matched by a number. The terms missing may be revealed by a diagram, thus:

Quantity	Number
Weight	Pound
Length	Foot
Duration	Hour
Quality	( )
Excellence	( )
Inferiority	( )

Often the strategy of concealment is accomplished by an ambiguity, as the critic sometimes uses the term "poetry" to designate good poetry, and sometimes uses it to designate "poetry, any poetry, good, bad, or indifferent." I do, however, strongly sympathize with the formalists, as against the sociologists, when the sociologist treats poetry simply as a kind of haphazard sociological survey—a report about world-conditions that often shows commendable intuitive insight but is handicapped by a poor methodology of research and controls.

the poet that it is doing for no one else. For instance, I think it can be shown by analysis of the imagery in Coleridge's "Mystery Poems" that one of the battles being fought there is an attempt to get self-redemption by the poet's striving for the vicarious or ritualistic redemption of his drug. It is obvious that this aspect of the equational structure is private and would best merit discussion when one is discussing the strategy of one man in its particularities. Readers in general will respond only to the sense of guilt, which was sharpened for Coleridge by his particular burden of addiction, but which may be sharpened for each reader by totally different particularities of experience. But if you do not discuss the poem's structure as a function of symbolic redemption at all (as a kind of private-enterprise Mass, with important ingredients of a black Mass), the observations you make about its structure are much more likely to be gratuitous and arbitrary (quite as only the most felicitous of observers could relevantly describe the distribution of men and postures in a football game if he had no knowledge of the game's purpose and did not discuss its formations as oppositional tactics for the carrying-out of this purpose, but treated the spectacle simply as the manifestation of a desire to instruct and amuse).

Thus, in the case of "The Ancient Mariner," knowledge of Coleridge's personal problems may enlighten us as to the particular burdens that the Pilot's boy ("who now doth crazy go") took upon himself as scapegoat for the poet alone. But his appearance in the poem cannot be understood at all, except in superficial terms of the interesting or the picturesque, if we do not grasp his function as a scapegoat of some sort—a victimized vessel for drawing off the most malign aspects of the curse that afflicts the "greybeard loon" whose cure had been effected under the dubious aegis of moonlight. And I believe that such a functional approach is the only one that can lead into a profitable analysis of a poem's structure even on the purely technical level. I remember how, for instance, I had pondered for years the reference to the "silly buckets" filled with curative rain. I noted the epithet as surprising, picturesque, and interesting. I knew that it was doing something, but I wasn't quite sure what. But as soon as I looked upon the Pilot's boy as a scapegoat, I saw that the word *silly* was a technical foreshadowing of the fate that befell this figure in the poem. The structure itself became more apparent: the "loon"-atic Mariner begins his cure from drought under the aegis of a moon that causes a silly rain, thence by synecdoche to silly buckets, and the most malignant features of this problematic cure are transferred to the Pilot's boy who now doth crazy go. Now, if you want to confine your observations to the one poem, you have a structural-functional-technical analysis of some important relationships within the poem itself. If you wish to trail the matter farther afield, into the equational structure of other work by Coleridge, you can back your interpretation of the moon by such reference as that to "moon-blasted madness," which gives you increased authority to discern lunatic ingredients in the lunar. His letters, where he talks of his addiction in imagery like that of the "Mystery Poems" and contemplates entering an insane asylum for a cure, entitle you to begin looking for traces of the drug as an ingredient in the redemptive problem. His letters also explicitly place the drug in the same cluster with the serpent; hence, we begin to discern what is going on when the Mariner transubstantiates the water snakes, in removing them from the category of the loathsome and accursed to the category of the blessed and beautiful. So much should be enough for the moment. Since the poem is constructed about an opposition between punishments under the aegis of the sun and cure under the aegis of the moon, one could proceed in other works to disclose the two sets of equations clustered about these two principles. Indeed, even in "The Ancient Mariner" itself we get a momentous cue, as the sun is explicitly said to be "like God's own head." But, for the moment, all I would maintain is that, if we had but this one poem by Coleridge, and knew not one other thing about him, we could not get an insight into its structure until we began with an awareness of its function as a symbolic redemptive process.

I can imagine a time when the psychological picture will be so well known and taken into account—when we shall have gone so far beyond Freud's initial concerns—that a reference to the polymorphous perverse of the infantile, for instance, will seem far too general—a mere first approximation. Everyone provides an instance of the polymorphous perverse, in attenuated form, at a moment of hesitancy; caught in the trackless maze of an unresolved, and even undefined, conflict, he regresses along this channel and that, in a formless experimentation that "tries anything and everything, somewhat." And in so far as his puzzle is resolved into pace, and steady rhythms of a progressive way out are established, there is always the likelihood that this solution will maintain continuity with the past of the poet's personality by a covert drawing upon analogies with this past. Hence the poet or speculator, no matter how new the characters with which he is now concerned, will give them somewhat the roles of past characters; whereat I see nothing unusual about the thought that a mature and highly complex philosophy might be so organized as to be surrogate for, let us say, a kind of adult breast-feeding—or, in those more concerned with alienation, a kind of adult weaning. Such categories do not by any means encompass the totality of a communicative structure; but they are part of it, and the imagery and transitions of the poem itself cannot disclose their full logic until such factors are taken into account.

However, I have spoken of pace. And perhaps I might conclude with some words on the bearing that the Freudian technique has upon the matter of pace. The Freudian procedure is primarily designed to break down a rhythm grown obsessive, to confront the systematic pieties of the patient's misery with systematic impieties of the clinic.[10] But the emphasis here is more upon the breaking of a malign rhythm than upon the upbuilding of a benign one. There is no place in this technique for examining the available resources whereby the adoption of total dramatic enactment may lead to correspondingly proper attitude. There is no talk of games, of dance, of manual and physical actions, of historical role, as a "way in" to this new upbuilding. The sedentary patient is given a sedentary cure. The theory of rhythms—work rhythms, dance rhythms, march rhythms—is no explicit part of this scheme, which is primarily designed to break old rhythms rather than to establish new ones.

The establishing of a new pace, beyond the smashing of the old puzzle, would involve in the end a rounded philosophy of the drama. Freud, since his subject is conflict, hovers continually about the edges of such a philosophy; yet it is not dialectical enough. For this reason Marxists properly resent his theories, even though one could, by culling incidental sentences from his works, fit him comfortably into the Marxist perspective. But the Marxists are wrong, I think, in resenting him as an irrationalist, for there is nothing more rational than the systematic recognition of irrational and non-rational factors. And I should say that both Freudians and Marxists are wrong in so far as they cannot put their theories together, by an over-all theory of drama itself (as they should be able to do, since Freud gives us the material of the closet drama, and Marx the material of the problem play, the one worked out in terms of personal conflicts, the other in terms of public conflicts).

The approach would require explicitly the analysis of rôle: salvation via change or purification of identity (purification in either the moral or chemical sense); different typical relationships between individual and group (as charted attitudinally in proverbs, and in complex works treated as sophisticated variants); modes of acceptance, rejection, self-acceptance, rejection of rejection[11] ("the enemies of my enemies are my friends"); transitional disembodiment as intermediate step between old self and new self (the spirituality of Shelley and of the Freudian cure itself); monasticism in the development of methods that fix a transitional or other-worldly stage, thereby making the evanescent itself into a kind of permanency—with all

[10]There are styles of cure, shifting from age to age, because each novelty becomes a common-place, so that the patient integrates his conflict with the ingredients of the old cure itself, thus making them part of his obsession. Hence, the need for a new method of jolting. Thus, I should imagine that a patient who had got into difficulties after mastering the Freudian technique would present the most obstinate problems for a Freudian cure. He would require some step beyond Freud. The same observation would apply to shifting styles in a poetry and philosophy, when considered as cures, as the filling of a need.

[11]I am indebted to Norbert Gutermann for the term "self-acceptance" and to William S. Knickerbocker for the term "rejection of rejection."

these modes of enactment finally employing, as part of the gesture idiom, the responses of the body itself as actor. (If one sought to employ Freud, as is, for the analysis of the poem, one would find almost nothing on poetic posture or pantomime, tonality, the significance of different styles and rhythmic patterns, nothing of this behaviorism.) Such, it seems to me, would be necessary, and much more in that direction, before we could so extend Freud's perspective that it revealed the major events going on in art.

But such revisions would by no means be anti-Freudian. They would be the kind of extensions required by reason of the fact that the symbolic act of art, whatever its analogies with the symbolic act of neurosis, also has important divergencies from the symbolic act of neurosis. They would be extensions designed to take into account the full play of communicative and realistic ingredients that comprise so large an aspect of poetic structure.

Freud and Literature

By Lionel Trilling

I

The Freudian psychology is the only systematic account of the human mind which, in point of subtlety and complexity, of interest and tragic power, deserves to stand beside the chaotic mass of psychological insights which literature has accumulated through the centuries. To pass from the reading of a great literary work to a treatise of academic psychology is to pass from one order of perception to another, but the human nature of the Freudian psychology is exactly the stuff upon which the poet has always exercised his art. It is therefore not surprising that the psychoanalytical theory has had a great effect upon literature. Yet the relationship is reciprocal, and the effect of Freud upon literature has been no greater than the effect of literature upon Freud. When, on the occasion of the celebration of his seventieth birthday. Freud was greeted as the "discoverer of the unconscious," he corrected the speaker and disclaimed the title. "The poets and philosophers before me discovered the unconscious," he said. "What I discovered was the scientific method by which the unconscious can be studied."

A lack of specific evidence prevents us from considering the particular literary "influences" upon the founder of psychoanalysis; and, besides, when we think of the men who so clearly anticipated many of Freud's own ideas—Schopenhauer and Nietzsche, for example—and then learn that he did not read their works until after he had formulated his own theories, we must see that particular influences cannot be in question here but that what we must deal with is nothing less than a whole *Zeitgeist,* a direction of thought. For psychoanalysis is one of the culminations of the Romanticist literature of the nineteenth century. If there is perhaps a contradiction in the idea of a science standing upon the shoulders of a literature which avows

"Freud and Literature," from *The Liberal Imagination* (1950) by Lionel Trilling, is reprinted by permission of Charles Scribner's Sons. Copyright 1950 Lionel Trilling; renewal copyright © 1978 Diana Trilling and James Trilling. The essay first appeared in *The Kenyon Review* (Spring 1940), 152-73; and in revised form in *Horizon* (September 1947).

itself inimical to science in so many ways, the contradiction will be resolved
if we remember that this literature, despite its avowals, was itself scientific
in at least the sense of being passionately devoted to a research into the self.

In showing the connection between Freud and this Romanticist tradition, it is difficult to know where to begin, but there might be a certain apt-
ness in starting even back of the tradition, as far back as 1762 with Diderot's
Rameau's Nephew. At any rate, certain men at the heart of nineteenth-
century thought were agreed in finding a peculiar importance in this brilliant little work: Goethe translated it, Marx admired it, Hegel—as Marx
reminded Engels in the letter which announced that he was sending the
book as a gift—praised and expounded it at length, Shaw was impressed by
it, and Freud himself, as we know from a quotation in his *Introductory
Lectures,* read it with the pleasure of agreement.

The dialogue takes place between Diderot himself and a nephew of the
famous composer. The protagonist, the younger Rameau, is a despised,
outcast, shameless fellow; Hegel calls him the "disintegrated consciousness"
and credits him with great wit, for it is he who breaks down all the normal
social values and makes new combinations with the pieces. As for Diderot,
the deuteragonist, he is what Hegel calls the "honest consciousness," and
Hegel considers him reasonable, decent, and dull. It is quite clear that the
author does not despise his Rameau and does not mean us to. Rameau is
lustful and greedy, arrogant yet self-abasing, perceptive yet "wrong," like
a child. Still, Diderot seems actually to be giving the fellow a kind of
superiority over himself, as though Rameau represents the elements which,
dangerous but wholly necessary, lie beneath the reasonable decorum of
social life. It would perhaps be pressing too far to find in Rameau Freud's
id and in Diderot Freud's ego; yet the connection does suggest itself; and
at least we have here the perception which is to be the common characteristic
of both Freud and Romanticism, the perception of the hidden element of
human nature and of the opposition between the hidden and the visible.
We have too the bold perception of just what lies hidden: "If the little
savage [i.e., the child] were left to himself, if he preserved all his foolish-
ness and combined the violent passions of a man of thirty with the lack of
reason of a child in the cradle, he'd wring his father's neck and go to bed
with his mother."

From the self-exposure of Rameau to Rousseau's account of his own
childhood is no great step; society might ignore or reject the idea of the
"immorality" which lies concealed in the beginning of the career of the
"good" man, just as it might turn away from Blake struggling to expound
a psychology which would include the forces beneath the propriety of social
man in general, but the idea of the hidden thing went forward to become
one of the dominant notions of the age. The hidden element takes many
forms and it is not necessarily "dark" and "bad"; for Blake the "bad" was

the good, while for Wordsworth and Burke what was hidden and unconscious was wisdom and power, which work in despite of the conscious intellect.

The mind has become far less simple; the devotion to the various forms of autobiography—itself an important fact in the tradition—provides abundant examples of the change that has taken place. Poets, making poetry by what seems to them almost a freshly discovered faculty, find that this new power may be conspired against by other agencies of the mind and even deprived of its freedom; the names of Wordsworth, Coleridge, and Arnold at once occur to us again, and Freud quotes Schiller on the danger to the poet that lies in the merely analytical reason. And it is not only the poets who are threatened; educated and sensitive people throughout Europe become aware of the depredations that reason might make upon the affective life, as in the classic instance of John Stuart Mill.

We must also take into account the preoccupation—it began in the eighteenth century, or even in the seventeenth—with children, women, peasants, and savages, whose mental life, it is felt, is less overlaid than that of the educated adult male by the proprieties of social habit. With this preoccupation goes a concern with education and personal development, so consonant with the historical and evolutionary bias of the time. And we must certainly note the revolution in morals which took place at the instance (we might almost say) of the *Bildungsroman,* for in the novels fathered by *Wilhelm Meister* we get the almost complete identification of author and hero and of the reader with both, and this identification almost inevitably suggests a leniency of moral judgment. The autobiographical novel has a further influence upon the moral sensibility by its exploitation of all the modulations of motive and by its hinting that we may not judge a man by any single moment in his life without taking into account the determining past and the expiating and fulfilling future.

It is difficult to know how to go on, for the further we look the more literary affinities to Freud we find, and even if we limit ourselves to bibliography we can at best be incomplete. Yet we must mention the sexual revolution that was being demanded—by Shelley, for example, by the Schlegel of *Lucinde,* by George Sand, and later and more critically by Ibsen; the belief in the sexual origin of art, baldly stated by Tieck, more subtly by Schopenhauer; the investigation of sexual maladjustment by Stendhal, whose observations on erotic feeling seem to us distinctly Freudian. Again and again we see the effective, utilitarian ego being relegated to an inferior position and a plea being made on behalf of the anarchic and self-indulgent id. We find the energetic exploitation of the idea of the mind as a divisible thing, one part of which can contemplate and mock the other. It is not a far remove from this to Dostoevski's brilliant instances of ambivalent feeling. Novalis brings in the preoccupation with the death wish, and this is linked on the one hand with sleep and on the other hand with the perception of the perverse, self-destroying impulses, which in turn leads us to that fascination by the horrible which we find in Shelley, Poe, and Baudelaire. And always there is the profound interest in the dream— "Our dreams," said Gerard de Nerval, "are a second life"—and in the nature of metaphor, which reaches its climax in Rimbaud and the later Symbolists, metaphor becoming less and less communicative as it approaches the relative autonomy of the dream life.

But perhaps we must stop to ask, since these are the components of the *Zeitgeist* from which Freud himself developed, whether it can be said that Freud did indeed produce a wide literary effect. What is it that Freud added that the tendency of literature itself would not have developed without him? If we were looking for a writer who showed the Freudian influence, Proust would perhaps come to mind as readily as anyone else; the very title of his novel, in French more than in English, suggests an enterprise of psychoanalysis and scarcely less so does his method—the investigation of sleep, of sexual deviation, of the way of association, the almost obsessive interest in metaphor; at these and at many other points the "influence" might be shown. Yet I believe it is true that Proust did not read Freud. Or again, exegesis of *The Waste Land* often reads remarkably like the psychoanalytic interpretation of a dream, yet we know that Eliot's methods were prepared for him not by Freud but by other poets.

Nevertheless, it is of course true that Freud's influence on literature has been very great. Much of it is so pervasive that its extent is scarcely to be determined; in one form or another, frequently in perversions or absurd simplifications, it has been infused into our life and become a component of our culture of which it is now hard to be specifically aware. In biography its first effect was sensational but not fortunate. The early Freudian biographers were for the most part Guildensterns who seemed to know the pipes but could not pluck out the heart of the mystery, and the same condemnation applies to the early Freudian critics. But in recent years, with the acclimatization of psychoanalysis and the increased sense of its refinements and complexity, criticism has derived from the Freudian system much that is of great value, most notably the license and the injunction to read the work of literature with a lively sense of its latent and ambiguous meanings, as if it were, as indeed it is, a being no less alive and contradictory than the man who created it. And this new response to the literary work has had a corrective effect upon our conception of literary biography. The literary critic or biographer who makes use of the Freudian theory is no less threatened by the dangers of theoretical systematization than he was in the early days, but he is likely to be more aware of these dangers; and I think it is true to say that now the motive of his interpretation is not that of exposing the secret shame of the writer and limiting the meaning of his work, but, on the contrary, that of finding grounds for sympathy with the writer and for increasing the possible significances of the work.

The names of the creative writers who have been more or less Freudian in tone or assumption would of course be legion. Only a relatively small number, however, have made serious use of the Freudian ideas. Freud himself seems to have thought this was as it should be: he is said to have expected very little of the works that were sent to him by writers with inscriptions of gratitude for all they had learned from him. The Surrealists have, with a certain inconsistency, depended upon Freud for the "scientific" sanction of their program. Kafka, with an apparent awareness of what he was doing, has explored the Freudian conceptions of guilt and punishment, of the dream, and of the fear of the father. Thomas Mann, whose tendency, as he himself says, was always in the direction of Freud's interests, has been most susceptible to the Freudian anthropology, finding a special charm in the theories of myths and magical practices. James Joyce, with his interest in the numerous states of receding consciousness, with his use of words as things and of words which point to more than one thing, with his pervading sense of the interrelation and interpenetration of all things, and, not least important, his treatment of familial themes, has perhaps most thoroughly and consciously exploited Freud's ideas.

II

It will be clear enough how much of Freud's thought has significant affinity with the anti-rationalist element of the Romanticist tradition. But we must see with no less distinctness how much of his system is militantly rationalistic. Thomas Mann is at fault when, in his first essay on Freud, he makes it seem that the "Apollonian," the rationalistic, side of psychoanalysis is, while certainly important and wholly admirable, somehow secondary and even accidental. He gives us a Freud who is committed to the "night side" of life. Not at all: the rationalistic element of Freud is foremost; before everything else he is positivistic. If the interpreter of dreams came to medical science through Goethe, as he tells us he did, he entered not by way of the *Walpurgisnacht* but by the essay which played so important a part in the lives of so many scientists of the nineteenth century, the famous disquisition on Nature.

This correction is needed not only for accuracy but also for any understanding of Freud's attitude to art. And for that understanding we must see how intense is the passion with which Freud believes that positivistic rationalism, in its golden-age pre-Revolutionary purity, is the very form and pattern of intellectual virtue. The aim of psychoanalysis, he says, is the control of the night side of life. It is "to strengthen the ego, to make it more independent of the super-ego, to widen its field of vision, and so to extend the organization of the id." "Where id was,"—that is, where all the irrational, non-logical, pleasure-seeking dark forces were—"there shall ego be,"—that is, intelligence and control. "It is," he concludes, with a reminiscence of Faust, "reclamation work, like the draining of the Zuyder Zee." This passage is quoted by Mann when, in taking up the subject of Freud a second time, he does indeed speak of Freud's positivistic program; but even here the bias induced by Mann's artistic interest in the "night side" prevents him from giving the other aspect of Freud its due emphasis. Freud would never have accepted the role which Mann seems to give him as the legitimizer of the myth and the dark irrational ways of the mind. If Freud discovered the darkness for science he never endorsed it. On the contrary, his rationalism supports all the ideas of the Enlightenment that deny validity to myth or religion; he holds to a simple materialism, to a simple determinism, to a rather limited sort of epistemology. No great scientist of our day has thundered so articulately and so fiercely against all those who would sophisticate with metaphysics the scientific principles that were good enough for the nineteenth century. Conceptualism or pragmatism is anathema to him through the greater part of his intellectual career, and this, when we consider the nature of his own brilliant scientific methods, has surely an element of paradox in it.

From his rationalistic positivism comes much of Freud's strength and what weakness he has. The strength is the fine, clear tenacity of his positive aims, the goal of therapy, the desire to bring to men a decent measure of earthly happiness. But upon the rationalism must also be placed the blame for the often naive scientific principles which characterize his early thought —they are later much modified—and which consist largely of claiming for his theories a perfect correspondence with an external reality, a position which, for those who admire Freud and especially for those who take seriously his views on art, is troublesome in the extreme.

Now Freud has, I believe, much to tell us about art, but whatever is suggestive in him is not likely to be found in those of his works in which he deals expressly with art itself. Freud is not insensitive to art—on the contrary—nor does he ever intend to speak of it with contempt. Indeed, he speaks of it with a real tenderness and counts it one of the true charms of the good life. Of artists, especially of writers, he speaks with admiration and even a kind of awe, though perhaps what he most appreciates in literature are specific emotional insights and observations; as we have noted, he speaks of literary men, because they have understood the part played in life by the hidden motives, as the precursors and coadjutors of his own science.

And yet eventually Freud speaks of art with what we must indeed call contempt. Art, he tells us, is a "substitute gratification," and as such is "an illusion in contrast to reality." Unlike most illusions, however, art is "almost always harmless and beneficent" for the reason that "it does not seek to be anything but an illusion. Save in the case of a few people who are, one might say, obsessed by Art, it never dares make any attack on the realm of reality." One of its chief functions is to serve as a "narcotic." It shares the characteristics of the dream, whose element of distortion Freud calls a "sort of inner dishonesty." As for the artist, he is virtually in the same category with the neurotic. "By such separation of imagination and intellectual capacity," Freud says of the hero of a novel, "he is destined to be a poet or a neurotic, and he belongs to that race of beings whose realm is not of this world."

Now there is nothing in the logic of psychoanalytical thought which requires Freud to have these opinions. But there is a great deal in the practice of the psychoanalytical therapy which makes it understandable that Freud, unprotected by an adequate philosophy, should be tempted to take the line he does. The analytical therapy deals with illusion. The patient comes to the physician to be cured, let us say, of a fear of walking in the street. The fear is real enough, there is no illusion on that score, and it produces all the physical symptoms of a more rational fear, the sweating palms, pounding heart, and shortened breath. But the patient knows that there is no cause for the fear, or rather that there is, as he says, no "real cause": there are no machine guns, man traps, or tigers in the street. The physician knows, however, that there is indeed a "real" cause for the fear, though it has nothing at all to do with what is or is not in the street; the cause is within the patient, and the process of the therapy will be to discover, by gradual steps, what this real cause is and so free the patient from its effects.

Now the patient in coming to the physician, and the physician in accepting the patient, make a tacit compact about reality; for their purpose they agree to the limited reality by which we get our living, win our loves, catch our trains and our colds. The therapy will undertake to train the patient in proper ways of coping with this reality. The patient, of course, has been dealing with this reality all along, but in the wrong way. For Freud there are two ways of dealing with external reality. One is practical, effective, positive; this is the way of the conscious self, of the ego which must be made independent of the super-ego and extend its organization over the id, and it is the right way. The antithetical way may be called, for our purpose now, the "fictional" way. Instead of doing something about, or to, external reality, the individual who uses this way does something to, or about, his affective states. The most common and "normal" example of this is daydreaming, in which we give ourselves a certain pleasure by imagining our difficulties solved or our desires gratified. Then, too, as Freud discovered, sleeping dreams are, in much more complicated ways, and even though quite unpleasant, at the service of this same "fictional" activity. And in ways yet more complicated and yet more unpleasant, the actual neurosis from which our patient suffers deals with an external reality which the mind considers still more unpleasant than the painful neurosis itself.

For Freud as psychoanalytic practitioner there are, we may say, the polar extremes of reality and illusion. Reality is an honorific word, and it means what is *there;* illusion is a pejorative word, and it means a response to what is *not there.* The didactic nature of a course of psychoanalysis no doubt requires a certain firm crudeness in making the distinction; it is after all aimed not at theoretical refinement but at practical effectiveness. The polar extremes are practical reality and neurotic illusion, the latter judged by the former. This, no doubt, is as it should be; the patient is not being trained in metaphysics and epistemology.

This practical assumption is not Freud's only view of the mind in its relation to reality. Indeed what may be called the essentially Freudian view assumes that the mind, for good as well as bad, helps create its reality by selection and evaluation. In this view, reality is malleable and subject to creation; it is not static but is rather a series of situations which are dealt with in their own terms. But beside this conception of the mind stands the conception which arises from Freud's therapeutic-practical assumptions; in this view, the mind deals with a reality which is quite fixed and static, a reality that is wholly "given" and not (to use a phrase of Dewey's) "taken." In his epistemological utterances, Freud insists on this second view, although it is not easy to see why he should do so. For the reality to which he wishes to reconcile the neurotic patient is, after all, a "taken" and not a "given" reality. It is the reality of social life and of value, conceived and maintained by the human mind and will. Love, morality, honor, esteem— these are the components of a created reality. If we are to call art an illusion then we must call most of the activities and satisfactions of the ego illusions; Freud, of course, has no desire to call them that.

What, then, is the difference between, on the one hand, the dream and the neurosis, and, on the other hand, art? That they have certain common elements is of course clear; that unconscious processes are at work in both would be denied by no poet or critic; they share too, though in different degrees, the element of fantasy. But there is a vital difference between them which Charles Lamb saw so clearly in his defense of the sanity of true genius: "The...poet dreams being awake. He is not possessed by his subject but he has dominion over it."

That is the whole difference: the poet is in command of his fantasy, while it is exactly the mark of the neurotic that he is possessed by his fantasy. And there is a further difference which Lamb states; speaking of the poet's relation to reality (he calls it Nature), he says, "He is beautifully loyal to that sovereign directress, even when he appears most to betray her"; the illusions of art are made to serve the purpose of a closer and truer relation with reality. Jacques Barzun, in an acute and sympathetic discussion of Freud, puts the matter well: "A good analogy between art and *dreaming* has led him to a false one between art and *sleeping*. But the difference between a work of art and a dream is precisely this, that the work of art *leads us back to the outer reality by taking account of it.*" Freud's assumption of the almost exclusively hedonistic nature and purpose of art bars him from the perception of this.

Of the distinction that must be made between the artist and the neurotic Freud is of course aware; he tells us that the artist is not like the neurotic in that he knows how to find a way back from the world of imagination and "once more get a firm foothold in reality." This however seems to mean no more than that reality is to be dealt with when the artist suspends the practice of his art; and at least once when Freud speaks of art dealing with reality he actually means the rewards that a successful artist can win. He does not deny to art its function and its usefulness; it has a therapeutic effect in releasing mental tension; it serves the cultural purpose of acting as a "substitute gratification" to reconcile men to the sacrifices they have made for culture's sake; it promotes the social sharing of highly valued emotional experiences; and it recalls men to their cultural ideals. This is not everything that some of us would find that art does, yet even this is a good deal for a "narcotic" to do.

III

I started by saying that Freud's ideas could tell us something about art, but so far I have done little more than try to show that Freud's very conception of art is inadequate. Perhaps, then, the suggestiveness lies in the application of the analytic method to specific works of art or to the artist himself? I do not think so, and it is only fair to say that Freud himself was aware both of the limits and the limitations of psychoanalysis in art, even though he does not always in practice submit to the former or admit the latter.

Freud has, for example, no desire to encroach upon the artist's autonomy; he does not wish us to read his monograph on Leonardo and then say of the "Madonna of the Rocks" that it is a fine example of homosexual, autoerotic painting. If he asserts that in investigation the "psychiatrist cannot yield to the author," he immediately insists that the "author cannot yield to the psychiatrist," and he warns the latter not to "coarsen everything" by using for all human manifestations the "substantially useless and awkward terms" of clinical procedure. He admits, even while asserting that the sense of beauty probably derives from sexual feeling, that psychoanalysis "has less to say about beauty than about most other things." He confesses to a theoretical indifference to the form of art and restricts himself to its content. Tone, feeling, style, and the modification that part makes upon part he does not consider. "The layman," he says, "may expect perhaps too much from analysis...for it must be admitted that it throws no light upon the two problems which probably interest him the most. It can do nothing toward elucidating the nature of the artistic gift, nor can it explain the means by which the artist works—artistic technique."

What, then, does Freud believe that the analytical method can do? Two things: explain the "inner meanings" of the work of art and explain the temperament of the artist as man.

A famous example of the method is the attempt to solve the "problem" of *Hamlet* as suggested by Freud and as carried out by Dr. Ernest Jones, his early and distinguished follower. Dr. Jones's monograph is a work of painstaking scholarship and of really masterly ingenuity. The research undertakes not only the clearing up of the mystery of Hamlet's character, but also the discovery of "the clue to much of the deeper workings of Shakespeare's mind." Part of the mystery in question is of course why Hamlet, after he had so definitely resolved to do so, did not avenge upon his hated uncle his father's death. But there is another mystery to the play—what Freud calls "the mystery of its effect," its magical appeal that draws so much interest toward it. Recalling the many failures to solve the riddle of the play's charm, he wonders if we are to be driven to the conclusion "that its magical appeal rests solely upon the impressive thoughts in it and the splendor of its language." Freud believes that we can find a source of power beyond this.

We remember that Freud has told us that the meaning of a dream is its intention, and we may assume that the meaning of a drama is its intention, too. The Jones research undertakes to discover what it was that Shakespeare intended to say about Hamlet. It finds that the intention was wrapped by the author in a dreamlike obscurity because it touched so deeply both his personal life and the moral life of the world; what Shakespeare intended to say is that Hamlet cannot act because he is incapacitated by the guilt he feels at his unconscious attachment to his mother. There is, I think, nothing to be quarreled with in the statement that there is an Oedipus situation in *Hamlet;* and if psychoanalysis has indeed added a new point of interest to the play, that is to its credit.[1] And, just so, there is no reason to quarrel

[1]However, A. C. Bradley, in his discussion of Hamlet *(Shakespearean Tragedy),* states clearly the intense sexual disgust which Hamlet feels and which, for Bradley, helps account for his uncertain purpose; and Bradley was anticipated in this view by Löning. It is well known, and Dover Wilson has lately emphasized the point, that to an Elizabethan audience Hamlet's mother was not merely tasteless, as to a modern audience she seems, in hurrying to marry Claudius, but actually adulterous in marrying him at all because he was, as her brother-in-law, within the forbidden degrees.

with Freud's conclusion when he undertakes to give us the meaning of *King Lear* by a tortuous tracing of the mythological implications of the theme of the three caskets, of the relation of the caskets to the Norns, the Fates, and the Graces, of the connection of these triadic females with Lear's daughters, of the transmogrification of the death goddess into the love goddess and the identification of Cordelia with both, all to the conclusion that the meaning of *King Lear* is to be found in the tragic refusal of an old man to "renounce love, choose death, and make friends with the necessity of dying." There is something both beautiful and suggestive in this, but it is not *the* meaning of *King Lear* any more than the Oedipus motive is *the* meaning of *Hamlet*.

It is not here a question of the validity of the evidence, though that is of course important. We must rather object to the conclusions of Freud and Dr. Jones on the ground that their proponents do not have an adequate conception of what an artistic meaning is. There is no single meaning to any work of art; this is true not merely because it is better that it should be true, that is, because it makes art a richer thing, but because historical and personal experience show it to be true. Changes in historical context and in personal mood change the meaning of a work and indicate to us that artistic understanding is not a question of fact but of value. Even if the author's intention were, as it cannot be, precisely determinable, the meaning of a work cannot lie in the author's intention alone. It must also lie in its effect. We can say of a volcanic eruption on an inhabited island that it "means terrible suffering," but if the island is uninhabited or easily evacuated it means something else. In short, the audience partly determines the meaning of the work. But although Freud sees something of this when he says that in addition to the author's intention we must take into account the mystery of *Hamlet's* effect, he nevertheless goes on to speak as if, historically, *Hamlet's* effect had been single and brought about solely by the "magical" power of the Oedipus motive to which, unconsciously, we so violently respond. Yet there was, we know, a period when *Hamlet* was relatively in eclipse, and it has always been scandalously true of the French, a people not without filial feeling, that they have been somewhat indifferent to the "magical appeal" of *Hamlet*.

I do not think that anything I have said about the inadequacies of the Freudian method of interpretation limits the number of ways we can deal with a work of art. Bacon remarked that experiment may twist nature on the rack to wring out its secrets, and criticism may use any instruments upon a work of art to find its meanings. The elements of art are not limited to the world of art. They reach into life, and whatever extraneous knowledge of them we gain—for example, by research into the historical context of the work—may quicken our feelings for the work itself and even enter legitimately into those feelings. Then, too, anything we may learn about the artist himself may be enriching and legitimate. But one research into the mind of the artist is simply not practicable, however legitimate it may theoretically be. That is, the investigation of his unconscious intention as it exists apart from the work itself. Criticism understands that the artist's statement of his conscious intention, though it is sometimes useful, cannot finally determine meaning. How much less can we know from his unconscious intention considered as something apart from the whole work? Surely very little that can be called conclusive or scientific. For, as Freud himself points out, we are not in a position to question the artist; we must apply the technique of dream analysis to his symbols, but, as Freud says with some heat, those people do not understand his theory who think that a dream may be interpreted without the dreamer's free association with the multitudinous details of his dream.

We have so far ignored the aspect of the method which finds the solution to the "mystery" of such a play as *Hamlet* in the temperament of Shakespeare himself and then illuminates the mystery of Shakespeare's temperament by means of the solved mystery of the play. Here it will be amusing to remember that by 1935 Freud had become converted to the theory that it was not Shakespeare of Stratford but the Earl of Oxford who wrote the plays, thus invalidating the important bit of evidence that Shakespeare's father died shortly before the composition of *Hamlet*. This is destructive enough to Dr. Jones's argument, but the evidence from which Dr. Jones draws conclusions about literature fails on grounds more relevant to literature itself. For when Dr. Jones, by means of his analysis of *Hamlet,* takes us into "the deeper workings of Shakespeare's mind," he does so with a perfect confidence that he knows what *Hamlet* is and what its relation to Shakespeare is. It is, he tells us, Shakespeare's "chief masterpiece," so far superior to all his other works that it may be placed on "an entirely separate level." And then, having established his ground on an entirely subjective literary judgment, Dr. Jones goes on to tell us that *Hamlet* "probably expresses the core of Shakespeare's philosophy and outlook as no other work of his does." That is, all the contradictory or complicating or modifying testimony of the other plays is dismissed on the basis of Dr. Jones's acceptance of the peculiar position which, he believes, *Hamlet* occupies in the Shakespeare canon. And it is upon this quite inadmissible judgment that Dr. Jones bases his argument: "It may be expected *therefore* that anything which will give us the key to the inner meaning of the play will *necessarily* give us the clue to much of the deeper workings of Shakespeare's mind." (The italics are mine.)

I should be sorry if it appeared that I am trying to say that psychoanalysis can have nothing to do with literature. I am sure that the opposite is so. For example, the whole notion of rich ambiguity in literature, of the interplay between the apparent meaning and the latent—not "hidden"—meaning, has been reinforced by the Freudian concepts, perhaps even received its first impetus from them. Of late years, the more perceptive psychoanalysts have surrendered the early pretensions of their teachers to deal "scientifically" with literature. That is all to the good, and when a study as modest and precise as Dr. Franz Alexander's essay on *Henry IV* comes along, an essay which pretends not to "solve" but only to illuminate the subject, we have something worth having. Dr. Alexander undertakes nothing more than to say that in the development of Prince Hal we see the classic struggle of the ego to come to normal adjustment, beginning with the rebellion against the father, going on to the conquest of the super-ego (Hotspur, with his rigid notions of honor and glory), then to the conquests of the *id* (Falstaff, with his anarchic self-indulgence), then to the identification with the father (the crown scene) and the assumption of mature responsibility. An analysis of this sort is not momentous and not exclusive of other meanings; perhaps it does no more than point up and formulate what we all have already seen. It has the tact to *accept* the play and does not, like Dr. Jones's study of *Hamlet,* search for a "hidden motive" and a "deeper working," which implies that there is a reality to which the play stands in the relation that a dream stands to the wish that generates it and from which it is separable; it is this reality, this "deeper working," which, according to Dr. Jones, produced the play. But *Hamlet* is not merely the product of Shakespeare's thought, it is the very instrument of his thought, and if meaning is intention, Shakespeare did not intend the Oedipus motive or anything less than *Hamlet;* if meaning is effect then it is *Hamlet* which affects us, not the Oedipus motive. *Coriolanus* also deals, and very terribly, with the Oedipus motive, but the effect of the one drama is very different from the effect of the other.

IV

If, then, we can accept neither Freud's conception of the place of art in life nor his application of the analytical method, what is it that he contributes to our understanding of art or to its practice? In my opinion, what he contributes outweighs his errors; it is of the greatest importance, and it lies in no specific statement that he makes about art but is, rather, implicit in his whole conception of the mind.

For, of all mental systems, the Freudian psychology is the one which makes poetry indigenous to the very constitution of the mind. Indeed, the mind, as Freud sees it, is in the greater part of its tendency exactly a poetry-making organ. This puts the case too strongly, no doubt, for it seems to make the working of the unconscious mind equivalent to poetry itself, forgetting that between the unconscious mind and the finished poem there supervene the social intention and the formal control of the conscious mind. Yet the statement has at least the virtue of counterbalancing the belief, so commonly expressed or implied, that the very opposite is true, and that poetry is a kind of beneficent aberration of the mind's right course.

Freud has not merely naturalized poetry; he has discovered its status as a pioneer settler, and he sees it as a method of thought. Often enough he tries to show how, as a method of thought, it is unreliable and ineffective for conquering reality; yet he himself is forced to use it in the very shaping of his own science, as when he speaks of the topography of the mind and tells us with a kind of defiant apology that the metaphors of space relationship which he is using are really most inexact since the mind is not a thing of space at all, but that there is not other way of conceiving the difficult idea except by metaphor. In the eighteenth century Vico spoke of the metaphorical, imagistic language of the early stages of culture; it was left to Freud to discover how, in a scientific age, we still feel and think in figurative formations, and to create, what psychoanalysis is, a science of tropes, of metaphor and its variants, synecdoche and metonymy.

Freud showed, too, how the mind, in one of its parts, could work without logic, yet not without that directing purpose, that control of intent from which, perhaps it might be said, logic springs. For the unconscious mind works without the syntactical conjunctions which are logic's essence. It recognizes no *because,* no *therefore,* no *but;* such ideas as similarity, agreement, and community are expressed in dreams imagistically by compressing the elements into a unity. The unconscious mind in its struggle with the conscious always turns from the general to the concrete and finds the tangible trifle more congenial than the large abstraction. Freud discovered in the very organization of the mind those mechanisms by which art makes its effects, such devices as the condensations of meanings and the displacement of accent.

All this is perhaps obvious enough and, though I should like to develop it in proportion both to its importance and to the space I have given to disagreement with Freud, I will not press it further. For there are two other elements in Freud's thought which, in conclusion, I should like to introduce as of great weight in their bearing on art.

Of these, one is a specific idea which, in the middle of his career (1920), Freud put forward in his essay *Beyond the Pleasure Principle.* The essay itself is a speculative attempt to solve a perplexing problem in clinical analysis, but its relevance to literature is inescapable, as Freud sees well enough, even though his perception of its critical importance is not sufficiently strong to make him revise his earlier views of the nature and function of art. The idea is one which stands besides Aristotle's notion of the catharsis, in part to supplement, in part to modify it.

Freud has come upon certain facts which are not to be reconciled with his earlier theory of the dream. According to this theory, all dreams, even the unpleasant ones, could be understood upon analysis to have the intention of fulfilling the dreamer's wishes. They are in the service of what Freud calls the pleasure principle, which is opposed to the reality principle. It is, of course, this explanation of the dream which had so largely conditioned Freud's theory of art. But now there is thrust upon him the necessity for reconsidering the theory of the dream, for it was found that in cases of war neurosis—what we once called shellshock—the patient, with the utmost anguish, recurred in his dreams to the very situation, distressing as it was, which had precipitated his neurosis. It seemed impossible to interpret these dreams by any assumption of a hedonistic intent. Nor did there seem to be the usual amount of distortion in them: the patient recurred to the terrible initiatory situation with great literalness. And the same pattern of psychic behavior could be observed in the play of children; there were some games which, far from fulfilling wishes, seemed to concentrate upon the representation of those aspects of the child's life which were most unpleasant and threatening to his happiness.

To explain such mental activities Freud evolved a theory for which he at first refused to claim much but to which, with the years, he attached an increasing importance. He first makes the assumption that there is indeed in the psychic life a repetition-compulsion which goes beyond the pleasure principle. Such a compulsion cannot be meaningless, it must have an intent. And that intent, Freud comes to believe, is exactly and literally the developing of fear. "These dreams," he says, "are attempts at restoring control of the stimuli by developing apprehension, the pretermission of which caused the traumatic neurosis." The dream, that is, is the effort to reconstruct the bad situation in order that the failure to meet it may be recouped; in these dreams there is no obscured intent to evade but only an attempt to meet the situation, to make a new effort of control. And in the play of children it seems to be that "the child repeats even the unpleasant experiences because through his own activity he gains a far more thorough mastery of the strong impression than was possible by mere passive experience."

Freud, at this point, can scarcely help being put in mind of tragic drama; nevertheless, he does not wish to believe that this effort to come to mental grips with a situation is involved in the attraction of tragedy. He is, we might say, under the influence of the Aristotelian tragic theory which emphasizes a qualified hedonism through suffering. But the pleasure involved in tragedy is perhaps an ambiguous one; and sometimes we must feel that the famous sense of cathartic resolution is perhaps the result of glossing over terror with beautiful language rather than an evacuation of it. And sometimes the terror even bursts through the language to stand stark and isolated from the play, as does Oedipus's sightless and bleeding face. At any rate, the Aristotelian theory does not deny another function for tragedy (and for comedy, too) which is suggested by Freud's theory of the traumatic neurosis—what might be called the mithridatic function, by which tragedy is used as the homeopathic administration of pain to inure ourselves to the greater pain which life will force upon us. There is in the cathartic theory of tragedy, as it is usually understood, a conception of tragedy's function which is too negative and which inadequately suggests the sense of active mastery which tragedy can give.

In the same essay in which he sets forth the conception of the mind embracing its own pain for some vital purpose, Freud also expresses a provisional assent to the idea (earlier stated, as he reminds us, by Schopenhauer) that there is perhaps a human drive which makes of death the final and desired goal. The death instinct is a conception that is rejected by many of even the most thoroughgoing Freudian theorists (as, in his last book, Freud mildly noted); the late Otto Fenichel in his authoritative work on the neurosis argues cogently against it. Yet even if we reject the theory as not fitting the facts in any operatively useful way, we still cannot miss its grandeur, its ultimate tragic courage in acquiescence to fate. The idea of the reality principle and the idea of the death instinct form the crown of Freud's broader speculation on the life of man. Their quality of grim poetry is characteristic of Freud's system and the ideas it generates for him.

And as much as anything else that Freud gives to literature, this quality of his thought is important. Although the artist is never finally determined in his work by the intellectual systems about him, he cannot avoid their influence; and it can be said of various competing systems that some hold more promise for the artist than others. When, for example, we think of the simple humanitarian optimism which, for two decades, has been so pervasive, we must see that not only has it been politically and philosophically inadequate, but also that it implies, by the smallness of its view of the varieties of human possibility, a kind of check on the creative faculties. In Freud's view of life no such limitation is implied. To be sure, certain elements of his system seem hostile to the usual notions of man's dignity. Like every great critic of human nature—and Freud is that—he finds in human pride the ultimate cause of human wretchedness, and he takes pleasure in knowing that his ideas stand with those of Copernicus and Darwin in making pride more difficult to maintain. Yet the Freudian man is, I venture to think, a creature of far more dignity and far more interest than the man which any other modern system has been able to conceive. Despite popular belief to the contrary, man, as Freud conceives him, is not to be understood by any simple formula (such as sex) but is rather an inextricable tangle of culture and biology. And not being simple, he is not simply good; he has, as Freud says somewhere, a kind of hell within him from which rise everlastingly the impulses which threaten his civilization.

He has the faculty of imagining for himself more in the way of pleasure and satisfaction than he can possibly achieve. Everything that he gains he pays for in more than equal coin; compromise and the compounding with defeat constitute his best way of getting through the world. His best qualities are the result of a struggle whose outcome is tragic. Yet he is a creature of love; it is Freud's sharpest criticism of the Adlerian psychology that to aggression it gives everything and to love nothing at all.

One is always aware in reading Freud how little cynicism there is in his thought. His desire for man is only that he should be human, and to this end his science is devoted. No view of life to which the artist responds can insure the quality of his work, but the poetic qualities of Freud's own principles, which are so clearly in the line of the classic tragic realism, suggest that this is a view which does not narrow and simplify the human world for the artist but on the contrary opens and complicates it.

The Language of Pundits

By Alfred Kazin

It is curious that Freud, the founder of psychoanalysis, remains the only first-class writer identified with the psychoanalytic movement. It was, of course, Freud's remarkable literary ability that gave currency to his once difficult and even "bestial" ideas; it was the insight he showed into concrete human problems, the discoveries whose force is revealed to us in a language supple, dramatic, and charged with the excitement of Freud's mission as a "conquistador" into realms hitherto closed to scientific inquiry, that excited and persuaded so many readers of his books. Even the reader who does not accept all of Freud's reasoning is aware, as he reads his interpretation of dreams, of the horror associated with incest, of the Egyptian origins of Moses, that this is a writer who is bent on making the most mysterious and unmentionable matters entirely clear to himself, and that this fundamental concern to get at the truth makes dramatis personae out of his symbols and dramatic episodes out of the archetypal human struggles he has described. It is certainly possible to read Freud, even to enjoy his books, without being convinced by him, but anyone sensitive to the nuances and playfulness of literary style, to the shaping power of a great intellectual conception, is not likely to miss in Freud the peculiar urgency of the great writer; for myself, I can never read him without carrying away a deeply engraved, an unforgettable sense of the force of human desire.

By contrast, many of the analysts who turn to writing seem to me not so much writers as people clutching at a few ideas. Whenever I immerse myself, very briefly, in the magisterial clumsiness of Dr. Gregory Zilboorg, or the slovenly looseness of Dr. Theodore Reik, or the tensely inarticulate essays of Dr. Harry Stack Sullivan, or the purringly complacent formulas of Dr. Edmund Bergler, or even the smoothly professional pages of Dr. Erich Fromm, I have a mental picture of a man leaping up from his chair, crying with exultation, "I have it! The reason for frigidity in the middle-aged female is the claustrophobic constitution!," and straightway rushing to his publisher. Where Freud really tried to give an explanation to himself of one specific human difficulty after another, and then in his old-fashioned way tried to show the determination of one new fact by another, it is enough these days for Dr. Bergler to assert why all writers are blocked, or for Dr. Theodore Reik, in his long-winded and inconsequential trek into love and lust, to announce that male and female are so different as to be virtually of different species. The vital difference between a writer and someone who merely is published is that the writer seems always to be saying to himself, as Stendhal actually did, "If I am not clear, the world around me collapses." In a very real sense, the writer writes in order to teach himself, to understand himself, to satisfy himself; the publishing of his ideas, though it brings gratifications, is a curious anticlimax.

Of course, there are psychoanalyst-writers who aim at understanding for themselves, but don't succeed. Even in Freud's immediate circle, several of the original disciples, having obtained their system from the master, devoted themselves to specialties and obsessions that, even if they were more than private *idées fixes*, like Otto Rank's belief in the "birth-trauma," were simply not given the hard and lucid expression necessary to convince the world of their objectivity. Lacking Freud's striking combination of intellectual zeal and common sense, his balanced and often rueful sense of the total image presented by the human person, these disciples wrote as if they could draw upon Freud's system while expanding one or two favorite notions out of keeping with the rest. But so strongly is Freud's general conception the product of his literary ability, so much is it held together only in Freud's own books, by the force of his own mind, that it is extraordinary how, apart from Freud, Freudianism loses its general interest and often becomes merely an excuse for wild-goose chases.

Obviously these private concerns were far more important to certain people in Freud's own circle than was the validity of Freudianism itself. When it came to a conflict between Freudianism and their own causes (Otto Rank) or their desire to be uninhibited in mystical indefiniteness (C. G. Jung), the body of ideas which they had inherited, not earned, no longer existed for them. Quite apart from his personal disposition to remain in control of the movement which he had founded, Freud was objectively right in warning disciples like Ferenczi, Rank, Adler, and Stekel not to break away from his authority. For the analyst's interest in psychoanalysis is likely to have its origin in some personal anxiety, and some particularly unstable people (of whom there were several in Freud's circle), lacking Freud's unusual ability not only to work through his own neuroses but to sublimate everything into the grand creative exultation of founding a movement, committed themselves fruitlessly to the development of their unsystematic ideas, found it impossible to heal themselves by the *ad hoc* doctrines they had advanced for this purpose, and even relapsed into serious mental illness and suicide.

Until fairly recently, it was perfectly possible for anyone with a Ph.D. (in literature or Zen or philology) to be a "psychotherapist" in New York State. I have known several such therapists among the intellectuals of New York, and I distinguish them very sharply from the many skillful and devoted lay analysts, with a direct training in psychoanalysis, who are likely to have an objective concern with the malady of their patients. The intellectuals with Ph.D.s who transferred from other professions to the practice of psychoanalysis still seem to me an extreme and sinister example of the tendency of psychoanalysis to throw up the pundit as a type. Like modern intellectuals everywhere, intellectuals as self-made analysts are likely to have one or two ruling ideas which bear obvious relation to their private history, but which, unlike intellectuals generally, they have been able to impose upon people who came to them desperately eager for orientation in their difficulties. In short, the ruling weakness of intellectuals, which is to flit from idea to idea in the hope of finding some instrument of personal or world salvation, has often become a method of indoctrination. All the great figures in psychoanalysis have been egotists of the most extreme sort; all the creative ones, from Freud himself to the late unfortunate Dr. Wilhelm Reich, were openly exasperated with the necessity of having to deal with patients at all. They were interested only in high thinking, though Freud at least tempered his impatience enough to learn from his patients; the objective power, the need to examine symptoms in others, never left him.

By contrast, the intellectual who is looking for an audience or a disciple has often, as a psychotherapist, found one in his patient. And the obvious danger of exploiting the credulous, the submissive, the troubled (as someone said, it is the analyst's love that cures the patient, and certain intellectuals love no one so much as a good listener), which starts from a doctrine held by the analyst in good faith but which may be no less narrow-minded or fanatical for all that, seems to me only an extension of the passion for explaining everything by psychoanalysis which literary intellectuals have indulged in so long. When I think of some of the intellectuals who have offered their services as therapists, I cannot but believe that to them the patient is irrelevant to their own passion for intellectual indoctrination. My proof of this is the way they write. Ever since Freud gave the word to so many people less talented than himself, it has become increasingly clear that, whatever psychoanalysis may have done for many troubled people, it has encouraged nonwriters to become bad writers and mediocre writers to affect the style of pundits. For the root of all bad writing is to be distracted, to be self-conscious, not to have your eye on the ball, not to confront a subject with entire directness, with entire humility, and with concentrated passion. The root of all bad writing is to compose what you have not worked out, *de haut en bas*, for yourself. Unless words come into the writer's mind as fresh coinages for what the writer himself knows that he knows, knows to be true, it is impossible for him to give back in words that direct quality of experience which is the essence of literature.

Now, behind the immense power and authority of psychoanalytical doctrines over contemporary literature—which expresses itself in the motivation of characters, the images of poetry, the symbol hunting of critics, the immense congregation of psychiatric situations and of psychiatrists in contemporary plays and novels—lies the urgent conviction, born with modern literature in the romantic period, the seedbed of Freudian ideas, that literature can give us knowledge. The Romantic poets believed in the supremacy of imagination over logic exactly as we now believe that the unconscious has stories to tell which ordinary consciousness knows nothing of. And just as the analyst looks to free association on the part of the patient to reveal conflicts buried too deep in the psyche to be revealed to the ordinarily conscious mind, so the Romantic poets believed that what has been buried in us, far from the prying disapprovals of culture, stands for "nature," our true human nature. A new world had been revealed to the Romantics, a world accessible through the imagination that creates art. And Freud, who also felt that he had come upon a new world, said that his insights had been anticipated by literary men in particular; he felt that he had confirmed, as scientific doctrine, profound discoveries about our buried, our archetypal, our passionate human nature that philosophers and poets had made as artists.

Had made as artists. Nietzsche, who also anticipated many of Freud's psychological insights, said that Dostoevsky was the only psychologist who had ever taught him anything. No doubt he meant that the characters Dostoevsky had created, the freshness of Dostoevsky's perceptions, the powerful but ironic rationality of Dostoevsky's style had created new facts for him to think of in comparison with the stale medical formulas of psychiatry in his time. Similarly, Freud said of Dostoevsky that "before genius, analysis lays down its arms," indicating that with the shaping power of the artist who can create characters like old Karamazov and Prince Myshkin, with the genius that in its gift of creation actually parallels life instead of merely commenting on it, analysis cannot compete. And in point of fact we do learn more about the human heart from a stupendous creation like the Karamazov family than we ever do from all the formulary "motivations" of human nature. Just as each human being, in his uniqueness, escapes all the dry formulas and explanations about human nature, so a great new creation in imaginative literature, a direct vision of the eternal like William Blake's or an unprecedented and unassimilable human being like old

Karamazov, automatically upsets and rearranges our hardened conceptions
of human nature.

There is no substitute for life, for the direct impression of life; there is
no deep truth about life, such as writers bring home to us, that does not
come in the form of more life. To anyone who really knows how rare and
precious imaginative creation is—how small, after all, is that procession
which includes Dante's Paolo and Francesca, Shakespeare's Othello, and
Tolstoy's Natasha—how infinitely real in suggestion is the character that
has been created in and through imagination, there is something finally
unbearable, the very opposite of what literature is for, in the kind of metallic
writing which now so often serves in a novel to "motivate" a character.

Maybe the only tenable literary role which novelists and poets, as well
as critics and psychologists, now want to play is that of the expert—the
explainer, the commentator, the analyst. Just as so many psychoanalysts
want to be writers, so many writers now want to be analysts. And whenever
I rise up at intervals from my dutiful immersion in certain specimens of
contemporary literature, I find it hard to say who has less to contribute to
literature, the psychiatrist who wants to push a few small ideas into a book
or the novelist who in the course of a story breaks down into writing like a
psychoanalyst.

II

The deterioration of language in contemporary fiction into the language
of pundits is not often noticed by critics—perhaps because the novelists
have taken to writing like critics. But it is by no means the highbrow or
intellectual novelist—like Mary McCarthy, who in a single story for *Partisan Review* is likely to produce so many deliberate symbols—who is the
only offender against art. John O'Hara in *From the Terrace* wrote, of the
mother of his hero, that "What had happened to her was that she unconsciously abandoned the public virginity and, again unconsciously, began
to function as a woman." Of the Eaton brothers, O'Hara made it clear that
"If William slapped Alfred or otherwise punished him, the difference in
ages was always mentioned while William himself was being punished; and
each time that that occurred the age separation contributed to a strengthening of the separation that was already there because of, among other considerations, the two distinct personalities." This is a novelist? Frankly, I
have the impression that many of the younger novelists have learned to
write fiction from reading the New Critics, the anthropologists and psychologists. I cannot begin to enumerate all the novels of recent years, from
Ralph Ellison's *Invisible Man* to Vance Bourjaily's recent *Confessions of a
Spent Youth*, which describe American social customs, from college up, as

fulfilling the prescription of tribal rites laid down by the anthropologists. But whereas an angry and powerful novelist, as Ellison is in *Invisible Man,* whatever helpful hints he may get from psychiatrically oriented literary critics, will aim at the strongest possible image of Negro suffering and confusion in a hostile society, Vance Bourjaily, in his recent novel, has his hero preface his description of a business smoker by apologizing that "it would take the calm mind of an anthropologist to describe objectively the rites with which the advertising tribe sent its bachelor to meet his bride."

I don't know what repels me more in such writing, the low spirits behind such prosiness or the attempted irony that is meant to disguise the fact that the writer is simply not facing his subject directly but is looking for something to say about it. No wonder that a passage like this sounds not like fiction but a case history: "I had a good time with Vicky during those two or three months; at the same time, I was learning about the social structure of the town and that of the school which, with certain exceptions for unusual individuals, reflected it; Vicky was more or less middle middle. As a friend of hers, since my own status was ambiguous, it seemed to me that I must acquire hers by association." And Mr. Bourjaily's book *is* a case history, though so meanderingly self-absorbed, for the most part, that it comes splendidly alive when the hero describes a visit to his relatives in the Near East; for a few pages we are onto people whom Mr. Bourjaily has to describe for us, since they are new types, and then we get free of the motivational analysis that is the novelist's desperate response to people who he thinks are too familiar to be conveyed directly. This is a curious idea of a novel — as if it were the subject, rather than the point of view, which made it boring.

The true writer starts from autobiography, but he does not end there; and it is not himself he is interested in, but the use he can make of self as a literary creation. Of course, it is not the autobiographical subject that makes such books as Mr. Bourjaily's flat; it is the relatively shallow level from which the author regards his own experience. The mark of this is that the writer does not even bother to turn his hero into a character; he is just a focus for the usual "ironic" psychological comment. If the writer nowadays sees himself as a pundit, he sees his hero as a patient. What, in fact, one sees in many contemporary American novelists today is the author as analyst confronting his alter ego as analysand. The novel, in short, becomes simply an instrument of self-analysis, which may be privately good for the writer (I doubt it) but is certainly boring to his readers.

III

The deterioration of language in contemporary "imaginative" literature —this reduction of experience to flat, vaguely orphic loose statements—

seems to me most serious whenever, in our psychiatrically centered culture, spontaneity becomes an arbitrary gesture which people can simulate. Among the Beat writers, spontaneity becomes a necessary convention of metal health, a way of simulating vitality, directness, rough informality, when in fact the literary works produced for this pose have no vitality, are not about anything very significant, and are about as rough as men ever are using dirty words when they cut themselves shaving. The critic Harold Rosenberg once referred scathingly to the "herd of independent minds"; when I read the Beat and spontaneous poets en bloc, as I have just done in Donald Allen's anthology of the "new" American poetry, I feel that I am watching a bunch of lonely Pagliaccis making themselves up to look gay. To be spontaneous on purpose, spontaneous all the time, spontaneous on demand is bad enough; you are obeying not yourself but some psychiatric commandment. But to convert this artificial, constant, unreal spontaneity into poetry as a way of avoiding the risks and obligations of an objective literary work is first to make a howling clown out of yourself and then deliberately to cry up your bad literature as the only good literature.

The idea of the Beat poets is to write so quickly that they will not have to stand up for the poem itself; it is enough to be caught in the act of writing. The emphasis is not on the poem but on themselves being glimpsed in the act of creation. In short, they are functioning, they are getting out of the prison house of neurosis, they are positive and free. "Look, Ma, no hands!" More than this, they are shown in the act of writing poems which describe them in the act of living, just about to write poems. *"Morning again, nothing has to be done / maybe buy a piano or make fudge / At least clean the room up, for sure like my farther / I've done flick the ashes & buts over the bedside on the floor."* This is Peter Orlovsky, "Second Poem."

Elsewhere, the hysterical demand for spontaneity as an absolute value means that everything in the normal social world becomes an enemy of your freedom. You want to destroy it so as to find an image of the ecstasy that has become the only image of reality the isolated mind will settle for. It is a wish for the apocalypse that lies behind the continued self-righteous muttering that the world is about to blow up. The world is not about to blow up, but behind the extreme literary pose that everything exists to stifle and suppress and exterminate us perhaps lies the belief, as Henry Miller plainly put it in *Tropic of Cancer,* that "For a hundred years or more the world, *our* world, has been dying. ... The world is rotting away, dying piecemeal. But it needs the *coup de grâce,* it needs to be blown to smithereens. ... We are going to put it down—the evolution of this world which has died but which has not been buried. We are swimming on the face of time and all else has drowned, is drowning, or will drown."

The setting of this apocalyptic wish is the stated enmity between the self and the world, between the literary imagination and mere reality—a tension which was set up by Romanticism and which Freudianism has sharpened and intensified to the point where the extreme Romantic, the Beat writer, confesses that the world must be destroyed in order that the freedom of his imagination proceed to its infinite goal. Romanticism put so much emphasis on the personal consciousness that eventually the single person came to consider himself prior to the world and, in a sense, replacing it; under Romanticism, the self abandoned its natural ties to society and nature and emphasized the will. The more the single conscious mind saw the world as an object for it to study, the more consciousness was thrown back on itself in fearful isolation; the individual, alone now with his consciousness, preoccupied in regarding himself and studying himself, had to exercise by more and more urgent exertions of will that relationship to the world which made consciousness the emperor of all it could survey—the world was merely raw material to the inquiring mind.

Freud, himself a highly conservative and skeptical thinker with a deeply classical bias in favor of limitation, restraint, and control, could not have anticipated that his critique of repression, of the admired self-control of the bourgeoisie, would in time, with the bankruptcy of bourgeois values, become a philosophy for many of his followers. Freudianism is a critique of Victorian culture; it is not a prescription for living in the twentieth century, in a world where the individual finds himself increasingly alienated from the society to which he is physically tied. Freud once wrote in a letter to Romain Rolland: "Psychoanalysis also has its scale of values, but its sole aim is the enhanced harmony of the ego, which is expected successfully to mediate between the claims of the instinctual life [the id] and those of the external world; thus between inner and outer reality.

"We seem to diverge rather far in the role we assign to intuition. Your mystics rely on it to teach them how to solve the riddle of the universe; we believe that it cannot reveal to us anything but primitive, instinctual impulses and attitudes...worthless for orientation in the alien, external world."

It was the Romantics who handed down to modern writers the necessity to think of the world as "alien and external." By now so many writers mechanically think of it this way that it is no wonder that they look for a philosophy of life to the "primitive, instinctual impulses and attitudes," though, as Freud knew, they are "worthless for orientation in the alien, external world." Man cannot cheat his own mind; he cannot bypass the centrality of his own intelligence. Yet is not sole reliance on the "primitive, instinctual impulses" exactly the *raison d'être* of so many Beat poems and novels; of neurotic plays dealing with people whose only weakness, *they* think, is that they are repressed; of literary studies whose whole thesis is that the American novel has always been afraid of sex? What is wrong with such works is not that the single points they make are incorrect, but that they rely upon a single point for a positive philosophy of life. It is impossible to write well and deeply in this spirit of Sisyphus, pushing a single stone up the mountain. It is impossible to write well if you start from an arbitrary point of view, and in the face of everything that is human, complex, and various, push home your *idée fixe*. It is impossible for the haunted, the isolated, the increasingly self-absorbed and self-referring self to transcend itself sufficiently to create works of literature.

Literature grows out of a sense of abundant relationships with the world, out of a sense that what is ugly to everyone else is really beautiful to you, that what is invisible to many men is pressingly alive and present to your writer's eye. We can no longer, by taking thought, transcend the life that consists in taking thought. The English novelist and philosopher Iris Murdoch has recently helped clear the air of desperate self-pity by saying that "We need to return from the self-centered concept to the other-centered concept of truth. We are not isolated free choosers, monarchs of all we survey, but benighted creatures sunk in a reality whose nature we are constantly and overwhelmingly tempted to deform by fantasy. Our current picture of freedom encourages a dream-like facility; whereas what we require is a renewed sense of the difficulty and complexity of the moral life and the opacity of persons."

By now the self-centered mind fashioned by romanticism, constantly keeping itself open only to adjurations of absolute freedom and spontaneity, has traveled about as far along the road of self-concern as it can; it has nothing to discover further of itself but fresh despair. The immediate proof of this is in the quality of so much of the literature that has been shaped by Freudianism—only because all other creeds have failed it. It is not possible to write well with one's own wishes as the only material. It is not possible any longer to think anything out without a greater reality than oneself constantly pressing one's words into dramatic shape and unexpected meaning. All our words now are for our own emotions, none for the world that sustains the writer. And this situation is impossible, for it was never the self that literature was about, but what transcended the self, what comes home to us through experience.

On *The Interpretation of Dreams*

By Stanley Edgar Hyman

Freud's masterwork, *The Interpretation of Dreams,* was published late in 1899, postdated 1900. Freud had discovered the core of the theory, that dreams are wish-fulfilments, early in 1895, and in July, 1895, he first fully analyzed a dream of his own in the new terms, the dream he called "Irma's injection." Freud later recognized the book as his most important, and in his preface to the third English edition in 1931, he writes:

> It contains, even according to my present-day judgement, the most valuable of all the discoveries it has been my good fortune to make. Insight such as this falls to one's lot but once in a lifetime.

The book, then, at least on the surface, is an account of the origin, structure, and function of dreams, along with a method for their interpretation.

In Freud's view, the dream is a distortion of unsuitable thoughts to make them unrecognizable. The processes of distortion, elaborately described in the book's longest chapter, "The Dream-Work," are principally four. They are: "condensation," a combining of a number of thoughts into economical composites, so that each element of a dream will have several meanings and be what Freud called "overdetermined"; "displacement," a substitution of one identification for another; "considerations of representability," the replacement of abstractions by concrete images; and "secondary revision," a further tendentious disguising. All this complicated labor results from a conflict between two psychical forces ("or," as Freud says, "we may describe them as currents or systems"), which he first calls the "unconscious" and the "preconscious," and later the "repressed" and the "ego" (a quarter of a century later, he called the "repressed" the "id."). The motive for the labor lies in two major factors Freud named "repression," the act of refusing infantile impulses and related material admission to consciousness, and "resistance," the visible effort that

"The Interpretation of Dreams," by Stanley Edgar Hyman. Used by permission of Atheneum Publishers from *The Tangled Bank: Darwin, Marx, Frazer and Freud as Imaginative Writers* by Stanley Edgar Hyman (New York: Atheneum, 1962), pp. 310-38. Copyright © 1962 by Stanley Edgar Hyman.

keeps them unconscious. In "The History of the Psychoanalytic Movement," published in 1914, Freud wrote: "The theory of repression is the pillar upon which psychoanalysis rests," and the observed fact of resistance is its principal evidence.

The other principal discovery in *The Interpretation of Dreams* is the "Oedipus complex," which Freud first noticed in his patients, confirmed in analyzing his own dreams in 1897, and promptly recognized as universal. He explains it fully in the book, without the term (which he did not use until 1910). The Oedipus complex, as it is described in *The Interpretation of Dreams* (the theory was later modified in the case of girls), is an infantile erotic attachment to the parent of the opposite sex and rivalry with the parent of the same sex. Freud discusses Sophocles' *Oedipus the King* (which he had translated for his secondary-school graduation examination), and says of its protagonist, for whom he named the complex:

> His destiny moves us only because it might have been ours — because the oracle laid the same curse upon us before our birth as upon him. It is the fate of all of us, perhaps, to direct our first sexual impulse towards our mother and our first hatred and our first murderous wish against our father. Our dreams convince us that that is so. King Oedipus, who slew his father Laius and married his mother Jocasta, merely shows us the fulfilment of our own childhood wishes.

All dreams are thus wish-fulfilments, Freud says, and wish-fulfilment is the "key" to the understanding of dreams. The simplest wish dreams fulfill is the wish-to sleep, which by the distorting processes of the dream-work they guard from inner and outer disturbances that would awaken the sleeper. On a deeper level, dreams gratify the greedy wishful impulses of the unconscious in a symbolic form, and their function is to serve as a safety-valve discharging its excitation. In their deepest meaning, dreams fulfill the infantile Oedipal wish, repressed and unconscious. Freud writes: "Dreaming is a piece of infantile mental life that has been superseded."

The form of *The Interpretation of Dreams* is a controlled gradual revelation of Freud's theory, progressing from didactic oversimplification to full and rich complexity, like *The Origin of Species* or *Capital*. Freud will state a principle, then move on to "a first denial of this assertion," or write, "my earlier statement requires correction." He reminds us each time that things are still being kept too simple, with such remarks as "Later on I shall have to disclose a factor in dream-formation which I have not yet mentioned." We can see the development most neatly in the series of summary formulations, of progressive complication, of the book's main point. The second chapter concludes: "When the work of interpretation has been completed, we perceive that a dream is the fulfilment of a wish." The fourth chapter concludes: "a dream is a (disguised) fulfilment of a (suppressed or repressed) wish." The fifth chapter adds: "a succession of meanings or wish-fulfilments may be superimposed on one another, the bottom one being the fulfilment of a wish dating from earliest childhood." By the last chapter, this becomes: "a wish which is represented in a dream must be an infantile one." Thus the simple formula, a dream is the disguised fulfilment of a repressed infantile wish, gradually unfolds over hundreds of pages. If we had any doubt that this form was the work of conscious craft, it would be dissipated by Freud's statement about Sophocles' play:

> The action of the play consists in nothing other than the process of revealing, with cunning delays and ever-mounting excitement—a process that can be likened to the work of a psychoanalysis—that Oedipus himself is the murderer of Laius, but further that he is the son of the murdered man and of Jocasta.

The Interpretation of Dreams is thoroughly dramatistic, sometimes in the form of debate, sometimes in other fashions. Freud writes a running dialogue with an imaginary critic: "I shall meet with the most categorical contradiction," "I shall be told," "an objection may be raised," "Is it not more probable," "I can give only limited assent to this argument," "I cannot accept this objection," and so on. Dreams themselves are dramatic, as Freud notes, in that they reproduce an idea as though we were experiencing it. Neurosis is even more dramatic, in that hysterics "act all the parts in a play single-handed"; and Freud in fact defines hysteria as the conflict of two incompatible wishes, as Hegel defined tragedy as the conflict of two incompatible necessities. Freud quotes Havelock Ellis approvingly in an account of secondary revision that is a little playlet. Ellis writes:

> Sleeping consciousness we may even imagine as saying to itself in effect: "Here comes our master, Waking Consciousness, who attaches such mighty importance to reason and logic and so forth. Quick! gather things up, put them in order—any order will do—before he enters to take possession."

With the psyche full of agonists, Freud's psychology must be comparably dramatic, and as we might expect it is full of voices, struggles, soliloquies and colloquies, and stage movement.

As he follows the quicksilver associations of dreams, Freud's style is sometimes a kaleidoscope of verbal puns, what he calls "syllabic chemistry," perhaps reminding the reader of *Finnegans Wake*. In a footnote, Freud quotes the criticism of Fliess when he read the proofs, that "the dreamer seems to be too ingenious and amusing" (Freud does not quote his own reply, that "All dreamers are insufferably witty"). The dream-work is in fact very like the composition of poetry. One dream has "a particularly amusing and elegant form"; another, "remarkable among other things for its form," alternates idea and image as a poem does. Like the poem-work the dream-work "does not think, calculate or judge in any way at all; it restricts itself to giving things a new form." Freud was not pleased with his book's style. He writes to Fliess:

> The matter about dreams I believe to be unassailable; what I dislike about it is the style. I was quite unable to express myself with noble simplicity, but lapsed into a facetious, circumlocutory straining after the picturesque. I know that, but the part of me that knows it and appraises it is unfortunately not the part that is productive.

In answer to Fliess' reassurances, Freud replies ten days later:

> But I do not think that my self-criticism was wholly unjustified. Somewhere inside me there is a feeling for form, an appreciation of beauty as a kind of perfection; and the tortuous sentences of the dream-book, with its high-flown, indirect phraseology, its squinting at the point, has sorely offended one of my ideals.

A more interesting matter than the book's style (which is, by general agreement, much better than Freud thought) is its tone. There are in fact two tones. The first is the tone of Sherlock Holmes, the Great Detective: assured, intolerant, firm and strong. Of a difference of opinion between himself and a patient, Freud remarks: "Soon afterwards it turned out that I was right." When a dreamer protests over revealing a delicate circumstance behind the dream, Freud says with all of Holmes' forcefulness: "Nevertheless I shall have to hear it." His comment on an "innocent" dream he interprets as a masturbation fantasy is: "Altogether *far* from innocent." He announces vigorously, "Whatever interrupts the progress of analytic work is a resistance," recognizing no calamities or catastrophes, from a broken leg to a war, that are not the patient's devilment. We can see Conan Doyle's hand in the titles Freud gives the dreams, so like Holmes cases: The Dream of Irma's Injection, The Dream of the Botanical Monograph; and Doyle as well as Sophocles has had a clear influence on Freud's form of delayed revelation and suspense.[1] Freud writes typically: "We shall find later that the enigma of the formation of dreams can be solved by the revelation of an unsuspected psychical source of stimulation." The book's contrasting tone is a modest, scientific humility, rather like Darwin's in the *Origin*. Freud writes: "I shall further endeavour to elucidate," "I have been driven to realize," "I did not expect to find my guess at an interpretation justified," and so on. It is as though behind the manifest book, like the manifest dream-content, there were a latent book, like the latent dream-content, making a very different sort of statement.

---

[1]When Theodor Reik suggested this comparison with Holmes (for Freud's technique, not his tone) in 1913, Freud said he would prefer a comparison with Giovanni Morelli, a nineteenth-century art scholar who specialized in detecting fakes.

Of course there is. Only on the surface is this a book about the objective interpretation of dreams. Not only is there a subjective book beneath the surface, the account of Freud's own neurosis, self-analysis and cure, but Freud clearly calls our attention to it in *The Interpretation of Dreams,* with no more dissembling than an "as it were." Interpreting a dream about the dissection of his own pelvis, he writes:

> The dissection meant the self-analysis which I was carrying out, as it were, in the publication of this present book about dreams—a process which had been so distressing to me in reality that I had postponed the printing of the finished manuscript for more than a year.

In the preface to the second edition in 1908, Freud makes this even clearer. He writes:

> For this book has a further subjective significance for me personally—a significance which I only grasped after I had completed it. It was, I found, a portion of my own self-analysis, my reaction to my father's death—that is to say, to the most important event, the most poignant loss, of a man's life. Having discovered that this was so, I felt unable to obliterate the traces of the experience.

Despite these clear statements, to the best of my knowledge no one recognized the autobiographical extent of the book until the publication of Freud's letters to Fliess, in German in 1950 and in English as *The Origins of Psychoanalysis* in 1954.

Wilhelm Fliess was a Berlin nose-and-throat specialist and biological theorist,[2] with whom Freud had a close friendship in the years between 1895 and 1900. Freud destroyed his letters from Fliess, but Fliess kept his from Freud, and after his death in 1928 they were sold to a bookseller in Berlin and were eventually bought by Marie Bonaparte, who bravely defied Freud when he insisted they be destroyed, and published them after his death. The 284 documents, ranging in time from 1887 to 1902, are a uniquely fascinating one-sided correspondence to read, and a remarkable insight into the origins of psychoanalysis generally and the genesis of *The Interpretation of Dreams* specifically.

In his letters to Fliess we can see the agonized stages of Freud's self-analysis, which resulted in the emergence of what Jones in his biography calls "the serene and benign Freud" of the twentieth century. In June, 1897, Freud reports to Fliess: "I have never yet imagined anything like my present spell of intellectual paralysis. Every line I write is torture." He continues:

---

[2]Fliess' weird cyclic theories apparently still have followers. *Biorhythm,* by Hans J. Wernli, was published in this country in 1960. It is a popular account of the Fliess system, with instructions to the reader for making his own Biorhythmic chart, and it includes sample rhythmograms of Tyrone Power, Louis Bromfield, George Gershwin, and Henry Ford.

> Incidentally, I have been through some kind of a neurotic experience, with odd states of mind not intelligible to consciousness—cloudy thoughts and veiled doubts, with barely here and there a ray of light.

In July, he reports:

> I still do not know what has been happening to me. Something from the deepest depths of my own neurosis has ranged itself against my taking a further step in understanding of the neuroses, and you have somehow been involved.

... In October, things are going easier, and Freud reports:

> So far I have found nothing completely new, but all the complications to which by now I am used. It is no easy matter. Being entirely honest with oneself is a good exercise. Only one idea of general value has occurred to me. I have found love of the mother and jealousy of the father in my own case too, and now believe it to be a general phenomenon of early childhood.

... In November, Freud again hit trouble. He explains:

> My self-analysis is still interrupted. I have now seen why. I can only analyze myself with objectively-acquired knowledge (as if I were a stranger); self-analysis is really impossible, otherwise there would be no illness.

... By February of 1898 it was over, and Freud writes to Fliess: "Self-analysis has been dropped in favor of the dream book."

The Interpretation of Dreams constantly informs us of the author's reticence about revealing his dreams and their background. He writes:

> There is some natural hesitation about revealing so many intimate facts about one's mental life; nor can there be any guarantee against misinterpretation by strangers. But it must be possible to overcome such hesitation. ... And it is safe to assume that my readers too will very soon find their initial interest in the indiscretions which I am bound to make replaced by an absorbing immersion in the psychological problems upon which they throw light.

... At a sexually-suggestive detail in his dream of Irma's injection, Freud breaks off with "Frankly, I had no desire to penetrate more deeply at this point."[3] In a 1909 footnote to the interpretation of the dream, he adds:

> Though it will be understood that I have not reported everything that occurred to me during the process of interpretation.

---

[3]The dream of Irma's injection is brilliantly reanalyzed in terms of ego psychology by Erik H. Erikson in "The Dream Specimen of Psychoanalysis" in the *Journal of the American Psychoanalytic Association,* January 1954. Erikson goes much more fully into the dream than Freud did in the book, making explicit a good deal of the sexuality that Freud left implicit. [A partial and much condensed version of Erikson's essay appears in *Identity: Youth and Crisis* (New York: Norton, 1968). Ed.]

In concluding the chapter, he challenges the reader:

> But considerations which arise in the case of every dream of my own restrain me from pursuing my interpretive work. If anyone should feel tempted to express a hasty condemnation of my reticence, I would advise him to make the experiment of being franker than I am.

... We learn from a number of surprising letters to his fiancée the very considerable extent of Freud's own repression and prudishness. We must thus recognize Freud's impressive heroism in making these revelations. He is in fact the bravest sort of hero, a hero of the ludicrous. Men can confess with relative ease to rapes and murders they have committed, but it takes much more courage for Freud to begin the interpretation of one of his dreams with the announcement that at the time of the dream "a boil the size of an apple had risen at the base of my scrotum." At the same time that we recognize Freud's honesty, we must recognize its limits. He admits that he is not telling us the whole truth about himself, and that he is falsifying some of what he does tell. Explaining that "the politeness which I practise every day is to a large extent dissimulation," he adds, "and when I interpret my dreams for my readers I am obliged to adopt similar distortions." Freud acknowledges this more fully in the preface. He writes:

> But if I were to report my own dreams, it inevitably followed that I should have to reveal to the public gaze more of the intimacies of my mental life than I liked, or than is normally necessary for any writer who is a man of science and not a poet. Such was the painful but unavoidable necessity; and I have submitted to it rather than totally abandon the possibility of giving the evidence for my psychological findings. Naturally, however, I have been unable to resist the temptation of taking the edge off some of my indiscretions by omissions and substitutions.

In August of 1899, Freud writes to Fliess:

> I am deep in the chapter on the "dream-work" and have replaced—I think to advantage—the complete dream that you deleted by a small collection of dream-fragments.

The next month he assures Fliess: "I have avoided sex, but 'dirt' is unavoidable." In short, Freud has consciously disguised the material of the book as the dream-work unconsciously disguises, by a censoring process very like secondary revision.

Anyone who reread *The Interpretation of Dreams* after reading the Fliess correspondence must have had an uncanny experience: where Fliess had been invisible in the book before, he was suddenly omnipresent. In his superb new variorum translation of *The Interpretation of Dreams*, published in 1954, James Strachey identifies many of these references. What had on first reading seemed to be a hundred friends all turn out to be Wilhelm Fliess. As the hidden subject of the dream of Irma's injection, Fliess is: "another friend who had for many years been familiar with all my writings during the period of my gestation, just as I had with his"; "a person whose agreement I recalled with satisfaction whenever I felt isolated in my opinions"; "this friend who played so large a part in my life." As the disguised subject of the dream of the botanical monograph, Fliess is involved in a tender fantasy:

> If ever I got glaucoma, I had thought, I should travel to Berlin and get my-self operated on, incognito, in my friend's house, by a surgeon recommended by him.

One of the events inspiring the dream was "a letter from my friend in Berlin the day before." When Freud returns to Irma's injection, two more Fliesses turn up: "a friend who was seriously ill" in Munich a year before, and "my friend in Berlin, who *did* understand me, who would take my side, and to whom I owed so much valuable information, dealing, amongst other things, with the chemistry of the sexual processes."

... The relationship with Fliess seems to have had, as Freud recognized, a strong homosexual component. (In one letter, he even addresses Fliess as "Dearest.") For the self-analysis, the attachment performed the vital function of an analytic transference, enabling Freud to project onto Fliess his infantile relations with his parents and other relatives. The success of the self-analysis not only cured Freud of his neurosis, but of the trans-ference, and the friendship inevitably came to an end. During the com-position of *The Interpretation of Dreams*, Freud writes to Fliess:

> So you see what happens. I live gloomily and in darkness until you come, and then I pour out all my grumbles to you, kindle my flickering light at your steady flame and feel well again; and after your departure I have eyes to see again, and what I look upon is good.

In 1900 Freud writes: "But there can be no substitute for the close contact with a friend which a particular—almost a feminine—side of me calls for." When their friendship turned into bickering in 1901, Freud writes to Fliess, "I was sorry to lose my 'only audience.'" Nine years later, Freud showed in a letter to Sandor Ferenczi that he understood the Fliess relationship. He writes, somewhat over-optimistically:

> You not only noticed, but also understood, that I *no longer* have any need to uncover my personality completely, and you correctly traced this back to the traumatic reason for it. Since Fliess's case, with the overcoming of which you recently saw me occupied, that need has been extinguished. A part of homo-sexual cathexis has been withdrawn and made use of to enlarge my own ego. I have succeeded where the paranoic fails.

... According to *Glory Reflected,* a memoir by Freud's son Martin, Fliess' photograph continued to occupy a place of honor in his father's study after the break.

Beneath the attachment to Fliess in *The Interpretation of Dreams* is of course the Oedipus complex. ... When Alfred Adler and Wilhelm Stekel broke with Freud, Jones says, Ferenczi suggested that Freud was "living over again the unpleasant experience of Fliess's desertion of him ten years ago, and Freud confirmed this." "I had quite got over the Fliess affair," Freud writes to Ferenczi. "Adler is a little Fliess come to life again. And his appendage Stekel is at least called Wilhelm." In 1912, when C. G. Jung signalled his approaching break by remissness in answering Freud's letters, Freud was reminded, Jones says, "of the same course of events with Fliess where the first sign of Fliess's cooling towards him was his delay in answering Freud's letters" (although in the case of Fliess, Freud had cooled first).

Before Fliess there had been a number of such ambivalent or soon-souring attachments. One of them was with Freud's brother-in-law and old friend, Eli Bernays. Another was with Freud's teacher, Theodor Meynert, of whom Freud tells a very dramatic story in *The Interpretation of Dreams.* He writes:

> I had carried on an embittered controversy with him in writing, on the subject of male hysteria, the existence of which he denied. When I visited him during his fatal illness and asked after his condition, he spoke at some length about his state and ended with these words: "You know, I was always one of the clearest cases of male hysteria." He was thus admitting, to my satisfaction and astonishment, what he had for so long obstinately contested.

Another such was Breuer, who gets into a Fliess dream in the book. Freud broke with Breuer in 1896, at the beginning of the period Jones calls "the more passionate phase of his relations with Fliess," and in letters to Fliess at the time Freud reviles Breuer bitterly. Jones writes:

> Breuer was failing in his role as father-protector by repudiating Freud's researches and rejecting his conclusions. Yet how could one with an easy conscience turn against a person who for fifteen years had done so much to help and support one? In early life Freud had found it impossible to hate his father, and had concealed his hostility by love. The same solution was the only feasible one now, but the outer reality forbade it except by the device of "decomposing" the father-person into two, one "good," the other "bad." So hatred was directed against Breuer, and love towards Fliess—both in an excessive degree out of proportion to the merits or demerits of the persons themselves. We know that with Freud intense love and hate were specially apt to go hand in hand.

Without the intense hate, Freud was similarly swept off his feet by Charcot, of whom he writes his fiancée in 1885:

Charcot, who is one of the greatest of physicians and a man whose common sense borders on genius, is simply wrecking all my aims and opinions. I sometimes come out of his lectures as from out of Notre Dame, with an entirely new idea about perfection. But he exhausts me; when I come away from him I no longer have any desire to work at my own silly things; it is three whole days since I have done any work, and I have no feelings of guilt. My brain is sated as after an evening in the theater. Whether the seed will ever bear any fruit I don't know; but what I do know is that no other human being has ever affected me in the same way.

Less intensely, Freud had been similarly involved with another teacher, Ernst Bruecke, and with Bruecke's assistant, Ernst Fleischl von Marxow. After Fliess there were many others among the more imaginative of Freud's psychoanalytic followers, particularly Jung, Stekel, Otto Rank, and Ferenczi. The passionate letters to Jung are as embarrassing to read as the earlier ones to Fliess. Freud writes to Jung in 1907 "of the calm assurance that finally took possession of me and bade me wait until a voice from the unknown answered mine. That voice was yours." The successive editions of *The Interpretation of Dreams* are like a stratification of developing friendships and favoritisms: Jung appears in the second edition in 1909; Stekel dominates the third in 1911; and Ferenczi and Rank take over from the fourth in 1914 on.

The ambivalent relationship toward Stekel in the book is particularly interesting. Freud began as a relativist in dream interpretation, insisting that images have a unique meaning for each dreamer in the context of his associations. Stekel was an absolutist, insisting that dreams use universal symbols that can be listed in a handbook, as he did so list them in *Die Sprache des Traumes* in 1911 and in later works. Over the years Freud became more and more convinced by Stekel (who had first come to him as a patient), and *The Interpretation of Dreams* expanded to include more and more general dream symbolism. In the 1909 edition Freud lists all sorts of objections to the Stekel approach, admits "we shall feel tempted to draw up a new 'dream-book' on the decoding principle," and then writes: "Subject to these qualifications and reservations I will now proceed." He goes on to compile a moderate gypsy dream book: the emperor and empress "as a rule" are the father and mother, umbrellas "may" stand for the male organ, ovens usually represent the uterus, etc. In later editions this was enormously expanded, became a new section, and lost much of its tentative tone. In the 1925 collected edition, long after the break with Stekel, Freud wrote an acknowledgment of his influence, still deeply ambivalent: Stekel "has perhaps damaged psychoanalysis as much as he has benefited it," and the intuitive method by which he gets his readings "must be rejected as scientifically untrustworthy"; yet Stekel is ultimately right, and on the subject of absolute symbolism Freud concedes: "It was only by degrees and as my experience increased that I arrived at a full appreciation of its extent and significance, and I did so under the influence of the contributions of Wilhelm Stekel."

Years after the break with Fliess, International Psychoanalytic Congresses were held in four of the six towns where Freud and Fliess had held their "congresses," and a return to a fifth was scheduled but prevented by the first World War. At a meeting with Jung and a few other followers in Munich in 1912, while lunching at a hotel, Freud suddenly fainted. Two weeks later he had an explanation. He writes to Jones:

> I cannot forget that six and four years ago I suffered from very similar though not such intense symptoms in the *same* room of the Park Hotel. I saw Munich first when I visited Fliess during his illness and this town seems to have acquired a strong connection with my relation to that man. There is some piece of unruly homosexual feeling at the root of the matter.

One earlier fainting in the dining room of the Park, Jones says in *Free Associations,* was during a painful scene with Rie, Freud's lifelong friend, family doctor, and tarock-crony. Freud had also fainted at Bremen in 1909, in the presence of Jung and Ferenczi.

Even deeper in Freud's psyche...was the figure concealed by displacement, the figure of his father. As Freud says in the 1908 preface, it was guilts connected with his father's death in 1896 that inspired the self-analysis and the book. Freud discusses typical dreams "containing the death of some loved relative," and says of at least one group of them, those with a painful affect, that their meaning is "a wish that the person in question may die." As examples of absurd dreams he gives "two or three dreams which deal (by chance, as it may seem at first sight) with the dreamer's dead father." Freud introduces the second of them: "Here is another, almost exactly similar, example from a dream of my own. (I lost my father in 1896.)" Another is introduced:

> For instance, a man who had nursed his father during his last illness and had been deeply grieved by his death, had the following senseless dream some time afterwards.

The dream is a very brief one of the father being dead and not knowing it, and Freud goes on to interpret it. He writes:

> While he was nursing his father he had repeatedly wished his father were dead; that is to say, he had had what was actually a merciful thought that death might put an end to his sufferings. During his mourning, after his father's death, even this sympathetic wish became a subject of unconscious self-reproach, as though by means of it he had really helped to shorten the sick man's life. A stirring up of the dreamer's earliest infantile impulses against his father made it possible for this self-reproach to find expression

as a dream; but the fact that the instigator of the dream and the daytime thoughts were such worlds apart was precisely what necessitated the dream's absurdity.

If this is not Freud's own dream, it is one he powerfully identified with, since he repeats it in a 1911 paper, and tells another like it in his *Introductory Lectures*. Freud readily admits to such identification in *The Interpretation of Dreams*. He writes of a patient:

> I knew that the root of his illness had been hostile impulses against his father, dating from his childhood and involving a sexual situation. Insofar, therefore, as I was identifying myself with him, I was seeking to confess to something analogous.

Freud generalizes about absurd dreams and dead fathers, in a clearly autobiographical statement:

> Nor is it by any means a matter of chance that our first examples of absurdity in dreams related to a dead father. In such cases, the conditions for creating absurd dreams are found together in characteristic fashion. The authority wielded by a father provokes criticism from his children at an early age, and the severity of the demands he makes upon them leads them, for their own relief, to keep their eyes open to any weakness of their father's; but the filial piety called up in our minds by the figure of a father, particularly after his death, tightens the censorship which prohibits any such criticism from being consciously expressed.

He then begins "Here is another absurd dream about a dead father," and gives one more dream of his own. Freud's father seems to have been kind but somewhat strict. Jones writes:

> On the other hand, the father was after all a Jewish patriarch and so demanded corresponding respect. Moritz Rosenthal, the pianist, tells a story of how one day he was having an argument with his father in the street when they encountered Jakob Freud, who laughingly reproved him thus: "What, are you contradicting your father? My Sigmund's little toe is cleverer than my head, but he would never dare to contradict me!"

We know something of Freud's reaction to his father's death from a series of letters to Fliess. He writes the day after the funeral:

> The old man died on the night of the 23rd, and we buried him yesterday. He bore himself bravely up to the end, like the remarkable man he was.

In response to Fliess's letter of condolence, Freud writes:

> I find it so difficult to put pen to paper at the moment that I have even put off writing to you to thank you for the moving things you said in your letter. By one of the obscure routes behind the official consciousness the old man's

death affected me deeply. I valued him highly and understood him very well indeed, and with his peculiar mixture of deep wisdom and imaginative lightheartedness he meant a great deal in my life. By the time he died his life had long been over, but at a death the whole past stirs within one. I feel now as if I had been torn up by the roots.

He goes on to tell Fliess about "a very pretty dream I had on the night after the funeral." In 1899, while at work on *The Interpretation of Dreams*, Freud writes to Fliess, in connection with some thoughts about death: "My father knew that he was dying, did not speak about it and retained his composure to the end." A few weeks after the book was published, he reports to Fliess:

> Two of my patients have almost simultaneously arrived at self-reproach over the nursing and death of their parents, and shown me that my dreams about this were typical. The guilt is in such cases connected with revenge feelings, malicious pleasure at the patient's sufferings, the patient's excretory difficulties (both urine and stools). Truly an unsuspected corner of mental life.

This is the heart of Freud's revelation about his ambivalence toward his father. In explaining a dream inspired by his father in *The Interpretation of Dreams*, Freud gives us the traumatic childhood scene. He writes:

> When I was seven or eight years old there was another domestic scene, which I can remember very clearly. One evening before going to sleep I disregarded the rules which modesty lays down and obeyed the calls of nature in my parents' bedroom while they were present. In the course of his reprimand, my father let fall the words: "The boy will come to nothing." This must have been a frightful blow to my ambition, for references to this scene are still constantly recurring in my dreams and are always linked with an enumeration of my achievements and successes, as though I wanted to say: 'You see, I *have* come to something.'"[4] This scene, then, provided the material for the final episode of the dream, in which—in revenge, of course—the roles were interchanged. The older man (clearly my father, since his blindness in one eye referred to his unilateral glaucoma) was now micturating in front of me, just as I had in front of him in my childhood. In the reference to his glaucoma I was reminding him of the cocaine, which had helped him in the operation, as though I had in that way kept my promise. Moreover I was making fun of him; I had to hand him the urinal because he was blind, and I revelled in allusions to my discoveries in connection with the theory of hysteria, of which I felt so proud.

[4]Martin Freud tells an anecdote that shows how thoroughly Freud later came to fill all of his father's roles. When Martin's son Walter, Freud's grandson, was four, he cranked up a truck parked on the street and got the motor started. Furiously angry, Freud said that "there was not the slightest sense in becoming attached to a boy who must sooner or later kill himself in dangerous escapades."

Freud mentions in a footnote

> the tragic requital that lay in my father's soiling his bed like a child during the last days of his life.

In a sense, the whole of psychoanalysis stems from that bedroom scene at seven or eight. Freud later gives a dream of his own, about washing away feces with urine, with the introductory statement that it "will fill every reader with disgust." He interprets it as a boast about his scientific achievements, and sees himself in the role of the cleansing father: "I had discovered the infantile aetiology of the neuroses and had thus saved my own children from falling ill." The day before the dream he had "longed to be away from all this grubbing in human dirt," and the dream reassured him. Analyzing an absurd dream about his father, Freud writes:

> These elevated thoughts prepared the way for the appearance of something which was common in another sense. My father's *post mortem* rise of temperature corresponded to the words "after his death" in the dream. His most severe suffering had been caused by a complete paralysis *(obstruction)* of the intestines during his last weeks. Disrespectful thoughts of all kinds followed from this. One of my contemporaries who lost his father while he was still at his secondary school — on that occasion I myself had been deeply moved and had offered to be his friend — once told me scornfully of how one of his female relatives had had a painful experience. Her father had fallen dead in the street and had been brought home; when his body was undressed it was found that at the moment of death, or *post mortem,* he had passed a stool. His daughter had been so unhappy about this that she could not prevent this ugly detail from disturbing her memory of her father. Here we have reached the wish that was embodied in this dream. "To stand before one's children's eyes, after one's death, great and unsullied" — who would not desire this?

He continues:

> The little boy's right to appear in the context of this dream was derived from the fact that he had just had the same misadventure — easily forgivable both in a child and in a dying man — of soiling his bed-clothes.

Along with the major excretory theme, a few minor themes related to Freud's father run through *The Interpretation of Dreams.* One is gray hair. In reaction to the misdeeds of a brother, Freud believed, his father's hair "turned gray from grief in a few days." At the time of the self-analysis, Freud was displeased to find his own beard graying. In a dream, he writes, "the beard further involved an allusion to my father and myself through the intermediate idea of growing gray." In interpreting the dream of dissecting his own pelvis, he explains:

> But I should also have been very glad to miss growing gray — *"Grauen"* in the other sense of the word. I was already growing quite gray, and the gray

of my hair was another reminder that I must not delay any longer. And, as we have seen, the thought that I should have to leave it to my children to reach the goal of my difficult journey forced its way through to representation at the end of the dream.

Another father image is fur. Freud reports a story that his father told him when he was ten or twelve:

> "When I was a young man," he said, "I went for a walk one Saturday in the streets of your birthplace; I was well dressed, and had a new fur cap on my head. A Christian came up to me and with a single blow knocked off my cap into the mud and shouted "Jew! get off the pavement!'" "And what did you do?" I asked. "I went into the roadway and picked up my cap," was his quiet reply. This struck me as unheroic conduct on the part of the big, strong man who was holding the little boy by the hand.

A few pages later a *coat* trimmed with fur appears in a dream involving his mother, but Freud either does not recognize the image or does not comment on it. A third theme is his father's glaucoma, which comes up in the dream of the botanical monograph as well as in the revenge dream of handing his blind father the urinal, and in the fantasy of himself getting glaucoma and putting himself in the hands of Fliess.

The principal guilt dream involving Freud's father in the book is the dream of the burning child. It does not appear until the last chapter, although it is foreshadowed earlier by a dream of a patient about sitting before a child's coffin surrounded by candles. The dream of the burning child opens the last chapter, and Freud goes to great pains to make it clear that it is *not* his own dream. He begins:

> Among the dreams which have been reported to me by other people, there is one which has special claims upon our attention at this point. It was told to me by a woman patient who had herself heard it in a lecture on dreams: its actual source is still unknown to me. Its content made an impression on the lady, however, and she proceeded to "re-dream" it, that is, to repeat some of its elements in a dream of her own, so that, by taking it over in this way, she might express her agreement with it on one particular point.
>
> The preliminaries to this model dream were as follows. A father had been watching beside his child's sick-bed for days and nights on end. After the child had died, he went into the next room to lie down, but left the door open so that he could see from his bedroom into the room in which his child's body was laid out, with tall candles standing round it. An old man had been engaged to keep watch over it, and sat beside the body murmuring prayers. After a few hours' sleep, the father had a dream that *his child was standing beside his bed, caught him by the arm and whispered to him reproachfully: "Father, don't you see I'm burning?"* He woke up, noticed a bright glare of light from the next room, hurried into it and found that the old watchman had dropped off to sleep and that the wrappings and one of the arms of his be-

loved child's dead body had been burned by a lighted candle that had fallen on them.

If this dream was not Freud's originally (and the explanation of insistent denials as confirmations that he published in the 1925 paper "Negation" suggests that it was), or if he did not re-dream it, he indentified with it so strongly that it becomes the key image of his guilt. Applied to Freud, it would be the dream of the burning father, with Jakob Freud whispering reproachfully: "Son, don't you see I'm burning?"[5] Freud keeps returning to it all through the chapter: "Its interpretation was not given fully in our sense"; "The unusually subordinate part played in this dream by wish-fulfilment is remarkable"; "The dream of the burning child at the beginning of this chapter gives us a welcome opportunity of considering the difficulties with which the theory of wish-fulfilment is faced"; finally, "Other wishes, originating from the repressed, probably escape us, since we are unable to analyze the dream."

. . . The part of Freud's Oedipus complex more repressed than the hostility to the father in *The Interpretation of Dreams* is the erotic attachment to the mother. Freud describes it openly (except for the comic Latin) in a letter to Fliess written during the self-analysis. He writes:

> At certain points I have the impression of having come to the end, and so far I have always known where the next night of dreams would continue. To describe it in writing is more difficult than anything else, and besides it is far too extensive. I can only say that in my case my father played no active role, though I certainly projected on to him an analogy from myself; that my "primary originator" was an utly, elderly but clever woman who told me a great deal about God and hell, and gave me a high opinion of my own capacities; that later (between the ages of two and two-and-a-half) libido towards *matrem* was aroused; the occasion must have been the journey with her from Leipzig to Vienna, during which we spent a night together and I must have had the opportunity of seeing her *nudam* (you have long since drawn the conclusions from this for your own son, as a remark of yours revealed); and that I welcomed my one-year-younger brother (who died within a few months) with ill wishes and real infantile jealousy, and that his death left the germ of guilt in me.

We see a number of these themes in the book. The nurse's early role in giving Freud a high opinion of his own capacities clearly continued his mother's favoritism. Freud writes:

> What, then, could have been the origin of th⌐ ambitiousness which produced the dream in me? At that point I recalled an anecdote I had often heard repeated in my childhood. At the time of my birth an old peasant-woman had

---

[5]Richard Blake suggests additional confirmation: Freud's father's *post mortem* rise of temperature, and the urethral associations of fire.

prophesied to my proud mother that with her first-born child she had brought a great man into the world. Prophecies of this kind must be very common: there are so many mothers filled with happy expectations and so many old peasant-women and others of the kind who make up for the loss of their power to control things in the present world by concentrating it on the future. Nor can the prophetess have lost anything by her words. Could this have been the source of my thirst for grandeur?

To a discussion of Oedipus dreams, "in which the dreamer has sexual intercourse with his own mother," Freud adds the footnote in 1911:

> I have found that people who know that they are preferred or favored by their mother give evidence in their lives of a peculiar self-reliance and an unshakable optimism which often seem like heroic attributes and bring actual success to their possessors.

Less favorably, Freud later refers to his mother-induced self-confidence as "an absurd megalomania which had long been suppressed in my waking life."

On the actual Oedipal desire, he is more reticent in the book. "Love and hunger," writes Freud, who was himself breast-fed, meet at a woman's breast." If the account of undisguised Oedipus dreams does not admit to Freud's having any, Freud does tell a disguised Oedipus dream, which he says was his last true anxiety-dream, at the age of seven or eight. He writes:

> It was a very vivid one, and in it I saw *my beloved mother, with a peculiarly peaceful, sleeping expression on her features, being carried into the room by two (or three) people with birds' beaks and laid upon the bed.*

His brief and quite reticent analysis concludes:

> The anxiety can be traced back, when repression is taken into account, to an obscure and evidently sexual craving that had found appropriate expression in the visual content of the dream.

The other ingredient of the Oedipus complex, the child's fear that the forbidden indulgence with his mother will bring death or castration, comes in oddly, in an anecdote of how his mother taught him to accept mortality at six. Beneath its apparent triviality, it makes an intimate association of death with the mother's flesh. Freud writes:

> When I was six years old and was given my first lessons by my mother, I was expected to believe that we were all made of earth and must therefore return to earth. This did not suit me and I expressed doubts of the doctrine. My mother thereupon rubbed the palms of her hands together—just as she did in making dumplings, except that there was no dough between them—and showed me the blackish scales of *epidermis* produced by the friction as a proof that we were made of earth. My astonishment at this ocular demonstration knew no bounds and I acquiesced in the belief.

The whole of Freud's Oedipus complex is indirectly revealed in two adjacent cases a page or so from the end of the book. One is of a girl whose hysteria transparently mimed copulation, although the girl's mother could not recognize it. The other is of a boy whose daydream of a sickle and scythe concealed a wish to castrate his father. Freud is clearly a composite of both children: driven by an infantile sexuality his mother failed to recognize, torn by an infantile murderous hostility his father never discovered.

With the recognition comes release; with confession, absolution. Early in the book, Freud quotes Plato's idea "that the best men are those who only *dream* what other men *do* in their waking life." His positive slogan in *The Interpretation of Dreams* (anticipating the later "Where id was, there shall ego be") is: "Psychotherapy can pursue no other course than to bring the Unconscious under the domination of the Preconscious." When these repressed infantile guilty wishes were brought to consciousness by the ego, they could be dismissed: wishes are not omnipotent, they do not kill; my father did not die because I wished him dead as a child, or even as an adult. The last four paragraphs of the book finally get around to the ethical question and absolve Freud. Recalling Plato's formulation, Freud writes, "I think it is best, therefore, to acquit dreams." "Actions and consciously expressed opinions," he decides, "are as a rule enough for practical purposes in judging men's characters." Freud concludes: "It is in any case instructive to get to know the much trampled soil from which our virtues proudly spring."

The Interpretation of Dreams, we learn from a letter Freud wrote to Fliess in 1899, has a planned imaginative organization. He writes:

> The whole thing is planned on the model of an imaginary walk. First comes the dark wood of the authorities (who cannot see the trees), where there is no clear view and it is very easy to go astray. Then there is a cavernous defile through which I lead my readers—my specimen dream with its peculiarities, its details, its indiscretions, and its bad jokes—and then, all at once, the high ground and the prospect, and the question: "Which way do you want to go?"

Freud first makes the walk metaphor visible at the beginning of the third chapter, after the lengthy analysis in the second chapter of the dream of Irma's injection. He writes:

> When, after passing through a narrow defile, we suddenly emerge upon a piece of high ground, where the path divides and the finest prospects open up on every side, we may pause for a moment and consider in which direction we shall first turn our steps. Such is the case with us, now that we have surmounted the first interpretation of a dream. We find ourselves in the full day-light of a sudden discovery.

Beginning the fifth chapter, Freud writes:

> Having followed one path to its end, we may now retrace our steps and choose another starting-point for our rambles through the problems of dream-life.

The seventh chapter announces, near the beginning:

> But before starting off along this new path, it will be well to pause and look around, to see whether in the course of our journeys up to this point we have overlooked anything of importance. For it must be clearly understood that the easy and agreeable portion of our journey lies behind us. Hitherto, unless I am greatly mistaken, all the paths along which we have travelled have led us towards the light—towards elucidation and fuller understanding. But as soon as we endeavor to penetrate more deeply into the mental process involved in dreaming, every path will end in darkness.

Two things should be noticed. First, we are going circuitously only because dreams do, and we follow their movements. The "paths" leading to the unconscious cross "verbal bridges," and so forth. Freud writes:

> Superficial associations replace deep ones if the censorship makes the normal connecting paths impassable. We may picture, by way of analogy, a mountain region, where some general interruption of traffic (owing to floods, for instance) has blocked the main, major roads, but where communications are still maintained over inconvenient and steep footpaths normally used only by the hunter.

Second, all of these dark woods, narrow defiles, high grounds and deep penetrations are unconscious sexual imagery, and we are exploring a woman's body, that of Freud's mother. In the first chapter, Freud speaks of someone's failure to follow the path that would have led him to "the very heart" of an explanation, and we know that path that leads to the heart. If it seems unlikely that the discoverer of unconscious sexual imagery should have missed his own, we can only observe that such are the devious workings of the unconscious, remembering that Freud wrote innocently to Fliess, just after his father's death: "I am busy thinking out something which would cement our work together and put my column on your base."

As the book's paths leave the light for the darkness in the last chapter, lit only by the fitful flames of that curious torch, Freud's father, the organizing metaphor switches from walking to digging or mining. Freud had earlier remarked in a footnote: "There is at least one spot in every dream at which it is unplumbable—a navel, as it were, that is its point of contact with the unknown." In the last chapter Freud picks up that image and expands it in a tangle of metaphor (perhaps what he meant by "straining after the picturesque" in the letter to Fliess). Freud writes:

There is often a passage in even the most thoroughly interpreted dream which has to be left obscure; this is because we become aware during the work of interpretation that at that point there is a tangle of dream-thoughts which cannot be unravelled and which moreover adds nothing to our knowledge of the content of the dream. This is the dream's navel, the spot where it reaches down into the unknown. The dream thought to which we are led by interpretation cannot, from the nature of things, have any definite endings; they are bound to branch out in every direction into the intricate network of our world of thought. It is at some point where this meshwork is particularly close that the dream-wish grows up, like a mushroom out of its mycelium.

A few pages later he says:

It is true that in carrying out the interpretation in the waking state we follow a path which leads back from the elements of the dream to the dream-thoughts and that the dream-work followed one in the contrary direction. But it is highly improbable that these paths are passable both ways. It appears, rather, that in the daytime we drive shafts which follow along fresh chains of thought and that these shafts make contact with the intermediate thoughts and the dream-thoughts now at one point and now at another.

What we do down there in the tunnel or mine, oddly, is build. "We have been obliged," Freud writes movingly, "to build our way out into the dark," and adds that the time may come "when we shall find ourselves more at home in it." Freud talks of his psychological or conceptual "scaffolding," and warns us not to mistake it for the finished building; "our edifice is still uncompleted."

Freud qualifies his metaphors in a passage very reminiscent of Darwin's in *The Origin of Species*. He writes:

I see no necessity to apologize for the imperfections of this or any similar imagery. Analogies of this kind are only intended to assist us in our attempt to make the complications of mental functioning intelligible.

Later he remarks: "Let us replace these metaphors by something that seems to correspond better to the real state of affairs." Since this turns out to be only a better metaphor, we realize once again that his metaphors *are* his vision of reality.

Besides the key one of the walk that climbs down and then goes up again, there are a number of other thematic metaphors in *The Interpretation of Dreams*. Perhaps the most pervasive of them is of warfare. Freud says of the dream of the botanical monograph that it has "an indifferent ring about it," and explains: "This reminds one of the peace that has descended upon a battlefield strewn with corpses; no trace is left of the struggle which raged over it." Of another dream: "The state of things is what it was after some sweeping revolution in one of the republics of antiquity or the Renaissance." He speaks of where "our defensive weapons lie," of resistance as "guarding the frontier," and so forth. The warfare is seen primarily as the storming of a fortress: "The state of sleep guarantees the security of the citadel that must be guarded"; in psychosis "the watchman is overpowered"; a phobia "is like a frontier fortification"; the unconscious even has "a kind of sally-gate" so that it can take the offensive against the besiegers. Freud explains in summary that these images are "derived from a set of ideas relating to a struggle for a piece of ground." Again, in Freudian terms, we know what ground, what fortress.

Freud's theories were always deeply dualistic. Jones explains:

> One is naturally tempted to correlate this tendency with its manifestations in Freud's own personality. There was the fight between scientific discipline and philosophical speculation; his passionate love urge and his unusually great sexual repression; his vigorous masculinity, which shines through all his writings, and his feminine needs; his desire to create everything himself and his longing to receive stimulation from another; his love of independence and his needs of dependence. But such thoughts assuredly bring the risk of falsification from the lure of simplistic solutions.

For a divided personality dealing with an ambivalent subject-matter, what better metaphor than warfare?

Another metaphor, visible in many of the quotations above, is light. The book (like Freud's self-analysis) can be seen as an act of bringing that which attempts to "throw light" on something or enlighten, and at a key point Freud typically remarks: "We can now see our way a little further." If the paths that first led us toward the light end in darkness in the last chapter, it is a darkness that will eventually be lighted by knowledge, and the whole book (like Freud's self-analysis) can be seen as an act of bringing that which was buried in the dark up into the light. There is also a range of metaphors from natural science. Freud's hope was that his psychology would eventually be grounded in neurology, that "deeper research will one day trace the path further and discover an organic basis for the mental event," or "find a means of picturing the movements that accompany excitation of neurones." He produces a series of metaphors for the mind from mechanical instruments: "a compound microscope or a photographic apparatus, or something of that kind." The dream is "that most marvelous and most mysterious of all instruments," and seen in scientific imagery the censorship is no longer a watchman or guardian of a fortress, but is comparable to "the refraction which takes place when a ray of light passes into a new medium." Another metaphor is electricity, and dream formation makes new connections like "short-circuits," wishes are "currents in the apparatus," etc. Still another series of analogies is drawn from various sorts of picture language. Dream expression is "a pictographic script," "a picture-puzzle, a rebus," "hieroglyphic script," and so on. Dreams "present no greater difficulties to their translators than do the ancient hieroglyphic scripts to those who seek to read them."

A variety of minor metaphors enliven the book. Dream-thoughts are jammed up, "almost like pack-ice"; a dream is like a scrambled "algebraic equation"; analysis results in cure as though "the assertions made in the text are borne out by the accompanying illustrations"; day thoughts need unconscious wishes invested in them as entrepreneurs need capitalists; a repressed idea is like an American dentist in Austria, unable to practice without a local "front"; a dream "is like a firework, which takes hours to prepare but goes off in a moment."

Our best clue to the imaginative form of the book is the epigraph from *The Aeneid* on the title page, *Flectere si nequeo superos, Acheronta movebo* ("If I cannot bend the higher powers, I will stir up the infernal regions"). Freud borrowed it from a book by Ferdinand Lassalle, and first intended it, we learn from an 1896 letter to Fliess, to be the epigraph for a chapter on symptom-formation in a work of general psychology he intended to write. Freud explains in a note in his collected works: "This line of Virgil is intended to picture the efforts of the repressed instinctual impulses." When it is quoted near the end of *The Interpretation of Dreams,* that is its obvious reference, and Freud always denied that it had any other. Nevertheless, it clearly refers to Freud himself as well as to repressed wishes, and is his ultimate answer to his father's prophecy that he would never amount to anything. Freud is a mythic hero who has made the dangerous journey into the underworld and come back with the treasure, and in this aspect the book's form is that of a successful mythic quest.

Freud writes:

> The respect paid to dreams in antiquity is, however, based upon correct psychological insight and is the homage paid to the uncontrolled and indestructible forces in the human mind, to the "daemonic" power which produces the dream-wish and which we find at work in our unconscious.

The Interpretation of Dreams is full of these daemonic powers. Freud writes:

> These wishes in our unconscious, ever on the alert and, so to say, immortal, remind one of the legendary Titans, weighed down since primeval ages by the massive bulk of the mountains which were once hurled upon them by the victorious gods and which are still shaken from time to time by the convulsion of their limbs.

He adds in a footnote:

> If I may use a simile, they are only capable of annihilation in the same sense as the ghosts in the underworld of *The Odyssey* — ghosts which awoke to new life as soon as they tasted blood.

Freud continues: "Indeed it is a prominent feature of unconscious processes that they are indestructible. In the unconscious nothing can be brought to an end, nothing is past or forgotten." The last sentence of the book reminds us of "the indestructible wish."

Mircea Eliade, in *The Sacred and the Profane,* compares psychoanalysis to primitive initiation. He explains:

> The patient is asked to descend deeply into himself, to make his past live, to confront his traumatic experiences again; and, from the point of view of form, this dangerous operation resembles initiatory descents into hell, the realm of ghosts, and combats with monsters. Just as the initiate was expected to emerge from his ordeals victorious—in short, was to "die" and be "re-suscitated" in order to gain access to a fully responsible existence, open to spiritual values—so the patient undergoing analysis today must confront his own "unconscious," haunted by ghosts and monsters, in order to find psychic health and integrity and hence the world of cultural values.

As Freud's was the first analysis, so was he the proto-initiate, the primeval hero of the quest.

Some literary analogues immediately suggest themselves. Freud suggests the comparison with *Oedipus the King* of Sophocles, but since *The Interpretation of Dreams* ends in final triumphant affirmation, we would have to see it as somehow including both *Oedipus the King* and *Oedipus at Colonus,* or progressing from one to the other. Freud similarly brings up *Hamlet* (he quotes or refers to it at least six times in the book, even more often than *Faust*), but the same objection would make Shakespeare's progress from *Hamlet* to *The Tempest* a better analogy. Or, remembering the "dark wood" in which they both begin, we may compare *The Interpretation of Dreams* structurally with *The Divine Comedy;* at least *Inferno, Purgatorio,* and a page of the *Paradiso.* In another sense, recognizing the dream to be a kind of poem, the book is a poem about poetry, a highly imaginative sort of literary criticism. It is Freud's best book because it is his most intimate book, far more revealing than his *Autobiographical Study. The Interpretation of Dreams* was one of the two books *(Three Contributions to the Theory of Sex* was the other) that Freud regularly kept up to date. This was done almost entirely by additions, many in the form of footnotes, almost never by alteration of the text, even where the statement was absurdly outmoded. Freud explains in the preface to the fifth edition of *The Interpretation of Dreams,* in 1918:

> I have not been able to bring myself to embark upon any fundamental revision of this book, which might bring it up to the level of our present psychoanalytic views but would on the other hand destroy its historic character.

That "I have not been able to bring myself" is interesting. When we re-member Freud's reluctance to publish the book, the year's delay, and all his resistances in it, we realize its enormous importance to him. *The Inter-pretation of Dreams* is a relentless and unsparing *Confessions,* and its powerful self-revelation underlies its greatness.

Freud and the Scene of Writing

By Jacques Derrida

> Worin die Bahnung sonst besteht bleibt dahingestellt [In what pathbreaking consists remains undetermined]. *(Project for a Scientific Psychology, 1895)*

Our aim is limited: to locate in Freud's text several points of reference, and to isolate, on the threshhold of a systematic examination, those elements of psychoanalysis which can only uneasily be contained within logocentric closure, as this closure limits not only the history of philosophy but also the orientation of the "human sciences," notably of a certain linguistics. If the Freudian breakthrough has an historical originality, this originality is not due to its peaceful coexistence or theoretical complicity with this linguistics, at least in its congenital phonologism.[1]

It is no accident that Freud, at the decisive moments of his itinerary, has recourse to metaphorical models which are borrowed not from spoken language or from verbal forms, nor even from phonetic writing, but from a script which is never subject to, never exterior and posterior to, the spoken word. Freud invokes signs which do not transcribe living, full speech, master of itself and self-present. In fact, and this will be our problem, Freud *does not simply use* the metaphor of nonphonetic writing; he does not

"Freud and the Scene of Writing," by Jacques Derrida. Reprinted from *Writing and Difference* by Jacques Derrida, translated by Alan Bass (Chicago: University of Chicago Press, 1978), pp. 198-231, by permission of the University of Chicago Press and Routledge and Kegan Paul. Copyright © 1978 by the University of Chicago Press and Routledge and Kegan Paul, Ltd. *Writing and Difference* was first published in 1967 as *L'Ecriture et la différence* (Paris: Editions du Seuil).

[1]TN [Translator's Note]. Phonologism is Derrida's abbreviated fashion of describing one of the metaphysical gestures inherent in most linguistics: the privilege given to a model of language based on speech, because speech is the most *present* form of language, is presence in language. This is equivalent to the metaphysical repression of writing, i.e., of difference. Here, too, Derrida might be challenging Jacques Lacan, whose statement about the unconscious being structured like a language seems to depend upon many of the linguistic conceptions which Derrida considers to be uncritically metaphysical.

deem it expedient to manipulate scriptural metaphors for didactic ends. If such metaphors are indispensable, it is perhaps because they illuminate, inversely, the meaning of a trace in general, and eventually, in articulation with this meaning, may illuminate the meaning of writing in the popular sense. Freud, no doubt, is not manipulating metaphors, if to manipulate a metaphor means to make of the known an allusion to the unknown. On the contrary, through the insistence of his metaphoric investment he makes what we believe we know under the name of writing enigmatic. A movement unknown to classical philosophy is perhaps undertaken here, somewhere between the implicit and the explicit. From Plato and Aristotle on, scriptural images have regularly been used to *illustrate* the relationship between reason and experience, perception and memory. But a certain confidence has never stopped taking its assurance from the meaning of the well-known and familiar term: writing. The gesture sketched out by Freud interrupts that assurance and opens up a new kind of question about metaphor, writing, and spacing in general.

We shall let our reading be guided by this metaphoric investment. It will eventually invade the entirety of the psyche. Psychical *content* will be *represented* by a text whose essence is irreducibly graphic. The *structure* of the psychical *apparatus* will be *represented* by a writing machine. What questions will these representations impose upon us? We shall not have to ask if a writing apparatus—for example, the one described in the "Note on the Mystic Writing-Pad"—is a *good* metaphor for representing the working of the psyche, but rather what apparatus we must create in order to represent psychical writing; and we shall have to ask what the imitation, projected and liberated in a machine, of something like psychical writing might mean. And not if the psyche is indeed a kind of text, but: what is a text, and what must the psyche be if it can be represented by a text? For if there is neither machine nor text without psychical origin, there is no domain of the psychic without text. Finally, what must be the relationship between psyche, writing, and spacing for such a metaphoric transition to be possible, not only, nor primarily, within theoretical discourse, but within the history of psyche, text, and technology?

Breaching and Difference

From the *Project* (1895) to the "Note on the Mystic Writing-Pad" (1925), a strange progression: a problematic of breaching[2] is elaborated only to con-

---

[2]TN. "Breaching" is the translation we have adopted for the German word *Bahnung*. *Bahnung* is derived from *Bahn*, road, and literally means pathbreaking. Derrida's translation of *Bahnung* is *frayage*, which has an idiomatic connection to pathbreaking in the expression, *se frayer un chemin*. "Breaching" is clumsy, but it is crucial to maintain the sense of the *force* that breaks

form increasingly to a metaphorics of the written trace. From a system of traces functioning according to a model which Freud would have preferred to be a natural one, and from which writing is entirely absent, we proceed toward a configuration of traces which can no longer be represented except by the structure and functioning of writing. At the same time, the structural model of writing, which Freud invokes immediately after the *Project*, will be persistently differentiated and refined in its originality. All the mechanical models will be tested and abandoned, until the discovery of the *Wunderblock*, a writing machine of marvelous complexity into which the whole of the psychical apparatus will be projected. The solution to all the previous difficulties will be presented in the *Wunderblock*, and the "Note," indicative of an admirable tenacity, will answer precisely the questions of the *Project*. The *Wunderblock*, in each of its parts, will realize the apparatus of which Freud said, in the *Project:* "We cannot off-hand imagine an apparatus capable of such complicated functioning" *(SE,* I, 299) and which he replaced at that time with a neurological fable whose framework and intention, in certain respects, he will never abandon.

In 1895, the question was to explain memory in the manner of the natural sciences, in order "to furnish a psychology that shall be a natural science: that is, to represent psychical processes as quantitatively determined states of specifiable material particles" (I, 295). Now, a "main characteristic of nervous tissue is memory: that is, quite generally, a capacity for being permanently altered by single occurrences" (I, 299). And a "psychological theory deserving any consideration must furnish an explanation of 'memory' " (ibid.). The crux of such an explanation, what makes such an apparatus almost unimaginable, is the necessity of accounting simultaneously, as the "Note" will do thirty years later, for the permanence of the trace and for the virginity of the receiving substance, for the engraving of furrows and for the perennially intact bareness of the perceptive surface: in this case, of the neurones. "It would seem, therefore, that neurones must be both influenced and also unaltered, unprejudiced *(unvoreingenommen)"* (ibid.). Rejecting a distinction, which was common in his day, between "sense cells" and "memory cells," Freud then forges the hypothesis of "contact-barriers" and "breaching" *(Bahnung,* lit. pathbreaking), of the breaking open of a path *(Bahn).* Whatever may be thought of the continuities and ruptures to come, this hypothesis is remarkable as soon as it is considered as a metaphorical model and not as a neurological description. Breaching, the tracing of a trail, opens up a conducting path. Which pre-

---

open a pathway, and the *space* opened by this force; thus, "breaching" must be understood here as a shorthand for these meanings. In the Standard Edition *Bahnung* has been translated as "facilitation," and we have, of course, maintained this in all citations from the Standard Edition. Citations from *The Standard Edition of the Complete Psychological Works of Sigmund Freud,* London: Hogarth Press (abbreviated as *SE*), are by volume and page number.

supposes a certain violence and a certain resistance to effraction. The path is broken, cracked, *fracta*, breached. Now there would be two kinds of neurones: the permeable neurones (Φ), which offer no resistance and thus retain no trace of impression, would be the perceptual neurones; other neurones (Ψ), which would oppose contact-barriers to the quantity of excitation, would thus retain the printed trace: they "thus afford a possibility of representing *(darzustellen)* memory" (ibid.). This is the first representation, the first staging of memory. *(Darstellung* is representation in the weak sense of the word, but also frequently in the sense of visual depiction, and sometimes of theatrical performance. Our translation will vary with the inflection of the context.) Freud attributes psychical quality only to these latter neurones. They are the "vehicles of memory and so probably of psychical processes in general" (I, 300). Memory, thus, is not a psychical property among others; it is the very essence of the psyche: resistance, and precisely, thereby, an opening to the effraction of the trace.

Now assuming that Freud here intends to speak only the language of full and present quantity, assuming, as at least appears to be the case, that he intends to situate his work within the simple opposition of quantity and quality (the latter being reserved for the pure transparency of a perception without memory), we find that the concept of breaching shows itself intolerant of this intention. An equality of resistance to breaching, or an equivalence of the breaching forces, would eliminate any *preference* in the choice of itinerary. Memory would be paralyzed. It is the difference between breaches which is the true origin of memory, and thus of the psyche. Only this difference enables a "pathway to be preferred *(Wegbevorzugung)*": "Memory is represented *(dargestellt)* by the differences in the facilitations of the ψ-neurones" (I, 300). We then must not say that breaching without difference is insufficient for memory; it must be stipulated that there is no pure breaching without difference. Trace as memory is not a pure breaching that might be reappropriated at any time as simple presence; it is rather the ungraspable and invisible difference between breaches. We thus already know that psychic life is neither the transparency of meaning nor the opacity of force but the difference within the exertion of forces. As Nietzsche had already said.[3]

That quantity becomes *psychē* and *mnēmē* through differences rather than through plenitudes will be continuously confirmed in the *Project* itself. *Repetition* adds no quantity of present force, no *intensity;* it reproduces the same impression—yet it has the power of breaching. "The memory of an experience (that is, its continuing operative power) depends on a factor which is called the magnitude of the impression and on the frequency with which the same impression is repeated" (I, 300). The number

[3]TN. Cf. the end of Derrida's "Force and Signification" *(Writing and Difference,* chapter 1) for a discussion of differences of force in Nietzsche.

of repetitions is thus added to the quantity $(Q\eta)$ of the excitation, and these two quantities are of two absolutely heterogeneous types. There are only discrete repetitions, and they can act as such only through the diastem which maintains their separation. Finally, if breaching can supplement a quantity presently at work, or can be added to it, it is because breaching is certainly analogous to quantity, but is other than it as well: "*quantity* plus *facilitation* resulting from $Q\eta$ are at the same time something that can replace $Q\eta$" (I, 300-301). Let us not hasten to define this other of pure quantity as quality: for in so doing we would be transforming the force of memory into present consciousness and the translucid perception of present qualities. Thus, neither the difference between full quantities, nor the interval between repetitions of the identical, nor breaching itself, may be thought of in terms of the opposition between quantity and quality.[4] Memory cannot be derived from this opposition, and it escapes the grasp of "naturalism" as well as of "phenomenology."

All these differences in the production of the trace may be reinterpreted as moments of deferring. In accordance with a motif which will continue to dominate Freud's thinking, this movement is described as the effort of life to protect itself by *deferring* a dangerous cathexis, that is, by constituting a reserve *(Vorrat)*. The threatening expenditure or presence are deferred with the help of breaching or repetition. Is this not already the detour *(Aufschub,* lit. delay) which institutes the relation of pleasure to reality *(Beyond the Pleasure Principle, SE,* XVIII)? Is it not already death at the origin of a life which can defend itself against death only through an *economy* of death, through deferment, repetition, reserve? For repetition does not *happen to* an initial impression; its possibility is already there, in the resistance offered *the first time* by the psychical neurones. Resistance itself is possible only if the opposition of forces lasts and is repeated at the beginning. It is the very idea of a *first time* which becomes enigmatic. What we are advancing here does not seem to contradict what Freud will say further on: "Facilitation is probably the result of the single *(einmaliger)* passage of a large quantity." Even assuming that his affirmation does not lead us little by little to the problem of phylogenesis and of hereditary breaches, we may still maintain that in the *first time* of the contact between *two* forces, repetition has begun. Life is already threatened by the origin of the memory which constitutes it, and by the breaching which it resists, the

[4]Here more than elsewhere, concerning the concepts of difference, quantity, and quality, a systematic confrontation between Nietzsche and Freud is called for. Cf., for example, among many others, this fragment from *The Will to Power:* "Our 'knowing' limits itself to establishing quantities; but we cannot help feeling these differences in quantity as qualities. Quality is a perspective truth for *us;* not an 'in-itself.'...If we sharpened or blunted our senses tenfold, we should perish; i.e., with regard to making possible our existence we sense even relations between magnitudes as qualities" (Nietzsche: *The Will to Power,* trans. Walter Kaufmann [New York: Random House, 1967], p. 304).

effraction which it can contain only by repeating it. It is because breaching breaks open that Freud, in the *Project,* accords a privilege to pain. In a certain sense, there is no breaching without a beginning of pain, and "pain leaves behind it particularly rich breaches." But beyond a certain quantity, pain, the threatening origin of the psyche, must be deferred, like death, for it can "ruin" psychical "organization." Despite the enigmas of the "first time" and of originary repetition (needless to say, before any distinction between "normal" and "pathological" repetition), it is important that Freud attributes all this work to the primary function, and that he excludes any possible derivation of it. Let us observe this nonderivation, even if it renders only more dense the difficulty of the concepts of "primariness" and of the timelessness of the primary process, and even if this difficulty does not cease to intensify in what is to come. "Here we are almost involuntarily reminded of the endeavor of the nervous system, maintained through every modification, to avoid being burdened by a $Q\eta$ or to keep the burden as small as possible. Under the compulsion of the exigencies of life, the nervous system was obliged to lay up a store of $Q\eta$. This necessitated an increase in the number of its neurones, and these had to be impermeable. It now avoids, partly at least, being *filled* with $Q\eta$ (cathexis), by setting up *facilitations*. It will be seen, then, that *facilitations serve the primary function"* (I, 301).

No doubt life protects itself by repetition, trace, *différance* (deferral). But we must be wary of this formulation: there is no life present *at first* which would *then* come to protect, postpone, or reserve itself in *différance.* The later constitutes the essence of life. Or rather: as *differance* is not an essence, as it is not anything, it *is not* life, if Being is determined as *ousia,* presence, essence/existence, substance or subject. Life must be thought of as trace before Being may be determined as presence. This is the only condition on which we can say that life *is* death, that repetition and the beyond of the pleasure principle are native and congenital to that which they transgress. When Freud writes in the *Project* that "facilitations serve the primary function," he is forbidding us to be surprised by *Beyond the Pleasure Principle.* He complies with a dual necessity: that of recognizing *différance* at the origin, and at the same time that of crossing out the concept of *primariness:* we will not, then, be surprised by the *Traumdeutung,*

---

[5]The concepts of originary *différance* and of delay are unthinkable within the authority of the logic of identity or even within the concept of time. The very absurdity betrayed *by the terms* provides the possibility—if organized in a certain manner—of thinking beyond that logic and that concept. The word "delay" must be taken to mean something other than a relation between two "presents"; and the following model must be avoided: what was to happen (should have happened) in a (prior) present A, occurs only in a present B. The concepts of originary *différance* and originary "delay" were imposed upon us by a reading of Husserl.

which defines primariness as a "theoretical fiction" in a paragraph on the "delaying" *(Verspätung)* of the secondary process. It is thus the delay which is in the beginning.[5] Without which, *différance* would be the lapse which a consciousness, a self-presence of the present, accords itself. To defer *(différer)* thus cannot mean to retard a present possibility, to postpone an act, to put off a perception already now possible. That possibility is possible only through a *différance* which must be conceived of in other terms than those of a calculus or mechanics of decision.[6] To say that *différance* is originary is simultaneously to erase the myth of a present origin. Which is why "originary" must be understood as having been *crossed out*, without which *différance* would be derived from an original plenitude. It is a non-origin which is originary.

Rather than abandon it, we ought perhaps then to rethink the concept of *différer*. This is what we should like to do, and this is possible only if *différance* is determined outside any teleological or eschatological horizon. Which is not easy. Let us note in passing that the concepts of *Nachträglichkeit* and *Verspätung*, concepts which govern the whole of Freud's thought and determine all his other concepts, are already present and named in the *Project*. The irreducibility of the "effect of deferral"—such, no doubt, is Freud's discovery. Freud exploits this discovery in its ultimate consequences, beyond the psychoanalysis of the individual, and he thought that the history of culture ought to confirm it. In *Moses and Monotheism* (1937), the efficacy of delay and of action subsequent to the event is at work over large historical intervals. The problem of latency, moreover, is in highly significant contact with the problem of oral and written tradition in this text.

Although "breaching" is not named writing at any time in the *Project,* the contradictory requirements which the "Mystic Writing-Pad" will fulfill are already formulated in terms which are literally identical: "an unlimited receptive capacity and a retention of permanent traces" *(SE* XIX, 227).

Differences in the work of breaching concern not only forces but also locations. And Freud already wants to think force and place simultaneously.[7] He is the first not to believe in the descriptive value of his hypothetical representation of breaching. The distinction between the categories of neurones "has no recognized foundation, at least insofar as morphology (i.e., histology) is concerned." It is, rather, the index of a topographical description which external space, that is, familiar and constituted space,

---

[6]TN. In "Cogito and the History of Madness" *(Writing and Difference,* chapter 2), Derrida begins to elaborate on the metaphysical nature of the concept of decision. Decision in Greek is *krinein,* whence comes our "critic." The critic always *decides* on a meaning, which can be conceived only in terms of presence. Since *différance* subverts meaning and presence, it does not *decide.*

[7]TN. On the relation of force and place (site, *topos),* see "Force and Signification."

the exterior space of the natural sciences, cannot contain. This is why, under the heading of "the biological standpoint," a "difference in essence" *(Wesensverschiedenheit)* between the neurones is "replaced by a difference in the environment to which they are destined" *(Schicksals-Milieuver-schiedenheit)* (I, 304): these are pure differences, differences of situation, of connection, of localization, of structural relations more important than their supporting terms; and they are differences for which the relativity of outside and inside is always to be determined. The thinking of difference can neither dispense with topography nor accept the current models of spacing.

This difficulty becomes more acute when it becomes necessary to explain those differences that are pure par excellence: differences of quality, that is, for Freud, differences of consciousness. He must provide an explanation for "what we are aware of, in the most puzzling fashion *(rätselhaft)*, through our 'consciousness'" (I, 307). And "since this consciousness knows nothing of what we have so far been assuming—quantities and neurones—it [the theory] should explain this lack of knowledge to us as well" (I, 308). Now qualities are clearly pure differences: "Consciousness gives us what are called *qualities*—sensations which are *different (anders)* and whose difference *(Anders,* lit. otherness) is distinguished *(unterschieden wird,* lit. is differentiated) according to its relations with the external world. Within this difference there are series, similarities, and so on, but there are in fact no quantities in it. It may be asked *how* qualities originate and *where* qualities originate" (I, 308).

Neither outside nor inside. They cannot be in the external world, where the physicist recognizes only quantities, "masses in motion and nothing else" (I, 308). Nor in the interiority of the psyche (i.e., of memory), for "reproducing or remembering" are "without quality *(qualitätslos)*" (ibid.). Since rejection of the topographical model is out of the question, "we must summon up courage to assume that there is a third system of neurones—ω perhaps [perceptual neurones] —which is excited along with perception, but not along with reproduction, and whose states of excitation give rise to the various qualities—are, that is to say, *conscious sensations*" (I, 309). Foreshadowing in the interpolated sheet of the mystic writing-pad, Freud, annoyed by this "jargon," tells Fliess (letter 39, 1 Jan. 1896) that he is in-serting, "slipping" *(schieben)* the perceptual neurones (ω) between the ϕ- and ψ-neurones.

The last bit of daring results in "what seems like an immense difficulty": we have just encountered a permeability and a breaching which proceed from no quantity at all. From what then? From pure time, from pure temporalization in its conjunction with spacing: from periodicity. Only recourse to temporality and to a discontinuous or periodic temporality will

allow the difficulty to be resolved, and we must patiently consider its implications. "I can see only one way out. ...So far I have regarded it [the
passage of quantity] only as the transference of $Q\eta$ from one neurone to
another. It must have another characteristic, of a temporal nature" (I, 310).

If the discontinuity hypothesis "goes further," Freud emphasizes, than
the "physical clarification" due to its insistence on periods, it is because
in this case differences, intervals, and discontinuity are registered, "appropriated" without their quantitative support. Perceptual neurones, "incapable of receiving $Q\eta$ [quantities], appropriate the *period* of the excitation"
(ibid.). Pure difference, again, and difference between diastems. The concept of a *period in general* precedes and conditions the opposition between
quantity and quality, and everything governed by this opposition. For
"ψ-neurones too have their period, of course; but it is without quality, or
more correctly, monotonous" (ibid.). As we shall see, this insistence on discontinuity will faithfully become the occupation of the "Note on the Mystic
Writing-Pad"; as in the *Project,* it will be a last bold move resolving a final
logical difficulty.

The rest of the *Project* will depend in its entirety upon an incessant and
increasingly radical invocation of the principle of difference. Beneath an
indicial neurology, which plays the representational role of an artificial
model, we repeatedly find a persistent attempt to account for the psyche in
terms of spacing, a topography of traces, a map of breaches; and we repeatedly find an attempt to locate consciousness or quality in a space whose
structure and possibility must be rethought, along with an attempt to
describe the "functioning of the apparatus" in terms of pure differences and
locations, an attempt to explain how "quantity of excitation is expressed in
ψ by complexity and quality by topography." It is because the nature of this
system of differences and of this topography is radically new and must not
allow any omissions that Freud, in his setting up of the apparatus, multi-
plies "acts of boldness," "strange but indispensable hypotheses" (concerning
"secreting" neurones or "key" neurones). And when he renounces neurology
and anatomical localizations, it will be not in order to abandon his topographical preoccupations, but to transform them. Trace will become *gramme;*
and the region of breaching a ciphered spacing.

The Print and the Original Supplement

A few weeks after the *Project* is sent to Fliess, during a "night of work," all
the elements of the system arrange themselves into a "machine." It is not yet
a writing machine: "Everything fell into place, the cogs meshed, the thing

really seemed to be a machine which in a moment would run of itself."[8] In a moment: in thirty years. By itself: almost.

A little more than a year later, the trace starts to become writing. In letter 52 (6 Dec. 1896), the entire system of the *Project* is reconstituted in terms of a graphic conception as yet unknown in Freud. It is not surprising that this coincides with the transition from the neurological to the physical. At the heart of the letter: the words "sign" *(Zeichen)*, registration *(Niederschrift)*, transcription *(Umschrift)*. Not only is the communication between trace and delay (i.e., a present which does not constitute but is originally reconstituted from "signs" of memory) explicitly defined in this letter, but verbal phenomena are assigned a place within a system of stratified writing which these phenomena are far from dominating: "As you know, I am working on the assumption that our psychic mechanism has come into being by a process of stratification *(Aufeinanderschichtung)*; the material present in the form of memory-traces *(Errinerungsspuren)* being subjected from time to time to a *rearrangement (Umordnung)* in accordance with fresh circumstances to a *retranscription (Umschrift)*. Thus, what is essentially new about my theory is the thesis that memory is present not once but several times over, that it is laid down *(niederlegt)* in various species of indications [*Zeichen*, lit. signs] . . . . I cannot say how many of these registrations *(Niederschriften)* there are: at least three, probably more. . . . The different registrations are also separated (not necessarily topographically) according to the neurones which are their vehicles. . . . *Perception*. These are neurones in which perceptions originate, to which consciousness attaches, but which in themselves retain no trace of what has happened. *For consciousness and memory are mutually exclusive. Indication of perception:* the first registration of the perceptions; it is quite incapable of consciousness and arranged according to associations by simultaneity. . . . *Unconscious* is a second registration. . . . *Preconscious* is the third transcription, attached to word-presentations and corresponding to our official ego. . . . This secondary *thought-consciousness* is subsequent in time and probably linked to the hallucinatory activation of word-presentations" (I, 235).

This is the first move toward the "Note." From now on, starting with the *Traumdeutung* (1900), the metaphor of writing will *appropriate simultaneously the problems of the psychic apparatus in its structure and that of*

---

[8]Letter 32 (10 Oct. 1895). The machine: "The three systems of neurones, the 'free' and 'bound' states of quantity, the primary and secondary processes, the main trend and the compromise trend of the nervous system, the two biological rules of attention and defence, the indications of quality, reality and thought, the state of the psycho-sexual group, the sexual determination of repression, and finally the factors determining consciousness as a perceptual function—the whole thing held together, and still does. I can hardly contain myself with delight. If I had only waited a fortnight before setting it all down for you" (Freud: *The Origins of Psychoanalysis: Letters to Wilhelm Fliess. Drafts and Notes,* trans. Eric Mosbacher and James Strachey [New York: Basic Books, 1954] , p. 129).

the psychic text in its fabric. The solidarity of the two problems should make us that much more attentive: the two series of metaphors — text and machine — do not come on stage at the same time.

"Dreams generally follow old facilitations," said the *Project.* Topographical, temporal, and formal regression in dreams must thus be interpreted, henceforth, as a path back into a landscape of writing. Not a writing which simply transcribes, a stony echo of muted words, but a lithography before words: metaphonetic, nonlinguistic, alogical. (Logic obeys consciousness, or preconsciousness, the site of verbal images, as well as the principle of identity, the founding expression of a philosophy of presence. "It was only a logical contradiction, which does not have much import," we read in *The Wolf-Man.*) With dreams displaced into a forest of script, the *Traumdeutung,* the interpretation of dreams, no doubt, on the first approach will be an act of reading and decoding. Before the analysis of the Irma dream, Freud engages in considerations of method. In one of his familiar gestures, he opposes the old popular tradition to so-called scientific psychology. As always, it is in order to justify the profound intention which inspires the former. Popular tradition may err, of course, when according to a "symbolical" procedure, it treats dream content as an indivisible and unarticulated whole, for which a second, possibly prophetic whole may be substituted. But Freud is not far from accepting the "other popular method": "It might be described as the 'decoding' method *(Chiffriermethode),* since it treats dreams as a kind of cryptography *(Geheimschrift)* in which each sign can be translated into another sign having a known meaning, in accordance with a fixed key *(Schlüssel)"* (IV, 97). Let us retain the allusion to a permanent code: it is the weakness of a method to which Freud attributes, nevertheless, the merit of being analytic and of spelling out the elements of meaning one by one.

A strange example, the one chosen by Freud to illustrate this traditional procedure: a text of phonetic writing is cathected and functions as a discrete, specific, translatable and unprivileged element in the overall writing of the dream. Phonetic writing as writing within writing. Assume, for example, says Freud, that I have dreamed of a letter *(Brief / epistola),* then of a burial. Open a *Traumbuch,* a book in which the keys to dreams are recorded, an encyclopedia of dream signs, the dream dictionary which Freud will soon reject. It teaches us that letter must be translated *(übersetzen)* by spite, and burial by engagement to be married. Thus a letter *(epistola)* written with letters *(litterae),* a document composed of phonetic signs, the transcription of verbal discourse, may be translated by a nonverbal signifier which, inasmuch as it is a determined affect, belongs to the overall syntax of dream writing. The verbal is cathected, and its phonetic transcription is bound, far from the center, in a web of silent script.

Freud then borrows another example from Artemidorus of Daldis (second century), the author of a treatise on the interpretation of dreams. Let it be a pretext for recalling that in the eighteenth century an English theologian, known to Freud, had already invoked Artemidorus with an intention that is doubtless worthy of comparison.[9] Warburton describes the system of hieroglyphics, and discerns in it (rightly or wrongly—it is of no concern to us here) various structures (hieroglyphics strictly speaking or symbolical ones, each type being either curiological or tropological, the relation here being of analogy or of part to whole) which ought to be systematically confronted with the mechanisms of dream-work (condensation, displacement, overdetermination). Now Warburton, interested, for reasons of self-justification, in demonstrating, against Father Kircher, "the high antiquity of Egyptian learning," chooses the example of an Egyptian science which draws all its resources from hieroglyphic writing. That science is *Traumdeutung*, also known as oneirocriticism. When all is said and done, it was only a science of writing in priestly hands. God, the Egyptians believed, had made man a gift of writing just as he inspired dreams. Interpreters, like dreams themselves, then had only to draw upon the curiological or tropological storehouse. They would readily find there the key to dreams, which they would then pretend to divine. The hieroglyphic code itself served as a *Traumbuch*. An alleged gift of God, in fact constructed historically, it had become the common source from which was drawn oneiric discourse: the setting and the text of the dream's mise en scène. Since dreams are constructed like a form of writing, the kinds of transposition in dreams correspond to condensations and displacements already performed and enregistered in the system of hieroglyphics. Dreams would only manipulate elements *(stoicheia,* says Warburton, elements or letters) contained in the storehouse of hieroglyphics, somewhat as written speech would draw on a written language: "So that the question will be, on what grounds or rules of interpretation the Oneirocritics proceeded, when, if a man dreamt of a dragon, the Interpreter assured him it signified *majesty;* if of a serpent, a *disease;* a viper, *money;* frogs, *impostors.*"[10] What then did the hermeneuts of that age do? They consulted writing itself:

> Now the early *Interpreters of dreams* were not juggling impostors; but, like the early judicial *Astrologers,* more superstitious than their neighbors; and so the first who fell into their own delusions. However, suppose them to have

---

[9]Warburton, the author of *The Divine Legation of Moses.* The fourth part of his work was translated in 1744 under the title: *Essai sur les hiéroglyphes des Egyptiens, où l'on voit l'origine et le progrès du langage, l'antiquité des sciences en Egypte, et l'origine du culte des animaux.* This work, which we shall discuss elsewhere, had considerable influence. All of that era's reflections on language and signs bore its mark. The editors of the *Encyclopedia,* Condillac, and, through him, Rousseau all drew specific inspiration from it, borrowing in particular the theme of the originally metaphorical nature of language.

[10]William Warburton: *The Divine Legation of Moses Demonstrated,* 10th ed. (London: Thomas Tegg, 1846), 2:220.

been as arrant cheats as any of their successors, yet at their first setting up they must have had materials proper for their trade; which could never be the wild workings of each man's private fancy. Their customers would look to find a known analogy, become venerable by long application to mysterious wisdom, for the groundwork of their deciphering; and the Decipherers themselves would as naturally fly to some confessed authority, to support their pretended Science. But what ground or authority could this be, if not the mysterious learning of *symbolic characters?* Here we seem to have got a solution of the difficulty. The *Egyptian* priests, the first interpreters of dreams, took their rules for this species of *DIVINATION,* from their *symbolic* riddling, in which they were so deeply read: A ground of interpretation which would give the strongest credit to the Art; and equally satisfy the diviner and the Consulter; for by this time it was generally believed that their Gods have given them *hieroglyphic writing.* So that nothing was more natural than to imagine that these Gods, who in their opinion gave *dreams* likewise, had employed the same mode of expression in both revelations.[11]

It is here that the Freudian break occurs. Freud doubtless conceives of the dream as a displacement similar to an original form of writing which puts words on stage without becoming subservient to them; and he is thinking here, no doubt, of a model of writing irreducible to speech which would include, like hieroglyphics, pictographic, ideogrammatic, and phonetic elements. But he makes of psychical writing so originary a production that the writing we believe to be designated by the proper sense of the word—a script which is coded and visible "in the world"—would only be the metaphor of psychical writing. This writing, for example the kind we find in dreams which "follow old facilitations," a simple moment in a regression toward a "primary" writing, cannot be read in terms of any code. It works, no doubt, with a mass of elements which have been codified in the course of an individual or collective history. But in its operations, lexicon, and syntax a purely idiomatic residue is irreducible and is made to bear the burden of interpretation in the communication between unconsciousnesses. The dreamer invents his own grammar. No meaningful material or prerequisite text exists which he might *simply use,* even if he never deprives himself of them. Such, despite their interest, is the limitation of the *Chiffriermethode* and the *Traumbuch.* As much as it is a function of the generality and the rigidity of the code, this limitation is a function of an excessive preoccupation with *content,* and an insufficient concern for relations, locations, processes, and differences: "My procedure is not so convenient as the popular decoding method which translates any given piece of a dream's content by a fixed key. I, on the contrary, am prepared to find that the same piece of content may conceal a different meaning when it occurs in various people or in various contexts" (*SE* IV, 105). Elsewhere,

[11]Ibid., p. 221.

in support of that statement, Freud thinks it proper to adduce the case of Chinese writing: "They [the dream symbols] frequently have more than one or even several meanings, and, as with Chinese script, the correct interpretation can only be arrived at on each occasion from the context" (V, 353).

The absence of an exhaustive and absolutely infallible code means that in psychic writing, which thus prefigures the meaning of writing in general, the difference between signifier and signified is never radical. Unconscious experience, prior to the dream which "follows old facilitations," does not borrow but produces its own signifiers; does not create them in their materiality, of course, but produces their status-as-meaningful *(significance)*. Henceforth, they are no longer, properly speaking, signifiers. And the possibility of translation, if it is far from being eliminated—for experience perpetually creates distances between the points of identity or between the adherence of signifier to signified—is nevertheless in principle and by definition limited. Such, perhaps, is Freud's understanding, from another standpoint, in the article on "Repression": "Repression acts, therefore, in a *highly individual* manner" (XIV, 150). (Individuality here does not refer primarily to the repression practiced by individuals but to that of each "derivative of the repressed, which may have its own special vicissitude.") Translation, a system of translation, is possible only if a permanent code allows a substitution or transformation of signifiers while retaining the same signified, always present, despite the absence of any specific signifier. This fundamental possibility of substitution would thus be implied by the coupled concepts signified/signifier, and would consequently be implied by the concept of the sign itself. Even if, along with Saussure, we envisage the distinction between signified and signifier only as the two sides of a sheet of paper, nothing is changed. Originary writing, if there is one, must produce the space and the materiality of the sheet itself.

It will be said: and yet Freud translates all the time. He believes in the generality and the fixity of a specific code for dream writing: "When we have become familiar with the abundant use made by symbolism for representing sexual material in dreams, the question is bound to arise of whether many of these symbols do not occur with a permanently fixed meaning, like the 'grammalogues' in short; and we shall feel tempted to draw up a new 'dream-book' on the decoding principle" (V, 351). And, in fact, Freud never stopped proposing codes, rules of great generality. And the substitution of signifiers seems to be the essential activity of psychoanalytic interpretation. Certainly, Freud nevertheless stipulates an essential limitation on this activity. Or, rather, a double limitation.

If we consider first verbal expression, as it is circumscribed in the dream, we observe that its sonority, the materiality of the expression, does not disappear before the signified, or at least cannot be traversed and transgressed as it is in conscious speech. It acts as such, with the efficacy Artaud assigned it on the stage of cruelty.[12] The materiality of a word cannot be translated or carried over into another language. Materiality is precisely that which translation relinquishes. To relinquish materiality: such is the driving force of translation. And when that materiality is reinstated, translation becomes poetry. In this sense, since the materiality of the signifier constitutes the idiom of every dream scene, dreams are untranslatable: "Indeed, dreams are so closely related to linguistic expression that Ferenczi has truly remarked that every tongue has its own dream-language. It is impossible as a rule to translate a dream into a foreign language, and this is equally true, I fancy, of a book such as the present one" (IV, 99, n. 1). What is valid for a specific national language is a fortiori valid for a private grammar.

Moreover, this horizontal impossibility of translation without loss has its basis in a vertical impossibility. We are speaking here of the way in which unconscious thoughts become conscious. If a dream cannot be translated into another language, it is because within the psychical apparatus as well there is never a relation of simple translation. We are wrong, Freud tells us, to speak of translation or transcription in describing the transition of unconscious thoughts through the preconscious toward consciousness. Here again the metaphorical concept of translation *(Übersetzung)* or transcription *(Umschrift)* is dangerous, not because it refers to writing, but because it presupposes a text which would be already there, immobile: the serene presence of a statue, of a written stone or archive whose signified content might be harmlessly transported into the milieu of a different language, that of the preconscious or the conscious. It is thus not enough to speak of writing in order to be faithful to Freud, for it is then that we may betray him more than ever.

This is what the last chapter of the *Traumdeutung* explains. An entirely and conventionally topographical metaphor of the psychical apparatus is to be completed by invoking the existence of force and of two kinds of processes of excitation or modes of its discharge: "So let us try to correct some conceptions [intuitive illustrations: *Anschauungen*] which might be misleading so long as we looked upon the two systems in the most literal and crudest sense as two localities in the mental apparatus—conceptions which left their traces in the expressions 'to repress' and 'to force a way through.' Thus, we may speak of an unconscious thought seeking to convey itself into the preconscious so as to be able then to force its way through into consciousness. What we have in mind here is not the forming of a second thought situated in a new place, like a transcription *(Umschrift)* which

---

[12]TN. Derrida discusses Artaud's strikingly similar formulations about speech as but one element of language and representation among others in "The Theater of Cruelty and the Closure of Representation" *(Writing and Difference,* chapter 8); cf. especially note 7.

continues to exist alongside the original; and the notion of forcing a way through into consciousness must be kept carefully free from any idea of a change of locality" (V, 610).[13]

Let us interrupt our quotation for a moment. The conscious text is thus not a transcription, because there is no text *present elsewhere* as an unconscious one to be transposed or transported. For the value of presence can also dangerously affect the concept of the unconscious. There is then no unconscious truth to be rediscovered by virtue of having been written elsewhere. There is no text written and present elsewhere which would then be subjected, without being changed in the process, to an operation and a temporalization (the latter belonging to consciousness if we follow Freud literally) which would be external to it, floating on its surface. There is no present text in general, and there is not even a past present text, a text which is past as having been present. The text is not conceivable in an originary or modified form of presence. The unconscious text is already a weave of pure traces, differences in which meaning and force are united — a text nowhere present, consisting of archives which are *always already* transcriptions. Originary prints. Everything begins with reproduction. Always already: repositories of a meaning which was never present, whose signified presence is always reconstituted by deferral, *nachträglich,* belatedly, *supplementarily:* for the *nachträglich* also means *supplementary.* The call of the supplement is primary, here, and it hollows out that which will be reconstituted by deferral as the present. The supplement, which seems to be added as a plentitude to a plentitude, is equally that which compensates for a lack *(qui supplée).* "*Suppléer:* 1. To add what is missing, to supply a necessary surplus," says Littre, respecting, like a sleepwalker, the strange logic of that word. It is within its logic that the possibility of deferred action should be conceived, as well as, no doubt, the relationship between the primary and the secondary on all levels.[14] Let us note: *Nachtrag* has a precise meaning in the realm of letters: appendix, codicil, postscript. The text we call present may be deciphered only at the bottom of the page, in a footnote or postscript. Before the recurrence, the present is only the call for a footnote.[15] That the present in general is not primal but, rather, reconstituted, that it is not the absolute, wholly living form which constitutes experience, that there is no purity of the living present — such is the theme, formidable for metaphysics, which Freud, in a conceptual scheme unequal to the thing itself, would have us pursue. This pursuit is doubtless the only one which is exhausted neither within metaphysics nor within science.

[13]*The Ego and the Id (SE* XIX, chap. 2) also underscores the danger of a topographical representation of psychical facts.

[14]TN. Derrida's fullest discussion of supplementarity is in *De la grammatologie.*

[15]TN. Derrida fully develops the supplementary status of the footnote — *la greffe* — in *La double séance* in *La dissémination.*

Since the transition to consciousness is not a derivative or repetitive writing, a transcription duplicating an unconscious writing, it occurs in an original manner and, in its very secondariness, is originary and irreducible. Since consciousness for Freud is a surface exposed to the external world, it is here that instead of reading through the metaphor in the usual sense, we must, on the contrary, understand the possibility of a writing advanced as conscious and as acting in the world (the visible exterior of the graphism, of the literal, of the literal becoming literary, etc.) in terms of the labor of the writing which circulated like psychical energy between the unconscious and the conscious. The "objectivist" or "worldly" consideration of writing teaches us nothing if reference is not made to a space of psychical writing. (We might say: of transcendental writing in the event that, along with Husserl, we would see the psyche as a region of the world. But since this is also the case for Freud, who wants to respect simultaneously the Being-in-the-world of the psyche, its Being-situated, and the originality of its topology, which is irreducible to any ordinary intraworldliness, we perhaps should think that what we are describing here as the labor of writing erases the transcendental distinction between the origin of the world and Being-in-the-world. Erases it while producing it: the medium of the dialogue and misunderstanding between the Husserlian and Heideggerian concepts of Being-in-the-world.)

Concerning this nontranscriptive writing, Freud adds a fundamental specification. This specification will reveal: (1) the danger involved in immobilizing or freezing energy within a naive metaphorics of place; (2) the necessity not of abandoning but of rethinking the space or topology of this writing; (3) that Freud, who still insists on *representing* the psychical apparatus in an artificial model, has not yet discovered a mechanical model adequate to the graphematic conceptual scheme he is already using to describe the psychical text.

Again, we may speak of a preconscious thought being repressed or driven out and then taken over by the unconscious. These images, derived from a set of ideas *(Vorstellungskreis)* relating to a struggle for a piece of ground, may tempt us to suppose that it is literally true that a mental grouping *(Anordnung)* in one locality has been brought to an end and replaced by a fresh one in another locality. Let us replace these metaphors by something that seems to correspond better to the real state of affairs, and let us say that some particular mental grouping has had a cathexis of energy *(Energiebesetzung)* attached to it or withdrawn from it, so that the structure in question has come under the sway of a particular agency or been withdrawn from it. What we are doing here is once again to replace a topographical way of representing things by a dynamic one. What we regard as mobile *(das Bewegliche)* is not the psychical structure itself but its innervation [V, 610-11].

Let us once more interrupt our quotation. The metaphor of translation as the transcription of an original text would separate force and extension, maintaining the simple exteriority of the translated and the translating. This very exteriority, the static and topological bias of the metaphor, would assure the transparency of a neutral translation, of a phoronomic and non-metabolic process. Freud emphasizes this: psychic writing does not lend itself to translation because it is a single energetic system (however differentiated it may be), and because it covers the entirety of the psychical apparatus. Despite the difference of agencies, psychical writing in general is not a displacement of meanings within the limpidity of an immobile, pregiven space and the blank neutrality of discourse. A discourse which might be coded without ceasing to be diaphanous. Here energy cannot be reduced; it does not limit meaning, but rather produces it. The distinction between force and meaning is derivative in relation to an archi-trace; it belongs to the metaphysics of consciousness and of presence, or rather of presence in the word, in the hallucination of a language determined on the basis of the word or of verbal representation. The metaphysics of preconsciousness, Freud might say, since the preconscious is the place he assigns to the verbal. Without that, would Freud have taught us anything new?

Force produces meaning (and space) through the power of "repetition" alone, which inhabits it originarily as its death. This power, that is, this lack of power, which opens and limits the labor of force, institutes translatability, makes possible what we call "language," transforms an absolute idiom into a limit which is always already transgressed: a pure idiom is not language; it becomes so only through repetition; repetition always already divides the point of departure of the first time. Despite appearances, this does not contradict what we said earlier about untranslatability. At that time it was a question of recalling the origin of the movement of transgression, the origin of repetition, and the becoming- language of the idiom. If one limits oneself to the *datum or the effect of repetition,* to translation, to the obviousness of the distinction between force and meaning, not only does one miss the originality of Freud's aim, but one effaces the intensity of the relation to death as well.

We ought thus to examine closely—which we cannot do here—all that Freud invites us to think concerning writing as "breaching" in the *psychical* repetition of this previously *neurological* notion: opening up of its own space, effraction, breaking of a path against resistances, rupture and irruption becoming a route *(rupta, via rupta),* violent inscription of a form, tracing of a difference in a nature or a matter which are conceivable as such only in their *opposition* to writing. The route is opened in nature or matter, forest or wood *(hyle),* and in it acquires a reversibility of time and space.

We should have to study together, genetically and structurally, the history of the road and the history of writing.[16] We are thinking here of Freud's texts on the work of the memory-trace *(Erinnerungsspur)* which, though no longer the neurological trace, is not yet "conscious memory" ("The Unconscious," *SE* XIV, 188), and of the *itinerant* work of the trace, producing and following its route, the trace which traces, the trace which breaks open its own path. The metaphor of pathbreaking, so frequently used in Freud's descriptions, is always in communication with the theme of the *supplementary delay* and with the reconstitution of meaning through deferral, after a mole-like progression, after the subterranean toil of an impression. This impression has left behind a laborious trace which has never been *perceived*, whose meaning has never been lived in the present, i.e., has never been lived consciously. The postscript which constitutes the past present as such is not satisfied, as Plato, Hegel, and Proust perhaps thought, with reawakening or revealing the present past in its truth. It produces the present past. Is sexual deferral the best example or the essence of this movement? A false question, no doubt: the (presumably known) *subject* of the question—sexuality—is determined, limited, or unlimited only through inversion and through the answer itself. Freud's answer, in any event, is decisive. Take the Wolf-Man. It is by deferral that the perception of the primal scene—whether it be reality or fantasy hardly matters—is lived in its meaning, and sexual maturation is not the accidental form of this delay. "At age one and a half, he received impressions the deferred understanding of which became possible for him at the time of the dream through his development, exaltation and sexual investigations." Already in the *Project,* concerning repression in hysteria: "We invariably find that a memory is repressed which has become a trauma only after the event *(nur nachträglich)*. The reason for this state of things is the retardation *(Verspötung)* of puberty as compared with the remainder of the individual's development." That should lead, if not to the solution, at least to a new way of posing the formidable problem of the temporalization and the so-called "timelessness" of the unconscious. Here, more than elsewhere, the gap between Freud's intuition and his concepts is apparent. The timelessness of the unconscious is no doubt determined only in opposition to a common concept of time, a traditional concept, the metaphysical concept: the time of mechanics or the time of consciousness. We ought perhaps to read Freud

---

[16]TN. On roads, writing, and incest see "De la grammatologie," *Critique* 223-24, pp. 149ff. An English translation by Gayatri C. Spivak, *On Grammatology* (Baltimore: Johns Hopkins University Press, 1977), appeared after I had finished the present translation. All references are to the original French version.

the way Heidegger read Kant: like the *cogito,* the unconscious is no doubt timeless only from the standpoint of a certain vulgar conception of time.[17]

Dioptrics and Hieroglyphics

Let us not hasten to conclude that by invoking an energetics, as opposed to a topography, of translation Freud abandoned his efforts at localization. If, as we shall see, he persists in giving a projective and spatial—indeed, purely mechanical—representation of energetic processes, it is not simply for didactic reasons: a certain spatiality, inseparable from the very idea of system, is irreducible; its nature is all the more enigmatic in that we can no longer consider it as the homogeneous and serene milieu of dynamic and economic processes. In the *Traumdeutung,* the metaphoric machine is not yet adapted to the scriptural analogy which already governs—as shall soon be clear—Freud's entire descriptive presentation. It is an *optical machine.*

Let us return to our quotation. Freud does not want to abandon the topographical model against which he has just warned us: "Nevertheless, I consider it expedient and justifiable to continue to make use of the figurative image *(anschauliche Vorstellung:* intuitive representation, metaphor) of the two systems. We can avoid any possible abuse of this method of representation *(mode de mise en scène; Darstellungsweise)* by recollecting that ideas *(Vorstellungen:* representations), thoughts and psychical structures in general must never be regarded as localized in organic elements of the nervous system but rather, as one might say, *between* them, where resistance and facilitations provide the corresponding correlates. Everything that can be an object *(Gegenstand)* of our internal perception is *virtual,* like the image produced in a telescope by the passage of light rays. But we are justified in assuming the existence of the systems *(which are not in any way psychical entities themselves* [my italics] and can never be accessible to our psychical perception) like the lenses of the telescope, which cast the image. And, if we pursue this analogy, we compare the censorship between two systems to the refraction [the breaking of the ray: *Strahlenbrechung*] which takes place when a ray of light passes into a new medium" (V, 611).

This representation already cannot be understood in terms of the spatiality of a simple, homogenous structure. The change in medium and the movement of refraction indicate this sufficiently. Later, in a further reference to the same machine, Freud proposes an interesting differentiation. In the same chapter, in the section on "Regression," he attempts to explain the relation between memory and perception in the memory trace.

[17]TN. In *Being and Time,* and especially *Kant and the Problem of Metaphysics,* Heidegger "deconstructs" Kant's posited timelessness of the *cogito,* a position taken over from Descartes, in order to develop an "authentic" temporality.

What is presented to us in these words is the idea of *psychical locality*. I shall entirely disregard the idea that the mental apparatus with which we are here concerned is also known to us in the form of an anatomical preparation [*Preparat:* laboratory preparation] , and I shall carefully avoid the temptation to determine psychical locality in any anatomical fashion. I shall remain upon psychological ground, and I propose simply to follow the suggestion that we should picture the instrument which carries out our mental functions as resembling a compound microscope, or a photographic apparatus, or something of the kind. On that basis, psychical locality will correspond to a place *(Ort)* inside the apparatus at which one of the preliminary stages of an image comes into being. In the microscope and telescope, as we know, these occur in part at ideal points, regions in which no tangible component of the apparatus is situated. I see no necessity to apologize for the imperfections of this or of any similar imagery [V, 536] .

Beyond its pedagogical value, this illustration proves useful for its distinction between *system* and *psyche:* the psychical system is not psychical, and in this description only the system is in question. Next, it is the operation of the apparatus which interests Freud, how it runs and in what order, the regulated timing of its movements as it is *caught* and localized in the parts of the mechanism: "Strictly speaking, there is no need for the hypothesis that the psychical systems are actually arranged in a *spatial* order. It would be sufficient if a fixed order were established by the fact that in a given psychical process the excitation passes through the systems in a particular *temporal* sequence" (V, 537). Finally, these optical instruments *capture* light; in the example of photography they register it.[18] Freud wants to account for the photographic negative or inscription of light, and this is the differentiation *(Differenzierung)* which he introduces. It will reduce the "imperfections" of his analogy and perhaps "excuse" them. Above all it will throw into relief the apparently contradictory requirement which has haunted Freud since the *Project* and will be satisfied only by a writing machine, the "Mystic Pad":

Next, we have grounds for introducing a first differentiation at the sensory end [of the apparatus]. A trace *(Spur)* is left in our psychical apparatus of

[18]The metaphor of a photographic negative occurs frequently. Cf. "The Dynamics of Transference" *(SE* XII). The notions of negative and copy are the principal means of the analogy. In the analysis of Dora, Freud defines the transference in terms of editions. In "Notes on the Concept of the Unconscious in Psychoanalysis," 1913 *(SE* XII, 264), Freud compares the relations between the conscious and the unconscious to a photographic process: "The first stage of the photograph is the 'negative'; every photographic picture has to pass through the 'negative process,' and some of these negatives which have held good in examination are admitted to the 'positive process' ending in the picture." Hervey de Saint-Denys devotes an entire chapter of his book to the same analogy. The intentions are the same. They suggest a precaution that we will find again in the "Note on the Mystic Writing-Pad": "Memory, compared to a camera, has the marvelous superiority of natural forces: to be able to renew by itself its means of action."

the perceptions which impinge upon it. This we may describe as a "memory-trace" *(Errinerungsspur);* and to the function relating to it we give the name of "memory." If we are in earnest over our plan of attaching psychical processes to systems, memory-traces can only consist in permanent modifications of the elements of the systems. But, as has already been pointed out elsewhere, there are obvious difficulties involved in supposing that one and the same system can accurately retain modifications of its elements and yet remain perpetually open to the reception of fresh occasions for modification [V, 538].

Two systems will thus be necessary in a single machine. This double system, combining freshness of surface and depth of retention, could only distantly and "imperfectly" be represented by an optical machine. "By analysing dreams we can take a step forward in our understanding of the composition of that most marvelous and most mysterious of all instruments. Only a small step no doubt; but a beginning." Thus do we read in the final pages of the *Traumdeutung* (V, 608). Only a small step. The graphic representation of the (nonpsychical) system of the psychical is not yet ready at a time when such a representation of the psychical has already occupied, in the *Traumdeutung* itself, a large area. Let us measure this delay.

We have already defined elsewhere the fundamental property of writing, in a difficult sense of the word, as *spacing:* diastem and time becoming space; an unfolding as well, on an original site, of meanings which irreversible, linear consecution, moving from present point to present point, could only tend to repress, and (to a certain extent) could only fail to repress. In particular in so-called phonetic writing. The latter's complicity with logos (or the time of logic), which is dominated by the principle of noncontradiction, the cornerstone of all metaphysics or presence, is profound. Now in every silent or not wholly phonic spacing out of meaning, concatenations are possible which no longer obey the linearity of logical time, the time of consciousness or preconsciousness, the time of "verbal representations." The border between the non-phonetic space of writing (even "phonetic" writing) and the space of the stage *(scène)* of dreams is uncertain.

We should not be surprised, then, if Freud, in order to suggest the strangeness of the logico-temporal relations in dreams, constantly adduces writing, and the spatial synopses of pictograms, rebuses, hieroglyphics and nonphenetic writing in general. Synopsis and not stasis: scene and not tableau. The laconic, lapidary quality of dreams is not the impassive presence of petrified signs.[19]

Interpretation has spelled out the elements of dreams. It has revealed the work of condensation and displacement. It is still necessary to account for

[19]"Dreams are parsimonious, indigent, laconic." Dreams are "stenographic" (cf. above).

the synthesis which composes and stages the whole. The resources of the mise en scène *(die Darstellungsmittel)* must be questioned. A certain poly-centrism of dream representation is irreconcilable with the apparently linear unfolding of pure verbal representations. The logical and ideal structure of conscious speech must thus submit to the dream system and become subordinate to it, like a part of its machinery.

> The different portions of this complicated structure stand, of course, in the most manifold logical relations to one another. They can represent fore-ground and background, digressions and illustrations, conditions, chains of evidence and counter-arguments. When the whole mass of these dream-thoughts is brought under the pressure of the dream-work, and its elements are turned about, broken into fragments and jammed together—almost like pack-ice—the question arises of what happens to the logical connections which have hitherto formed its framework. What representation *(mise en scène)* do dreams provide for "if," "because," "just as," "although," "either-or," and all the other conjunctions without which we cannot understand sentences or speeches? [V, 312] .

This type of representation *(mise en scène)* may at first be compared to those forms of expression which are like the writing within speech: the painting or sculpture of signifiers which inscribe in a common space ele-ments which the spoken chain must suppress. Freud sets them off against poetry, "which can make use of speech *(Rede)*." But may the dream as well not use spoken language? "In dreams we see but we do not hear," said the *Project*. In point of fact, Freud, like Artaud later on, meant less the absence than the subordination of speech on the dream-stage.[20] Far from disap-pearing, speech then changes purpose and status. It is situated, surrounded, invested (in all senses of the word),[21] constituted. It figures in dreams much as captions do in comic strips, those picto-hieroglyphic combinations in which the phonetic text is secondary and not central in the telling of the tale: "Before painting became acquainted with the laws of expression by which it is governed...in ancient paintings small labels were hung from the mouths of the persons represented, containing in written char-acters *(als Schrift)* the speeches which the artist despaired of representing pictorially" (V, 312).

The overall writing of dreams exceeds phonetic writing and puts speech back in its place. As in hieroglyphics or rebuses, voice is circumvented. From the very beginning of the chapter on "The Dream-Work," we are left in no doubt on this subject, although Freud still uses the concept of trans-lation on which he will later cast suspicion. "The dream-thoughts and the

[20]TN. Cf. note 12 above.

[21]TN. "Invested in all senses of the word" includes the specifically Freudian sense of *Be-setzung* or libidinal investment, which has been translated into English as "cathexis." The French *investissement* is much closer to the original German.

dream-content (the latent and manifest) are presented to us like two ver-
sions *(mises en scène)* of the same subject-matter in two different languages.
Or, more properly, the dream-content seems like a transcript *(Übertragung)*
of the dream-thoughts into another mode of expression, whose characters
and syntactic laws it is our business to discover by comparing the original
and the translation. The dream-thoughts are immediately comprehensible,
as soon as we have learnt them. The dream-content, on the other hand, is
expressed as it were in a pictographic script *(Bilderschrift)*, the characters of which have to be transposed individually into the language of the
dream-thoughts" (IV, 277). *Bilderschrift:* not an inscribed image but a
figurative script, an image inviting not a simple, conscious, present perception of the thing itself—assuming it exists—but a reading. "If we attempted
to read these characters according to their symbolic relation *(Zeichen-
beziehung)*, we should clearly be led into error. . . . A dream is a picture
puzzle *(Bilderrätsel)* of this sort and our predecessors in the field of dream-
interpretation have made the mistake of treating the rebus as a pictorial
composition" (IV, 277-78). The figurative content is then indeed a form of
writing, a signifying chain in scenic form. In that sense, of course, it summarizes a discourse, it is the *economy of speech.* The entire chapter on
"Representability" *(Aptitude à la mise en scène; Darstellbarkeit)* shows
this quite well. But the reciprocal economic transformation, the total
reassimilation into discourse, is, in principle, impossible or limited. This
is first of all because words are also and "primarily" things. Thus, in
dreams they are absorbed, "caught" by the primary process. It is then not
sufficient to say that in dreams, words are condensed by "things"; and that
inversely, nonverbal signifiers may be interpreted to a certain degree in
terms of verbal representations. It must be seen that insofar as they are
attracted, lured into the dream, toward the fictive limit of the primary
process, words tend to become things pure and simple. An equally fictive
limit, moreover. Pure words and pure things are thus, like the idea of the
primary process, and consequently, the secondary process, "theoretical
fictions" (V, 603). The interval in "dreams" and the interval in "wakefulness" may not be distinguished *essentially* insofar as the nature of language
is concerned. "Words are often treated as things in dreams and thus undergo the same operations as thing presentations."[22] In the *formal regression* of dreams, words are not *overtaken* by the spatialization of representa-

---

[22]The "Metapsychological Supplement to the Theory of Dreams," 1916 *(SE* XIV) devotes
an important development to formal regression, which, according to *The Interpretation of
Dreams,* entails the substitution of "primitive methods of expression and representation
[which] takes the place of the usual ones" (V, 548). Freud insists above all on the role of verbal
representations: "It is very noteworthy how little the dream-work keeps to the word-presentations; it is always ready to exchange one word for another till it finds the expression most
handy for plastic representation" (XIV, 228). This passage is followed by a comparison, from
the point of view of word-representations and thing-representations, of the dreamer's lan-

tion *(mise en scène)*. Formal regression could not even succeed, moreover, if words had not always been subject in their materiality to the mark of their inscription or scenic capacity, their *Darstellbarkeit* and all the forms of their spacing. This last factor could only have been repressed by so-called living, vigilant speech, by consciousness, logic, the history of language, etc. Spatialization does not surprise the time of speech or the ideality of meaning, it does not happen to them like an accident. Temporalization presupposes the possibility of symbolism, and every symbolic synthesis, even before it falls into a space "exterior" to it, includes within itself spacing as difference. Which is why the pure phonic chain, to the extent that it implies differences, is itself not a pure continuum or flow of time. Difference is the articulation of space and time. The phonic chain or the chain of phonetic writing are always already distended by that minimum of essential spacing upon which the dream-work and any formal regression in general can begin to operate. It is not a question of a negation of time, of a cessation of time in a present or a simultaneity, but of a different structure, a different stratification of time. Here, once more, a comparison with writing—phonetic writing this time—casts light on writing as well as on dreams:

> They [dreams] reproduce *logical connection* by *simultaneity in time.* Here they are acting like the painter who, in a picture of the School of Athens or of Parnassus, represents in one group all the philosophers or all the poets who were never, in fact, assembled in a single hall or on a single mountain-top. . . . Dreams carry this mode of reproduction *(mise en scène)* down to details. Whenever they show us two elements close together, this guarantees that there is some specially intimate connection between what corresponds to them among the dream-thoughts. In the same way, in our system of writing, *"ab"* means that the two letters are to be pronounced in a single syllable. If a gap is left between the *"a"* and the *"b,"* it means that the *"a"* is the last letter of one word and the *"b"* is the first of the next one [IV, 314] .

The model of heiroglyphic writing assembles more strikingly—though we find it in every form of writing—the diversity of the modes and functions of signs in dreams. Every sign—verbal or otherwise—may be used at different levels, in configurations and functions which are never prescribed by its "essence," but emerge from a play of differences. Summarizing all these possibilities, Freud concludes: "Yet, in spite of all this ambiguity, it is fair to say that the productions *(mises en scène)* of the dream-work, which, it must be remembered, *are not made with the intention of being*

---

guage and the language of the schizophrenic. It should be analysed closely. We would perhaps find (against Freud?) that a rigorous determination of the anomaly is impossible. On the role of verbal representation in the preconscious and the (consequently) secondary character of visual elements, cf. *The Ego and the Id,* chap. 2.

understood, present no greater difficulties to their translators than do the ancient hieroglyphic scripts to those who seek to read them" (V, 341).

More than twenty years separate the first edition of the *Traumdeutung* from the "Note on the Mystic Writing-Pad." If we continue to follow the two series of metaphors—those concerning the nonpsychical system of the psychical and those concerning the psychical itself—what happens?

On the one hand, the *theoretical* import of the *psychographic* metaphor will be increasingly refined. A methodological inquiry will, to a certain extent, be devoted to it. It is with a graphematics still to come, rather than with a linguistics dominated by an ancient phonologism, that psychoanalysis sees itself as destined to collaborate. Freud recommends this *literally* in a text from 1913, and in this case we have nothing to add, interpret, alter.[23] The interest which psychoanalysis brings to linguistics presupposes an "overstepping of the habitual meaning of the word 'speech.' For in what follows 'speech' must be understood not merely to mean the expression of thought in words, but to include the speech of gesture and every other method, such, for instance, as writing, by which mental activity can be expressed" (XIII, 176). And having recalled the archaic character of expression in dreams, which accepts contradiction[24] and valorizes visibility, Freud specifies:

> It seems to us more appropriate to compare dreams with a system of writing than with a language. In fact, the interpretation of a dream is completely analogous to the decipherment of an ancient pictographic script such as Egyptian hieroglyphics. In both cases there are certain elements which are not intended to be interpreted (or read, as the case may be) but are only designed to serve as "determinatives," that is to establish the meaning of some other element. The ambiguity of various elements of dreams finds a parallel in these ancient systems of writing. ... If this conception of the method of representation in dreams *(mise en scéne)* has not yet been followed up, this, as will be readily understood, must be ascribed to the fact that psycho-analysts are entirely ignorant of the attitude and knowledge with which a philologist would approach such a problem as that presented by dreams [XIII, 177].

On the other hand, the same year, in the article on "The Unconscious," the problematic of the *apparatus* itself will begin to be taken up in terms of

[23] "The Claim of Psychoanalysis to Scientific Interest" (*SE* XIII). The second part of this text, devoted to "non-psychological sciences," is concerned first of all with the science of language (p. 176)—before philosophy, biology, history, sociology, pedagogy.

[24] As is known, the note on "The Antithetical Meaning of Primal Words," 1910 (*SE* XI) tends to demonstrate, after Abel, and with a great abundance of examples borrowed from hieroglyphic writing, that the contradictory or undetermined meaning of primal words could be determined, could receive its difference and its conditions of operation, only through gesture and writing. On this text and Abel's hypothesis, cf. Emile Benveniste, *Problèmes de linguistique générale* (Paris: Gallimard, 1964), chap. 7.

scriptural concepts: neither, as in the *Project,* in a topology of traces without writing, nor, as in the *Traumdeutung,* in the operations of optical mechanisms. The debate between the functional hypothesis and the topographical hypothesis concerns the locations of an *inscription (Niederschrift):* "When a psychical act (let us confine ourselves here to one which is in the nature of an idea [*Vorstellung,* lit. representation] is transposed from the systems Ucs. into the system Cs. (or Pcs.), are we to suppose that this transposition involves a fresh record—as it were, a second registration —of the idea in question which may thus be situated as well in a fresh psychical locality, and alongside of which the original unconscious registration continues to exist? Or are we rather to believe that the transposition consists in a change in the state of the idea, a change involving the same material and occurring in the same locality?" (XIV, 174). The discussion which follows does not directly concern us here. Let us simply recall that the economic hypothesis and the difficult concept of anticathexis (*Gegenbesetzung:* "the sole mechanism of primal repression," XIV, 181) which Freud introduces after refusing to decide on the last question, do not eliminate the topographical difference of the two inscriptions.[25] And let us note that the concept of inscription still remains simply the graphic *element* of an apparatus which is not itself a writing machine. The difference between the system and the psychical is still at work: the graphism itself is reserved for the description of psychical content or of an element in the machine. We might think that the machine itself is subject to another principle of organization, another destination than writing. This is perhaps the case as well, for the main thread of the article on "The Unconscious," its *example,* as we have emphasized, is the fate of a *representation* after it is first registered. When perception—the apparatus which originally enregistered and inscribes—is described, the "perceptual apparatus" can be nothing but a writing machine. The "Note on the Mystic Writing-Pad," twelve years later, will describe the perceptual apparatus and the origin of memory. Long disjointed and out of phase, the two series of metaphors will then be united.

Freud's Piece of Wax and the Three Analogies of Writing

In this six-page text, the analogy between a certain writing apparatus and the perceptual apparatus is demonstrated in progressive steps. Three stages in the description result each time in an increase in rigor, inwardness, and differentiation.

As has always been done—at least since Plato—Freud first considers

[25]This is the passage we quoted earlier, and in which the memory-trace was distinguished from "memory."

writing as a technique subservient to memory, an external, auxiliary technique of psychical memory which is not memory itself: *hypomnesis* rather than *mneme*, said the *Phaedrus*.[26] But here—something not possible for Plato—the psychical is caught up in an apparatus, and what is written will be more readily represented as a part extracted from the apparatus and "materialized." Such is the *first analogy:*

> If I distrust my memory—neurotics, as we know, do so to a remarkable extent, but normal people have every reason for doing so as well—I am able to supplement and guarantee *(ergänzen und versichern)* its working by making a note in writing *(schriftliche Anzeichnung)*. In that case the surface upon which this trace is preserved, the pocket-book or sheet of paper, is as it were a materialized portion *(ein materialisiertes Stück)* of my mnemic apparatus *(des Erinnerungsapparates)*, the rest of which I carry about with me invisible. I have only to bear in mind the place where this "memory" has been deposited and I can then "reproduce" it at any time I like, with the certainty that it will have remained unaltered and so have escaped the possible distortions to which it might have been subjected in my actual memory [XIX, 227].

Freud's theme here is not the absence of memory or the primal and normal finitude of the powers of memory; even less is it the structure of the temporalization which grounds that finitude, or this structure's essential relation to censorship and repression; nor is it the possibility and the necessity of the *Ergänzung*, the *hypomnemic supplement* which the psychical must project "into the world"; nor is it that which is called for, as concerns the nature of the psyche, in order for this supplementation to be possible. At first, it is simply a question of considering the conditions which customary writing surfaces impose on the operation of mnemic supplementation. Those conditions fail to satisfy the double requirement defined since the *Project:* a potential for indefinite preservation and an unlimited capacity for reception. A sheet of paper preserves indefinitely but is quickly saturated. A slate, whose virginity may always be reconstituted by erasing the imprints on it, does not conserve its traces. All the classical writing surfaces offer only one of the two advantages and always present the complementary difficulty. Such is the *res extensa* and the intelligible surface of classical writing apparatuses. In the processes which they substitute for our memory, "an unlimited receptive capacity and a retention of permanent traces seem to be mutually exclusive" (XIX, 227). Their extension belongs to classical geometry and is intelligible in its terms as pure exterior without relation to itself. A different writing space must be found, a space which writing has always claimed for itself.

[26]TN. For a complete discussion of *hypomnesis/mnesis* in Plato, cf. "La pharmacie de Platon," in *La dissémination.*

Auxiliary apparatuses *(Hilfsapparate)*, which, as Freud notes, are always constituted on the model of the organ to be supplemented (e.g., spectacles, camera, ear trumpet) thus seem particularly deficient when memory is in question. This remark makes even more suspect the earlier reference to optical apparatuses. Freud recalls, nevertheless, that the contradictory requirement he is presenting had already been recognized in 1900. He could have said in 1895: "As long ago as in 1900 I gave expression in *The Interpretation of Dreams* to a suspicion that this unusual capacity was to be divided between two different systems (or organs of the mental apparatus). According to this view, we possess a system *Pcpt.-Cs.*, which receives perceptions but retains no permanent trace of them, so that it can react like a clean sheet to every new perception; while the permanent traces of the excitations which have been received are preserved in 'mnemic systems' lying behind the perceptual system. Later, in *Beyond the Pleasure Principle* (1920), I added a remark to the effect that the inexplicable phenomenon of consciousness arises in the perceptual system *instead of* the permanent traces" (XIX, 228).[27]

A double system contained in a single differentiated apparatus: a perpetually available innocence and an infinite reserve of traces have at last been reconciled by the "small contrivance" placed "some time ago upon the market under the name of the Mystic Writing-Pad," and which "promises to perform more than the sheet of paper or the slate." Its appearance is modest, "but if it is examined more closely, it will be found that its construction shows a remarkable agreement with my hypothetical structure of our perceptual apparatus." It offers both advantages: "an ever-ready receptive surface and permanent traces of the inscriptions that have been made on it" (ibid.). Here is its description:

> The Mystic Pad is a slab of dark brown resin or wax with a paper edging; over the slab is laid a thin transparent sheet, the top end of which is firmly secured to the slab while its bottom end rests upon it without being fixed to it. This transparent sheet is the more interesting part of the little device. It itself consists of two layers which can be detached from each other except at their two ends. The upper layer is a transparent piece of celluloid; the lower layer is made of thin translucent waxed paper. When the apparatus is not in use, the lower surface of the waxed paper adheres lightly to the upper surface of the wax slab.
>
> To make use of the Mystic Pad, one writes upon the celluloid portion of the covering-sheet which rests upon the wax slab. For this purpose no pencil or chalk is necessary, since the writing does not depend on material being deposited upon the receptive surface. It is a return to the ancient method of writing upon tablets of clay or wax: a pointed stilus scratches the surface,

---

[27]Cf. chapter 4 of *Beyond the Pleasure Principle*.

the depressions upon which constitute the "writing." In the case of the Mystic Pad this scratching is not effected directly, but through the medium of the covering-sheet. At the points which the stilus touches, it presses the lower surface of the waxed paper on to the wax slab, and the grooves are visible as dark writing upon the otherwise smooth whitish-gray surface of the celluloid. If one wishes to destroy what has been written, all that is necessary is to raise the double covering-sheet from the wax slab by a light pull, starting from the free lower end.[28] The close contact between the waxed paper and the wax slab at the places which have been scratched (upon which the visibility of the writing depended) is thus brought to an end and it does not recur when the two surfaces come together once more. The Mystic Pad is now clear of writing and ready to receive fresh inscriptions [XIX, 228-29].

Let us note that the *depth* of the Mystic Pad is simultaneously a depth without bottom, an infinite allusion, and a perfectly superficial exteriority: a stratification of surfaces each of whose relation to itself, each of whose interior, is but the implication of another similarly exposed surface. It joins the two empirical certainties by which we are constituted: infinite depth in the implication of meaning, in the unlimited envelopment of the present, and, simultaneously, the pellicular essence of being, the absolute absence of any foundation.

Neglecting the device's "slight imperfections," interested only in the analogy, Freud insists on the essentially protective nature of the celluloid sheet. Without it, the fine waxed paper would be scratched or ripped. There is no writing which does not devise some means of protection, *to protect against itself*, against the writing by which the "subject" is himself threatened as he lets himself be written: *as he exposes himself.* "The layer of celluloid thus acts as a protective sheath for the waxed paper." It shields the waxed paper from "injurious effects from without." "I may at this point recall that in *Beyond the Pleasure Principle*,[29] I showed that the perceptual apparatus of our mind consists of two layers, of an external protective shield against stimuli whose task it is to diminish the strength of excitations coming in, and of a surface behind it which receives the stimuli, namely the system *Pcpt.-Cs.*" (XIX, 230).

But this still concerns only reception or perception, the most superficial surface's openness to the incision of a scratch. There is as yet no writing in the flatness of this *extensio*. We must account for writing as a trace which survives the scratch's present, punctuality, and *stigmē*. "This analogy," Freud continues, "would not be of much value if it could not be pursued further than this." This is the *second analogy:* "If we lift the entire covering-sheet—both the celluloid and the waxed paper—off the wax slab, the

[28]The *Standard Edition* notes here a slight infidelity in Freud's description. "The principle is not affected." We are tempted to think that Freud inflects his description elsewhere as well, in order to suit the analogy.

[29]This is still in chapter 4 of *Beyond the Pleasure Principle.*

writing vanishes, and, as I have already remarked, does not re-appear again. The surface of the Mystic Pad is clear of writing and once more capable of receiving impressions. But it is easy to discover that the permanent trace of what was written is retained upon the wax slab itself and is legible in suitable lights" (ibid.). The contradictory requirements are satisfied by this double system, and "this is precisely the way in which, according to the hypothesis which I mentioned just now, our psychical apparatus performs its perceptual function. The layer which receives the stimuli—the system *Pcpt.-Cs.*—forms no permanent traces; the foundations of memory come about in other, supplementary, systems" (ibid.). Writing supplements perception before perception even appears to itself [is conscious of itself]. "Memory" or writing is the opening of that process of appearance itself. The "perceived" may be read only in the past, beneath perception and after it.[30]

Whereas other writing surfaces, corresponding to the prototype of slate or paper, could represent only a materialized part of the mnemic system in the psychical apparatus, an abstraction, the Mystic Pad represents the apparatus in its entirety, not simply in its perceptual layer. The wax slab, in fact, represents the unconscious: "I do not think it is too far-fetched to compare the wax slab with the unconscious behind the system Pcpt.-Cs." (XIX, 230-31). The becoming-visible which alternates with the disappearance of what is written would be the flickering-up *(Aufleuchten)* and passing-away *(Vergehen)* of consciousness in the process of perception.

This introduces the *third and final analogy*. It is certainly the most interesting. Until now, it has been a question only of the space of writing, its extension and volume, reliefs and depressions. But there is as well a *time of writing*, and this time of writing is nothing other than the very structure of that which we are now describing. We must come to terms with the temporality of the wax slab. For it is not outside the slab, and the Mystic Pad includes in its structure what Kant describes as the three modes of time in the *three analogies of experience:* permanence, succession, simultaneity. Descartes, when he wonders *quaenam vero est haec cera,* can reduce its essence to the timeless simplicity of an intelligible object.[31] Freud, reconstructing an *operation,* can reduce neither time nor the multiplicity of sensitive layers. And he will link a discontinuist conception of time, as the periodicity and spacing of writing, to a whole chain of hypotheses which stretch from the *Letters to Fliess* to *Beyond the Pleasure Principle,*

---

[30]TN. In *La voix et le phénomène (The Voice and the Phenomenon),* trans. David Allison (Evanston: Northwestern University Press, 1973), there is a full "deconstruction" of perception as a past that was never present.

[31]TN. "Now what is this wax...?" The reference is to the *Second Meditation,* and Derrida is playing upon the fact that Freud's piece of wax, the mystic writing-pad, is irreducibly temporal and differentiated, while the timelessness of Descartes's piece of wax is symptomatic of the metaphysical repression of writing and difference. Cf. note 17 above.

and which, once again, are constructed, consolidated, confirmed, and solidified in the Mystic Pad. Temporality as spacing will be not only the horizontal discontinuity of a chain of signs, but also will be writing as the interruption and restoration of contact between the various depths of psychical levels: the remarkably heterogeneous temporal fabric of psychical work itself. We find neither the continuity of a line nor the homogeneity of a volume; only the differentiated duration and depth of a stage, and its spacing:

> But I must admit that I am inclined to press the comparison still further. On the Mystic Pad the writing vanishes every time the close contact is broken between the paper which receives the stimulus and the wax slab which preserves the impression. This agrees with a notion which I have long had about the method in which the perceptual apparatus of our mind functions, but which I have hitherto kept to myself [XIX, 231].

This hypothesis posits a discontinuous distribution — through rapid periodic impulses — of "cathectic innervations" *(Besetzungsinnervationen)*, from within toward the outside, toward the permeability of the system Pcpt.-Cs. These movements are then "withdrawn" or "removed." Consciousness fades each time the cathexis is withdrawn in this way. Freud compares this movement to the feelers which the *unconscious* would stretch out toward the external world, and which it would withdraw when these feelers had sampled the excitations coming from the external world in order to warn the unconscious of any threat. (Freud had no more reserved the image of the feeler for the unconscious — we find it in chapter 4 of *Beyond the Pleasure Principle*[32] — than he had reserved the notion of cathectic periodicity, as we noted above.) The "origin of our concept of time" is attributed to this "periodic non-excitability" and to this "discontinuous method of functioning of the system Pcpt.-Cs." Time is the economy of a system of writing.

The machine does not run by itself. It is less a machine than a tool. And it is not held with only one hand. This is the mark of its temporality.

---

[32]We find it again, the same year, in the article on "Negation" (*SE* XIX). In a passage which concerns us here for its recognition of the relation between negation in thought and *différance,* delay, detour *(Aufschub, Denkaufschub)* (*différance,* union of Eros and Thanatos), the sending out of feelers is attributed not to the unconscious but to the ego. On *Denkaufschub,* on thought as retardation, postponement, suspension, respite, detour, *différance* as opposed to — or rather *différante* (deferring, differing) from — the theoretical, fictive, and always already transgressed pole of the "primary process," cf. all of chapter 7 of *The Interpretation of Dreams.* The concept of the "circuitous path" *(Umweg)* is central to it. "Thought identity," entirely woven of memory, is an aim always already substituted for "perceptual identity," the aim of the "primary process," and *das ganze Denken ist nur ein Umweg*...("All thinking is no more than a circuitous path," *SE* V, 602). Cf. also the "Umwege zum Tode" in *Beyond the Pleasure Principle.* "Compromise," in Freud's sense, is always *différance.* But there is nothing before the compromise.

Its *maintenance* is not simple. The ideal virginity of the present *(maintenant)* is constituted by the work of memory. At least two hands are needed to make the apparatus function, as well as a system of gestures, a coordination of independent initiatives, an organized multiplicity of origins. It is at this stage that the "Note" ends: "If we imagine one hand writing upon the surface of the Mystic Writing-Pad while another periodically raises its covering sheet from the wax slab, we shall have a concrete representation of the way in which I tried to picture the functioning of the perceptual apparatus of our mind" (XIX, 232).

Traces thus produce the space of their inscription only by acceding to the period of their erasure. From the beginning, in the "present" of their first impression, they are constituted by the double force of repetition and erasure, legibility and illegibility. A two-handed machine, a multiplicity of agencies or origins—is this not the original relation to the other and the original temporality of writing, its "primary" complication: an originary spacing, deferring, and erasure of the simple origin, and polemics on the very threshold of what we persist in calling perception? The stage of dreams, "which follow old facilitations," was a stage of writing. But this is because "perception," the first relation of life to its other, the origin of life, had always already prepared representation. We must be several in order to write, and even to "perceive." The *simple* structure of maintenance and manuscription, like every intuition of an origin, is a myth, a "fiction" as "theoretical" as the idea of the primary process. For that idea is contradicted by the theme of primal repression.

Writing is unthinkable without repression. The condition for writing is that there be neither a permanent contact nor an absolute break between strata: the vigilance and failure of censorship. It is no accident that the metaphor of censorship should come from the area of politics concerned with the deletions, blanks, and disguises of writing, even if, at the beginning of the *Traumdeutung,* Freud seems to make only a conventional, didactic reference to it. The apparent exteriority of political censorship refers to an essential censorship which binds the writer to his own writing.

If there were only perception, pure permeability to breaching, there would be no breaches. We would be written, but nothing would be recorded; no writing would be produced, retained, repeated as legibility. But pure perception does not exist: we are written only as we write, by the agency within us which always already keeps watch over perception, be it internal or external. The "subject" of writing does not exist if we mean by that some sovereign solitude of the author. The subject of writing is a *system* of relations between strata: the Mystic Pad, the psyche, society, the world. Within that scene, on that stage, the punctual simplicity of the classical subject is not to be found. In order to describe the structure, it is not enough to recall that one always writes for someone; and the oppositions sender-receiver, code-message, etc., remain extremely coarse instruments. We would search the "public" in vain for the first reader: i.e., the first author of a work. And the "sociology of literature" is blind to the war and the ruses perpetrated by the author who reads and by the first reader who dictates, for at stake here is the origin of the work itself. The *sociality* of writing as *drama* requires an entirely different discipline.

That the machine does not run by itself means something else: a mechanism without its own energy. The machine is dead. It is death. Not because we risk death in playing with machines, but because the origin of machines is the relation to death. In a letter to Fliess, it will be recalled, Freud, evoking his representation of the psychical apparatus, had the impression of being faced with a machine which would soon run by itself. But what was to run by itself was the psyche and not its imitation or mechanical representation. For the latter does not live. Representation is death. Which may be immediately transformed into the following proposition: death is (only) representation. But it is bound to life and to the living present which it repeats originarily. A pure representation, a machine, never runs by itself. Such at least is the limitation which Freud recognizes in his analogy with the Mystic Pad. Like the first section of the "Note," his gesture at this point is extremely Platonic. Only the writing of the soul, said the *Phaedrus,* only the psychical trace is able to reproduce and to represent itself spontaneously. Our reading had skipped over the following remark by Freud: "There must come a point at which the analogy between an auxiliary apparatus of this kind and the organ which is its prototype will cease to apply. It is true, too, that once the writing has been erased, the Mystic Pad cannot 'reproduce' it from within; it would be a mystic pad indeed if, like our memory, it could accomplish that" (XIX, 230). Abandoned to itself, the multiplicity of layered surfaces of the apparatus is a dead complexity without depth. Life as depth belongs only to the wax of psychical memory. Freud, like Plato, thus continues to oppose hypomnemic writing and writing *en tei psychei,* itself woven of traces, empirical memories of a present truth outside of time. Henceforth, the Mystic Pad, separated from psychical responsibility, a representation abandoned to itself, still participates in Cartesian space and mechanics: *natural* wax, exteriority of the *memory aid.*

All that Freud had thought about the unity of life and death, however, should have led him to ask other questions here. And to ask them explicitly. Freud does not explicitly examine the status of the "materialized" supplement which is necessary to the alleged spontaneity of memory, even if that spontaneity were differentiated in itself, thwarted by a censorship of repression which, moreover, could not act on a perfectly spontaneous memory. Far from the machine being a pure absence of spontaneity, its *resemblance* to the psychical apparatus, its existence and its necessity bear witness to the finitude of the mnemic spontaneity which is thus supplemented. The machine—and, consequently, representation—is death and finitude *within* the psyche. Nor does Freud examine the possibility of this machine, which, in the world, has at least begun to *resemble* memory, and increasingly resembles it more closely. Its resemblance to memory is closer than that of the innocent Mystic Pad; the latter is no doubt infinitely more complex than slate or paper, less archaic than a palimpsest; but, compared to other machines for storing archives, it is a child's toy. This resemblance—i.e., necessarily a certain Being-in-the-world of the psyche—did not happen to memory from without, any more than death surprises life. It founds memory. Metaphor—in this case the analogy between two apparatuses and the possibility of this representational relation—raises a question which, despite his premises, and for reasons which are no doubt essential, Freud failed to make explicit, at the very moment when he had brought this question to the threshold of being thematic and urgent. Metaphor as a rhetorical or didactic device is possible here only through the solid metaphor, the "unnatural," historical production of a *supplementary* machine, *added to* the psychical organization in order to supplement its finitude. The very idea of finitude is derived from the movement of this supplementarity. The historico-technical production of this metaphor which survives individual (that is, generic) psychical organization, is of an entirely different order than the production of an intrapsychical metaphor, assuming that the latter exists (to speak about it is not enough for that), and whatever bond the two metaphors may maintain between themselves. Here the question of *technology* (a new name must perhaps be found in order to remove it from its traditional problematic) may not be derived from an assumed opposition between the psychical and the nonpsychical, life and death. Writing, here, is *technē* as the relation between life and death, between present and representation, between the two apparatuses. It opens up the question of technics: of the apparatus in general and of the analogy between the psychical apparatus and the nonpsychical apparatus. In this sense writing is the stage of history and the play of the world. It cannot be exhausted by psychology alone. That which, in Freud's discourse, opens itself to the theme of writing results in psychoanalysis being not simply psychology—nor simply psychoanalysis.

Thus are perhaps augured, in the Freudian breakthrough, a beyond and a beneath of the closure we might term "Platonic." In that moment of world history "subsumed" by the name of Freud, by means of an unbelievable mythology (be it neurological or metapsychological: for we never dreamed of taking it seriously, outside of the question which disorganizes and disturbs its literalness, the metapsychological fable, which marks perhaps only a minimal advance beyond the neurological tales of the *Project*), a relationship to itself of the historico-transcendental stage of writing was spoken without being said, thought without being thought:

was written and simultaneously erased, metaphorized; designating itself while indicating intrawordly relations, it *was represented*.

This may perhaps be recognized *(as an example and let this be understood prudently)* insofar as Freud too, with admirable scope and continuity, *performed for us the scene of writing*. But we must think of this scene in other terms than those of individual or collective psychology, or even of anthropology. It must be thought in the horizon of the scene/ stage of the world, as the history of that scene/stage. Freud's language is *caught up* in it.

Thus Freud performs for us the scene of writing. Like all those who write. And like all who know how to write, he let the scene duplicate, repeat, and betray itself within the scene. It is Freud then whom we will allow to say what scene he has played for us. And from him that we shall borrow the hidden epigraph which has silently governed our reading.

In following the advance of the metaphors of path, trace, breach, of the march treading down a track which was opened by effraction through neurone, light or wax, wood or resin, in order violently to inscribe itself in nature, matter, or matrix; and in following the untiring reference to a dry stilus and a writing without ink; and in following the inexhaustible inventiveness and dreamlike renewal of mechanical models—the metonymy perpetually at work on the same metaphor, obstinately substituting trace for trace and machine for machine—we have been wondering just what Freud was doing.

And we have been thinking of those texts where, better than anywhere else, he tells us *worin die Bahnung sonst besteht*. In what pathbreaking consists.

Of the *Traumdeutung:* "It is highly probable that all complicated machinery and apparatuses occurring in dreams stand for the genitals (and as a rule male ones), in describing which dream-symbolism is as indefatigable as the joke-work *(Witzarbeit)*" (V, 356).

Then, of *Inhibitions, Symptoms, and Anxiety:* "As soon as writing, which entails making a liquid flow out of a tube onto a piece of white paper, assumes the significance of copulation, or as soon as walking becomes a symbolic substitute for treading upon the body of mother earth, both writing and walking are stopped because they represent the performance of a forbidden sexual act" (XX, 90).

The last part of the lecture concerned the archi-trace as erasure: erasure of the present and thus of the subject, of that which is proper to the subject and of his proper name. The concept of a (conscious or unconscious) subject necessarily refers to the concept of substance—and thus of presence— out of which it is born.

Thus, the Freudian concept of trace must be radicalized and extracted from the metaphysics of presence which still retains it (particularly in the concepts of consciousness, the unconscious, perception, memory, reality, and several others).

The trace is the erasure of selfhood, of one's own presence, and is constituted by the threat or anguish of its irremediable disappearance, of the disappearance of its disappearance. An unerasable trace is not a trace, it is a full presence, an immobile and uncorruptible substance, a son of God, a sign of parousia and not a seed, that is, a mortal germ.

This erasure is death itself, and it is within its horizon that we must conceive not only the "present," but also what Freud doubtless believed to be the indelibility of certain traces in the unconscious, where "nothing ends, nothing happens, nothing is forgotten." This erasure of the trace is not only an accident that can occur here or there, nor is it even the necessary structure of a determined censorship threatening a given presence; it is the very structure which makes possible, as the movement of temporalization and pure *auto-affection*, something that can be called repression in general, the original synthesis of original repression and secondary repression, repression "itself."

Such a radicalization of the *thought of the trace* (a *thought* because it escapes binarism and makes binarism possible on the basis of *nothing*), would be fruitful not only in the deconstruction of logocentrism, but in a kind of reflection exercised more positively in different fields, at different levels of writing in general, at the point of articulation of writing in the current sense and of the trace in general.

These fields, whose specificity thereby could be opened to a thought fecundated by psychoanalysis, would be numerous. The problem of their respective limits would be that much more formidable to the extent that this problem could not be subsumed by any authorized conceptual opposition.

In question, first, would be:

1. *A psychopathology of everyday life* in which the study of writing would not be limited to the interpretation of the *lapsus calami*, and, moreover, would be more attentive to this latter and to its originality than Freud himself ever was. "*Slips of the pen*, to which I now pass, are so closely akin to slips of the tongue that we have nothing new to expect from them" (XV, 69). This did prevent Freud from raising the fundamental juridical problem of responsibility, before the tribunal of psychoanalysis, as concerns, for example, the murderous *lapsus calami* (ibid.).

2. *A history of writing*, an immense field in which only preparatory work has been done up to now; however admirable this work has been, it still gives way, beyond its empirical discoveries, to unbridled speculation.

3. *A becoming-literary of the literal*. Here, despite several attempts made by Freud and certain of his successors, a psychoanalysis of literature

respectful of the *originality of the literary signifier* has not yet begun, and this is surely not an accident. Until now, only the analysis of literary *signifieds,* that is, *nonliterary* signified meanings, has been undertaken. But such questions refer to the entire history of literary forms themselves, and to the history of everything within them which was destined precisely to authorize this disdain of the signifier.

4. Finally, to continue designating these fields according to traditional and problematic boundaries, what might be called a new *psychoanalytic graphology,* which would take into account the contributions of the three kinds of research we have just outlined roughly. Here, Melanie Klein perhaps opens the way. As concerns the forms of signs, even within phonetic writing, the cathexes of gestures, and of movements, of letters, lines, points, the elements of the writing apparatus (instrument, surface, substance, etc.), a text like *The Role of the School in the Libidinal Development of the Child* (1923) indicates the direction to be taken (cf. also, Strachey, *Some Unconscious Factors in Reading*).

Melanie Klein's entire thematic, her analysis of the constitution of good and bad objects, her genealogy of morals could doubtless begin to illuminate, if followed prudently, the entire problem of the archi-trace, not in its essence (it does not have one), but in terms of valuation and devaluation. Writing as sweet nourishment or as excrement, the trace as seed or mortal germ, wealth or weapon, detritus and/or penis, etc.

How, for example, on the stage of history, can writing as excrement separated from the living flesh and the sacred body of the hieroglyph (Artaud), be put into communication with what is said in *Numbers* about the parched woman drinking the inky dust of the law; or what is said in *Ezekiel* about the son of man who fills his entrails with the scroll of the law which has become sweet as honey in his mouth?

Freud and Dora: Story, History, Case History

By Steven Marcus

I

It is generally agreed that Freud's case histories are unique. Today more than half a century after they were written they are still widely read. Even more, they are still widely used for instruction and training in psychoanalytic institutes. One of the inferences that such a vigorous condition of survival prompts is that these writings have not yet been superseded. Like other masterpieces of literature or the arts, these works seem to possess certain transhistorical qualities—although it may by no means be easy to specify what those qualities are. The implacable "march of science" has not—or has not yet—consigned them to "mere" history. Their singular and mysterious complexity, density, and richness have thus far prevented such a transformation and demotion.

This state of affairs has received less attention than it merits. Freud's case histories—and his works in general—are unique as pieces or kinds of writing, and it may be useful to examine one of Freud's case histories from the point of view of literary criticism, to analyze it as a piece of writing, and to determine whether this method of proceeding may yield results that other means have not. My assumption—and conclusion—is that Freud is a great writer and that one of his major case histories is a great work of literature—that is to say it is both an outstanding creative and imaginative performance and an intellectual and cognitive achievement of the highest order. And yet this triumphant greatness is in part connected with the circumstance that it is about a kind of failure, and that part of the failure remains in fact unacknowledged and unconscious.

"Fragment of an Analysis of a Case of Hysteria," better known as the case of Dora, is Freud's first great case history—oddly enough he was to write only four others. It may be helpful for the reader if at the outset I refresh his memory by briefly reviewing some of the external facts of the case. In the autumn of 1900, Dora, an eighteen-year-old young woman, began treatment with Freud. She did so reluctantly and against her will, and, Freud writes, "it was only her father's authority which induced her to come to me at all." Neither Dora nor her father were strangers to Freud. He had made separate acquaintance with both of them in the past, during certain episodes of illness that characterized their lives if not the life of the family as a whole. (Freud knew other members of the family as well.)

As for Dora herself, her afflictions, both mental and physical, had begun in early childhood and had persisted and flourished with variations and fluctuating intensities until she was presented to Freud for therapy. Among the symptoms from which she suffered were to be found dyspnea, migraine, and periodic attacks of nervous coughing often accompanied by complete loss of voice during part of the episode. Dora had in fact first been brought by her father to Freud two years earlier, when she was sixteen and suffering from a cough and hoarseness; he had then "proposed giving her psychological treatment," but this suggestion was not adopted since "the attack in question, like the others, passed off spontaneously." In the course of his treatment of Dora, Freud also learned of further hysterical—or hysterically connected—productions on her part, such as a feverish attack that mimicked appendicitis, a periodic limp, and a vaginal catarrh or discharge. Moreover, during the two-year interval between Dora's first visit and the occasion on which her father brought her to Freud a second time, and "handed her over to me for psychotherapeutic treatment...Dora had grown unmistakably neurotic." Dora was now "in the first bloom of youth—a girl of intelligent and engaging looks." Her character had, however, undergone an alteration. She had become chronically depressed, and was generally dissatisfied with both herself and her family. She had become unfriendly toward the father whom she had hitherto loved, idealized, and identified with. She was "on very bad terms" with her mother, for whom she felt a good deal of scorn. "She tried to avoid social intercourse, and employed herself—so far as she was allowed to by the fatigue and lack of concentration of which she complained—with attending lectures for women and with carrying on more or less serious studies." Two further events precipitated the crisis which led to her being delivered to Freud. Her parents found a written note in which she declared her intention to commit suicide because "as she said, she could no longer endure her life." Following this there occurred one day "a slight passage of words" between Dora and her father, which ended with Dora suddenly losing consciousness—the attack, Freud believed, was "accompanied by convulsions and delirious states," although it was lost to amnesia and never came up in the analysis.

Having outlined this array of affections, Freud dryly remarks that such a case "does not upon the whole seem worth recording. It is merely a case of

'petite hysterie' with the commonest of all somatic and mental symptoms. ...
More interesting cases of hysteria have no doubt been published."

This disavowal of anything sensational to come is of course a bit of shrewd
disingenuousness on Freud's part, for what follows at once is his assertion
that he is going to elucidate the meaning, origin, and function of every one
of these symptoms by means of the events and experiences of Dora's life.
He is going in other words to discover the "psychological determinants"
that will account for Dora's illnesses; among these determinants he lists
three principal conditions: "a psychical trauma, a conflict of affects, and ...
a disturbance in the sphere of sexuality." And so Freud begins the treatment
by asking Dora to talk about her experiences. What emerges is the substance
of the case history, a substance which takes all of Freud's immense analytic,
expository, and narrative talents to bring into order. I will again very
roughly and briefly summarize some of this material.

Sometime after 1888, when the family had moved to B _____, the health
resort where the father's tuberculosis had sent them, an intimate and enduring friendship sprang up between them and a couple named K. Dora's
father was deeply unhappy in his marriage and apparently made no bones
about it. The K.'s too were unhappily married, as it later turned out. Frau
K. took to nursing Dora's father during these years of his illness. She also
befriended Dora, and they behaved toward one another in the most familiar
way and talked together about the most intimate subjects. Herr K., her
husband, also made himself a close friend of Dora's—going regularly for
walks with her and giving her presents. Dora in her turn befriended the
K.'s two small children, "and had been almost a mother to them." What
begins to be slowly if unmistakably disclosed is that Dora's father and
Frau K. had established a sexual liaison and that this relation had by the
time of Dora's entering into treatment endured for many years. At the same
time Dora's father and Frau K. had tacitly connived at turning Dora over
to Herr K., just as years later her father "handed her over to me [Freud]
for psychotherapeutic treatment." In some sense everyone was conspiring
to conceal what was going on; and in some yet further sense everyone was
conspiring to deny that anything was going on at all. What we have here, on
one of its sides, is a classical Victorian domestic drama, that is at the same
time a sexual and emotional can of worms.

Matters were brought to a crisis by two events that occurred to Dora at
two different periods of her adolescence. When she was fourteen, Herr K.
contrived one day to be alone with her in his place of business; in a state
of sexual excitement, he "suddenly clasped the girl to him and pressed a
kiss on her lips." Dora responded with a "violent feeling of disgust," and
hurried away. This experience, like those referred to in the foregoing
paragraph, was never discussed with or mentioned to anyone, and relations
continued as before. The second scene took place two years later in the

summer when Dora was sixteen (it was just after she had seen Freud for the first time). She and Herr K. were taking a walk by a lake in the Alps. In Dora's words, as they come filtered to us through Freud, Herr K. "had the audacity to make her a proposal." Apparently he had begun to declare his love for this girl whom he had known so well for so long. "No sooner had she grasped Herr K.'s intention than, without letting him finish what he had to say, she had given him a slap in the face and hurried away." The episode as a whole leads Freud quite plausibly to ask: "If Dora loved Herr K., what was the reason for her refusing him in the scene by the lake? Or at any rate, why did her refusal take such a brutal form, as though she were embittered against him? And how could a girl who was in love feel insulted by a proposal which was made in a manner neither tactless nor offensive?" It may occur to us to wonder whether in the extended context of this case that slap in the face was a "brutal form" of refusal; but as for the other questions posed by Freud they are without question rhetorical in character.

On this second occasion Dora did not remain silent. Her father was preparing to depart from the Alpine lake, and she declared her determination to leave at once with him. Two weeks later she told the story of the scene by the lake to her mother, who relayed it—as Dora had clearly intended—to her father. In due course Herr K. was "called to account" on this score, but he "denied in the most emphatic terms having on his side made any advances" and suggested that she "had merely fancied the whole scene she had described." Dora's father "believed" the story concocted by Herr— and Frau—K., and it is from this moment, more than two years before she came to Freud for treatment, that the change in Dora's character can be dated. Her love for the K.'s turned into hatred, and she became obsessed with the idea of getting her father to break off relations with them. She saw through the rationalizations and denials of her father and Frau K., and had "no doubt that what bound her father to this young and beautiful woman was a common love-affair." Nothing that could help to confirm this view had escaped her perception, which in this connection was pitilessly sharp. ..." Indeed, "the sharp-sighted Dora" was an excellent detective when it came to uncovering her father's clandestine sexual activities, and her withering criticisms of her father's character—that he was "insincere... had a strain of baseness in his character...only thought of his own enjoyment...had a gift for seeing things in the light which suited him best"— were in general concurred in by Freud. Freud also agreed with Dora that there was something in her embittered if exaggerated contention that "she had been handed over to Herr K. as the price of his tolerating the relations between her father and his wife." Nevertheless, the cause of her greatest embitterment seems to have been her father's "readiness to consider the scene by the lake as a product of her imagination." And although Freud was in his customary way skeptical about such impassioned protestations and repudiations—and surmised that something in the way of an opposite series of thoughts or self-reproaches lay behind them—he was forced to come to "the conclusion that Dora's story must correspond to the facts in every respect." If we try to put ourselves in the place of this girl between her sixteenth and eighteenth years, we can at once recognize that her situation was a desperate one. The three adults to whom she was closest, whom she loved the most in the world, were apparently conspiring—separately, in tandem, or in concert—to deny her the reality of her experience. They were conspiring to deny Dora her reality and reality itself. This betrayal touched upon matters that might easily unhinge the mind of a young person; for the three adults were not betraying Dora's love and trust alone; they were betraying the structure of the actual world. And indeed when Dora's father handed her over to Freud with the parting injunction "Please try and bring her to reason," there were no two ways of taking what he meant. Naturally he had no idea of the mind and character of the physician to whom he had dealt this leading remark.

II

Dora began treatment with Freud some time in October 1900. Freud wrote to Fliess that "the case has opened smoothly to my collection of picklocks," but the analysis was not proceeding well. The material produced was very rich, but Dora was there more or less against her will. Moreover, she was more than usually amnesic about events in her remote past and about her inner and mental life. The analysis found its focus and climax in two dreams. The first of these was the production by Dora of a dream that in the past she had dreamed recurrently. Among the many messages concealed by it, Freud made out one that he conveyed to his patient: "'You have decided to give up the treatment,'" he told her, adding, "'to which, after all, it is only your father who makes you come.'" It was a self-fulfilling interpretation. A few weeks after the first dream, the second dream occurred. Freud spent two hours elucidating it, and at the beginning of the third, which took place on December 31, 1900, Dora informed him that she was there for the last time. Freud pressed on during this hour and presented Dora with a series of stunning and outrageously intelligent interpretations. The analysis ended as follows: "Dora had listened to me without any of her usual contradictions. She seemed to be moved; she said good-bye to me very warmly, with the heartiest wishes for the New Year, and came no more." Dora's father subsequently called on Freud two or three times to reassure him that Dora was returning, but Freud knew better than to take him at his word. Fifteen months later, in April 1902, Dora returned for a single visit; what she had to tell Freud on that occasion was of some interest, but he knew that she was done with him, as indeed she was.

Dora was actuated by many impulses in breaking off the treatment; prominent among these partial motives was revenge — upon men in general and at that moment Freud in particular, who was standing for those other men in her life who had betrayed and injured her. He writes rather ruefully of Dora's "breaking off so unexpectedly, just when my hopes of a successful termination of the treatment were at their highest, and her thus bringing those hopes to nothing — this was an unmistakable act of vengeance on her part." And although Dora's "purpose of self-injury" was also served by this action, Freud goes on clearly to imply that he felt hurt and wounded by her behavior. Yet it could not have been so unexpected as all that, since as early as the first dream, Freud both understood and had communicated this understanding to Dora that she had already decided to give up the treatment. What is suggested by this logical hiatus is that although Dora had done with Freud, Freud had not done with Dora. And this supposition is supported by what immediately followed. As soon as Dora left him, Freud began writing up her case history — a proceeding that, as far as I have been able to ascertain, was not in point of immediacy a usual response for him. He interrupted the composition of *The Psychopathology of Everyday Life* on which he was then engaged and wrote what is substantially the case of Dora during the first three weeks of January 1901. On January 25, he wrote to Fliess that he had finished the work the day before and added, with that terrifying self-confidence of judgment that he frequently revealed, "Anyhow, it is the most subtle thing I have yet written and will produce an even more horrifying effect than usual." The title he had at first given the new work — "Dreams and Hysteria" — suggests the magnitude of ambition that was at play in him. At the same time, however, Freud's settling of his account with Dora took on the proportions of a heroic inner and intellectual enterprise.

Yet that account was still by no means settled, as the obscure subsequent history of this work dramatically demonstrates. In the first letter of January 25, 1901, Freud had written to Fliess that the paper had already been accepted by Ziehen, joint editor of the *Monatsschrift für Psychiatrie und Neurologie.* On the fifteenth of February, in another letter to Fliess, he remarks that he is now finishing up *The Psychopathology of Everyday Life,* and that when he has done so, he will correct it and the case history. About two months later, in March 1901, according to Ernest Jones, Freud showed "his notes of the case" to his close friend, Oscar Rie. The reception Rie gave to them was such, reports Freud, that "I thereupon determined to make no further effort to break down my state of isolation." On May 8, 1901, Freud wrote to Fliess that he had not yet "made up his mind" to send off the work. One month later, he made up his mind and sent it off, announcing to Fliess that "it will meet the gaze of an astonished public in the autumn." But nothing of the sort was to occur, and what happened next was, according to Jones, "entirely mysterious" and remains so. Freud either sent it off to Ziehen, the editor who had already accepted it, and then having sent it asked for it back. Or he sent it off to another magazine altogether, the *Journal für Psychologie und Neurologie*, whose editor, one Brodmann, refused to publish it. The upshot was that Freud returned the manuscript to a drawer for four more years. And when he did at last send it into print, it was in the journal that had accepted it in the first place.

But we are not out of the darkness and perplexities yet, for when Freud finally decided in 1905 to publish the case, he revised the work once again. There is one further touch of puzzlements. Freud got the date of his case wrong. When he wrote or rewrote it, either in January 1901 or in 1905, he assigned the case to the autumn of 1899 instead of 1900. And he continued to date it incorrectly, repeating the error in 1914 in the "History of the Psychoanalytic Movement" and again in 1923 when he added a number of new footnotes to the essay on the occasion of its publication in the eighth volume of his *Gesammelte Schriften*. Among the many things suggested by this recurrent error is that in some sense he had still not done with Dora, as indeed I think we shall see he had not. The modern reader may be inclined to remark that these questions of date, of revision, problems of textual status and authorial uncertainties of attitude would be more suitable to a discussion of a literary text—a poem, play, or novel—than to a work of "science." But such a conception of the nature of scientific discourse—particularly the modes of discourse that are exercised in those disciplines which are not preponderantly or uniformly mathematical or quantitative—has to undergo a radical revision.

The general form of what Freud has written bears certain suggestive resemblances to a modern experimental novel. Its narrative and expository course, for example, is neither linear nor rectilinear; instead its organization is plastic, involuted, and heterogeneous, and follows spontaneously an inner logic that seems frequently to be at odds with itself; it often loops back around itself and is multidimensional in its representation of both its material and itself. Its continuous innovations in formal structure seem unavoidably to be dictated by its substance, by the dangerous, audacious, disreputable, and problematical character of the experiences being represented and dealt with, and by the equally scandalous intentions of the author and the outrageous character of the role he has had the presumption to assume. In content, however, what Freud has written is in parts rather like a play by Ibsen, or more precisely like a series of Ibsen's plays. And as one reads through the case of Dora, scenes and characters from such works as *Pillars of Society, A Doll's House, Ghosts, An Enemy of the People, The*

Wild Duck, and *Rosmersholm* rise up and flit through the mind. There is, however, this difference. In this Ibsen-like drama, Freud is not only Ibsen, the creator and playwright; he is also and directly one of the characters in the action, and in the end suffers in a way that is comparable to the suffering of the others.

What I have been reiterating is that the case of Dora is first and last an extraordinary piece of writing, and it is to this circumstance in several of its most striking aspects that we should direct our attention. For it is a case history, a kind or genre of writing—that is to say a particular way of conceiving and constructing human experience in written language—that in Freud's hands became something that it never was before.

III

The ambiguities and difficulties begin with the very title of the work, "Fragment of an Analysis of a Case of Hysteria." It is a fragment in the sense that its "results" are "incomplete." The treatment was "broken off at the patient's own wish," at a time when certain problems "had not been attacked and others had only been imperfectly elucidated." It follows that the analysis itself is "only a fragment," as are "the following pages" of writing which present it. To which the modern reader, flushed with the superior powers of his educated irony, is tempted to reply: how is it that this fragment is also a whole, an achieved totality, an integral piece of writing called a case history? And how is it, furthermore, that this "fragment" is fuller, richer, and more complete than the most "complete" case histories of anyone else? But there is no more point in asking such questions of Freud—particularly at this preliminary stage of proceedings—than there would be in posing similar "theoretical" questions to Joyce or Proust.

The work is also fragmentary, Freud continues, warming to his subject, because of the very method he has chosen to pursue; on this plan, that of nondirectional free association, "everything that has to do with the clearing-up of a particular symptom emerges piecemeal, woven into various contexts, and distributed over widely separate periods of time." Freud's technique itself is therefore fragmentary; his way of penetrating to the micro-structure—the "finer structure" as he calls it—of a neurosis is to allow the material to emerge piecemeal. At the same time these fragments only *appear* to be incoherent and disparate; in actuality they eventually will be understood as members of a whole.

Furthermore, Freud goes on, there is still another "kind of incompleteness" to be found in this work, and this time it has been "intentionally introduced." He has deliberately chosen not to reproduce "the process of interpretation to which the patient's associations and communications had to be subjected, but only the results of that process." That is to say, what we have before us is not a transcription in print of a tape recording of eleven weeks of analysis but something that is abridged, edited, synthesized, and constructed from the very outset. And as if this were not enough, Freud introduces yet another context in which the work has to be regarded as fragmentary and incomplete. It is obvious, he argues, "that a single case history, even if it were complete and open to no doubt, cannot provide an answer to all questions arising out of the problem of hysteria." Thus, like a modernist writer—which in part he is—Freud begins by elaborately announcing the problematical status of his undertaking and the dubious character of his achievement.

Even more, like some familiar "unreliable narrator" in modernist fiction, Freud pauses at regular intervals to remind the reader of this case history that "my insight into the complex of events composing it [has] remained fragmentary," that his understanding of it remains in some essential sense permanently occluded. This darkness and constraint are the result of a number of converging circumstances, some of which have already been touched on and include the shortness of the analysis and its having been broken off by Dora at a crucial point. But it also includes the circumstance that the analysis—any analysis—must proceed by fragmentary methods, by analyzing thoughts and events bit by discontinuous bit. And at the end of one virtuoso passage in which Freud demonstrates through a series of referential leaps and juxtapositions the occurrence in Dora's past of childhood masturbation, he acknowledges that this is the essence of his procedure. "Part of this material," he writes, "I was able to obtain directly from the analysis, but the rest required supplementing. And, indeed, the method by which the occurrence of masturbation in Dora's case has been verified has shown us that material belonging to a single subject can only be collected piece by piece at various times and in different connections." In sum the process resembles "reality" itself, a word that, as contemporary writers like to remind us, should always be surrounded by quotation marks.

We are then obliged to ask—and Freud himself more than anyone else has taught us most about this obligation—*what else* are all these protestations of fragmentariness and incompleteness about? They refer in some measure, as Freud himself indicates in the Postscript, to a central inadequacy and determining incompleteness that he discovered only after it was too late—the "great defect" of the case was to be located in the undeveloped, misdeveloped, and equivocal character of the "transference," of the relation between patient and physician in which so much was focused. Something went wrong in the relation between Freud and Dora—or in the relation between Dora and Freud. But the protestations refer, I believe, to something else as well, something of which Freud was not entirely conscious. For the work is also fragmentary or incomplete in the sense of Freud's self-knowledge, both at the time of the actual case and at the time of his writing it. And he communicates in this piece of writing a less than complete understanding of himself, though like any great writer he provides us with the material for understanding some things that have escaped his own understanding, for filling in some gaps, for restoring certain fragments into wholes.

How else can we finally explain the fact that Freud chose to write up this particular history in such extensive detail? The reasons that he offers in both the Prefatory Remarks and the Postscript aren't entirely convincing— which doesn't of course deny them a real if fractional validity. Why should he have chosen so problematic a case, when presumably others of a more complete yet equally brief kind were available? I think this can be understood in part through Freud's own unsettled and ambiguous role in the case; that he had not yet, so to speak, "gotten rid" of it; that he had to write it out, in some measure, as an effort of self-understanding—an effort, I think we shall see, that remained heroically unfinished, a failure that nonetheless brought lasting credit with it.

IV

If we turn now to the Prefatory Remarks it may be illuminating to regard them as a kind of novelistic framing action, as in these few opening pages Freud rehearses his motives, reasons, and intentions and begins at the same time to work his insidious devices upon the reader. First, exactly like a novelist, he remarks that what he is about to let us in on is positively scandalous, for "the complete elucidation of a case of hysteria is bound to involve the revelation of intimacies and the betrayal of…secrets." Second, again like a writer of fiction, he has deliberately chosen persons, places, and circumstances that will remain obscure; the scene is laid not in metropolitan Vienna but "in a remote provincial town." He has from the beginning kept the circumstance that Dora was his patient such a close secret that only one other physician—"in whose discretion I have complete confidence"— knows about it. He has "postponed publication" of this essay for "four whole years," also in the cause of discretion, and in the same cause has "allowed no name to stand which could put a non-medical reader on the scent." Finally he has buried the case even deeper by publishing it "in a purely scientific and technical periodical" in order to secure yet another "guarantee against unauthorized readers." He has in short made his own mystery within a mystery, and one of the effects of such obscure preliminary goings-on is to create a kind of Nabokovian frame—what we have here is a history framed by an explanation which is itself slightly out of focus.

Third, he roundly declares, this case history is science and not literature: "I am aware that—in this city, at least—there are many physicians who (revolting though it may seem) choose to read a case history of this kind not as a contribution to the psychopathology of neuroses, but as a *roman à clef* designed for their private delectation." This may indeed be true; but it is equally true that nothing is more literary—and more modern—than the disavowal of all literary intentions. And when Freud does this again later on toward the end of "The Clinical Picture," the situation becomes even less credible. The passage merits quotation at length.

> I must now turn to consider a further complication to which I should certainly give no space if I were a man of letters engaged upon the creation of a mental state like this for a short story, instead of being a medical man engaged upon its dissection. The element to which I must now allude can only serve to obscure and efface the outlines of the fine poetic conflict which we have been able to ascribe to Dora. This element would rightly fall a sacrifice to the censorship of a writer, for he, after all, simplifies and abstracts when he appears in the character of a psychologist. But in the world of reality, which I am trying to depict here, a complication of motives, an accumulation and conjunction of mental activities—in a word, overdetermination—is the rule.

In this context it is next to impossible to tell whether Freud is up to another of his crafty maneuverings with the reader or whether he is actually simply unconscious of how much of a modern and modernist writer he is. For when he takes to describing the difference between himself and some hypothetical man of letters and writer of short stories he is in fact embarked upon an elaborate obfuscation. That hypothetical writer is nothing but a straw man; and when Freud in apparent contrast represents himself and his own activities he is truly representing how a genuine creative writer writes. And this passage, we must also recall, came from the same pen that only a little more than a year earlier had written passages about Oedipus and Hamlet that changed for good the ways in which the civilized world would henceforth think about literature and writers.[1] What might be

---

[1]Some years earlier Freud has been more candid and more innocent about the relation of his writing to literature. In *Studies on Hysteria* he introduces his discussion of the case of Fräulein Elisabeth von R. with the following disarming admission.

> I have not always been a psychotherapist. Like other neuropathologists, I was trained to employ local diagnoses and electro-prognosis, and it still strikes me myself as strange that the case histories I write should read like short stories and that, as one might say, they lack the serious stamp of science. I must console myself with the reflection that the nature of the subject is evidently responsible for this, rather than any preference of my own. The fact is

thought of as this sly unliterariness of Freud's turns up in other contexts as well.

If we return to the point in the Prefatory Remarks, we find that Freud then goes on to describe other difficulties, constraints, and problematical circumstances attaching to the situation in which he finds himself. Among them is the problem of "how to record for publication" even such a short case—the long ones are as yet altogether impossible. Moreover, since the material that critically illuminated this case was grouped about two dreams, their analysis formed a secure point of departure for the writing. (Freud is of course at home with dreams, being the unchallenged master in the reading of them.) Yet this tactical solution pushes the *entire problematic* back only another step further, since Freud at once goes on to his additional presupposition, that only those who are already familiar with "the interpretation of dreams"—that is, *The Interpretation of Dreams* (1900), whose readership in 1901 must have amounted to a little platoon indeed—are likely to be satisfied at all with the present account. Any other reader "will find only bewilderment in these pages." As much as it is like anything else, this is like Borges—as well as Nabokov. This off-putting and disconcerting quality, it should go without saying, is characteristically modern; the writer succumbs to no impulse to make it easy for the reader; on the contrary, he is by preference rather forbidding and does not extend a cordial welcome. The reader has been, as it were, "softened up" by his first encounter with this unique expository and narrative authority; he is thoroughly off balance and is as a consequence ready to be "educated," by Freud. By the same token, however, if he has followed these opening few pages carefully, he is certainly no longer as prepared as he was to assert the primacy and priority of his own critical sense of things. He is precisely where Freud—and any writer—wants him to be.

At the opening of Part I, "The Clinical Picture," Freud tells us that he begins his "treatment, indeed, by asking the patient to give me the whole story of his life and illness," and immediately adds that "the information I receive is never enough to let me see my way about the case." This inadequacy and unsatisfactoriness in the stories his patients tell is in distinct contrast to what Freud has read in the accounts rendered by his psychiatric contemporaries, and he continues by remarking that "I cannot help wondering how it is that the authorities can produce such smooth and exact histories in cases of hysteria. As a matter of fact the patients are incapable of giving such reports about themselves." There is a great deal going on here. In the first place there is the key assumption that everyone—that every

---

that local diagnosis and electrical reactions lead nowhere in the study of hysteria, whereas a detailed description of mental processes such as we are accustomed to find in the works of imaginative writers enables me, with the use of a few psychological formulas, to obtain at least some kind of insight into the course of that affection.

life, every existence—has a story, to which there is appended a corollary that most of us probably tell that story poorly. Furthermore, the relations at this point in Freud's prose between the words "story," "history," and "report" are unspecified, undifferentiated, and unanalyzed and in the nature of the case contain and conceal a wealth of material.

Freud proceeds to specify what it is that is wrong with the stories his patients tell him. The difficulties are in the first instance formal short-comings of *narrative:* the connections, "even the ostensible ones—are for the most part incoherent," obscured and unclear; "and the sequence of different events is uncertain." In short these narratives are disorganized and the patients are unable to tell a coherent story of their lives. What is more, he states, "the patients' inability to give an ordered history of their life in so far as it coincides with the history of their illness is not merely characteristic of the neurosis. It also possesses great theoretical significance." What we are led at this juncture to conclude is that Freud is implying that a coherent story is in some manner connected with mental health (at the very least with the absence of hysteria), and this in turn implies assumptions of the broadest and deepest kind about both the nature of coherence and the form and structure of human life. On this reading, human life is, ideally, a connected and coherent story, with all the details in explanatory place, and with everything (or as close to everything as is practically possible) accounted for, in its proper causal or other sequence. And inversely illness amounts at least in part to suffering from an incoherent story or an inadequate narrative account of oneself.

Freud then describes in technical detail the various types and orders of narrative insufficiency that he commonly finds; they range from dis-ingenuousness, both conscious and unconscious, to amnesias and par-amnesias of several kinds and various other means of severing connections and altering chronologies. In addition, he maintains, this discomposed memory applies with particular force and virulence to "the history of the illness" for which the patient has come for treatment. In the course of a successful treatment, this incoherence, incompleteness, and fragmentari-ness are progressively transmuted, as facts, events, and memories are brought forward into the forefront of the patient's mind. And he adds as a conclusion that these two aims "are coincident"—they are reached simul-taneously and by the same path. Some of the consequences that can be de-rived from these extraordinary observations are as follows. The history of any patient's illness is itself only a substory (or a subplot), although it is at the same time a vital part of a larger structure. Furthermore, in the course of psychoanalytic treatment, nothing less than "reality" itself is made, constructed, or reconstructed. A complete story—"intelligible, consistent, and unbroken"—is the theoretical, created end story. It is a story, or a fiction, not only because it has a narrative structure but also because the narrative account has been rendered in language, in conscious speech, and no longer exists in the deformed language of symptoms, the untranslated speech of the body. At the end—at the successful end—one has come into possession of one's own story. It is a final act of self-appropriation, the appropriation by oneself of one's own history. This is in part so because one's own story is in so large a measure a phenomenon of language, as psychoanalysis is in turn a demonstration of the degree to which language can go in the reading of all our experience. What we end with, then, is a fictional construction which is at the same time satisfactory to us in the form of the truth, and as the form of the truth.

No larger tribute has ever been paid to a culture in which the various narrative and fictional forms had exerted for centuries both moral and philosophical authority and which had produced as one of its chief climaxes the great bourgeois novels of the nineteenth century. Indeed we must see Freud's writings—and method—as themselves part of this culmination, and at the same moment, along with the great modernist novels of the first half of the twentieth century, as the beginning of the end of that tradition and its authority. Certainly the passages we have just dealt with contain heroic notions and offer an extension of heroic capabilities if not to all men then to most, at least as a possibility. Yet we cannot leave this matter so relatively unexamined, and must ask ourselves how it is that this "story" is not merely a "history" but a "case history" as well. We must ask ourselves how these associated terms are more intimately related in the nexus that is about to be wound and unwound before us. To begin to understand such questions we have to turn back to a central passage in the Prefatory Remarks. Freud undertakes therein "to describe the way in which I have overcome the *technical* difficulties of drawing up the report of this case history." Apparently "the report" and the "case history" referred to in this statement are two discriminable if not altogether discrete entities. If they are then we can further presume that, ideally at any rate, Dora (or any patient) is as much in possession of the "case history" as Freud himself. And this notion is in some part supported by what comes next. Freud mentions certain other difficulties, such as the fact that he "cannot make notes during the actual session...for fear of shaking the patient's confidence and of disturbing his own view of the material under observation." In the case of Dora, however, this obstacle was partly overcome because so much of the material was grouped about two dreams, and "the wording of these dreams was recorded immediately after the session" so that "they thus afforded a secure point of attachment for the chain of interpretations and recollections which proceeded from there." Freud then writes as follows:

> The case history itself was only committed to writing from memory after the treatment was at an end, but while my recollection of the case was still fresh

and was heightened by my interest in its publication. Thus the record is not absolutely—phonographically—exact, but it can claim to possess a high degree of trustworthiness. Nothing of any importance has been altered in it except in some places the order in which the explanations are given; and this has been done for the sake of presenting the case in a more connected form.

Such a passage raises more questions than it resolves. The first sentence is a kind of conundrum in which case history, writing, and memory dance about in a series of logical entwinements, of possible alternate combinations, equivalences, and semiequivalences. These are followed by further equivocations about "the record," "phonographic" exactitude, and so forth—the ambiguities of which jump out at one as soon as the terms begin to be seriously examined. For example, is "the report" the same thing as "the record," and if "the record" were "phonographically" exact would it be a "report"? Like the prodigious narrative historian that he is, Freud is enmeshed in an irreducible paradox of history: that the term itself refers to both the activity of the historian—the writing of history—and to the objects of his undertaking, what history is "about." I do not think, therefore, that we can conclude that Freud has created this thick context of historical contingency and ambiguity out of what he once referred to as Viennese *schlamperei*.

The historical difficulties are further compounded by several other sequential networks that are mentioned at the outset and that figure discernibly throughout the writing. First there is the virtual Proustian complexity of Freud's interweaving of the various strands of time in the actual account; or, to change the figure, his geological fusing of various time strata—strata which are themselves at the same time fluid and shifting. We observe this most strikingly in the palimpsestlike quality of the writing itself, which refers back to *Studies on Hysteria* of 1895; which records a treatment that took place at the end of 1900 (although it mistakes the date by a year); which then was written up in first form during the early weeks of 1901; which was then exhumed in 1905, and was revised and rewritten to an indeterminable extent before publication in that year; and to which additional critical comments in the form of footnotes were finally appended in 1923. All of these are of course held together in vital connection and interanimation by nothing else than Freud's consciousness. But we must take notice as well of the copresence of still further different time sequences in Freud's presentation—this copresence being itself a historical or novelistic circumstance of some magnitude. There is first the connection established by the periodically varied rehearsal throughout the account of Freud's own theory and theoretical notions as they had developed up to that point; this practice provides a kind of running applied history of psychoanalytic theory as its development is refracted through the embroiled medium of this particular case. Then there are the different time

strata of Dora's own history, which Freud handles with confident and lov-
ing exactitude. Indeed he is never more of a historical virtuoso than when
he reveals himself to us as moving with compelling ease back and forth
between the complex group of sequential histories and narrative accounts,
with divergent sets of diction and at different levels of explanation, that
constitute the extraordinary fabric of this work. He does this most conspicuously in his analytic dealings with Dora's dreams, for every dream,
he reminds us, sets up a connection between two "factors," an "event during
childhood" and an "event of the present day—and it endeavors to reshape
the present on the model of the remote past." The existence or recreation
of the past in the present is in fact "history" in more than one of its mani-
fold senses, and is one of Freud's many analogies to the following equally
celebrated utterance.

> Men make their own history, but they do not make it just as they please;
> they do not make it under circumstances chosen by themselves, but under
> circumstances directly encountered, given and transmitted from the past.
> The tradition of all the dead generations weighs like a nightmare on the
> brain of the living. And just when they seem engaged in revolutionising
> themselves and things, in creating something that has never yet existed,
> precisely in such periods of revolutionary crisis they anxiously conjure up
> the spirits of the past to their service and borrow from them names, battle
> cries and costumes in order to present the new scene of world history in this
> time-honored disguise and this borrowed language. *(The Eighteenth
> Brumaire of Louis Bonaparte.)*

And just as Marx regards the history-makers of the past as sleepwalkers,
"who required recollections of past world history in order to drug themselves concerning their own content," so Freud similarly regards the conditions of dream-formation, of neurosis itself, and even of the cure of
neurosis, namely the analytic experience of transference. They are all of
them species of living past history in the present. If the last of these works
out satisfactorily, then a case history is at the end transfigured. It becomes
an inseparable part of an integral life history. Freud is of course the master
historian of those transfigurations.

V

At the very beginning, after he had listened to the father's account of
"Dora's impossible behavior," Freud abstained from comment, for, he remarks, "I had resolved from the first to suspend my judgement of the true
state of affairs till I had heard the other side as well." Such a suspension
inevitably recalls an earlier revolutionary project. In describing the originating plan of *Lyrical Ballads,* Coleridge writes that it "was agreed that

my endeavours should be directed to persons and characters supernatural, or at least romantic; yet so as to transfer from our inward nature a human interest and a semblance of truth sufficient to procure for these shadows of imagination that willing suspension of disbelief for the moment, which constitutes poetic faith." We know very well that Freud had a more than ordinary capacity in this direction, and that one of the most dramatic moments in the prehistory of psychoanalysis had to do precisely with his taking on faith facts that turned out to be fantasies. Yet Freud is not only the reader suspending judgment and disbelief until he has heard the other side of the story; and he is not only the poet or writer who must induce a similar process in himself if he is to elicit it in his audience. He is also concomitantly a principal, an actor, a living character in the drama that he is unfolding in print before us. Moreover, that suspension of disbelief is in no sense incompatible with a large body of assumptions, many of them definite, a number of them positively alarming.

They have to do largely with sexuality and in particular with female sexuality. They are brought to a focus in the central scene of Dora's life (and case), a scene that Freud orchestrates with inimitable richness and to which he recurs thematically at a number of junctures with the tact and sense of form that one associates with a classical composer of music (or with Proust, Mann, or Joyce). Dora told this episode to Freud toward the beginning of their relation, after "the first difficulties of the treatment had been overcome." It is the scene between her and Herr K. that took place when she was fourteen years old—that is, four years before the present tense of the case—and acted Freud said as a "sexual trauma." The reader will recall that on this occasion Herr K. contrived to get Dora alone "at his place of business" in the town of B———, and then without warning or preparation "suddenly clasped the girl to him and pressed a kiss upon her lips." Freud then asserts that "this was *surely* just the situation to call up a *distinct* feeling of sexual excitement in a *girl* of *fourteen* who had *never before* been approached. But Dora had at that moment a violent feeling of disgust, tore herself free from the man, and hurried past him to the staircase and from there to the street door" (all italics are mine). She avoided seeing the K.'s for a few days after this, but then relations returned to "normal"—if such a term survives with any permissible sense in the present context. She continued to meet Herr K., and neither of them ever mentioned "the little scene." Moreover, Freud adds, "according to her account Dora kept it a secret till her confession during the treatment," and he pretty clearly implies that he believes this.

This episode preceded by two years the scene at the lake that acted as the precipitating agent for the severe stage of Dora's illness; and it was this later episode and the entire structure that she and others had elaborated about it that she had first presented to Freud, who continues thus:

> In this scene—second in order of mention, but first in order of time—the
> behavior of this child of fourteen was already entirely and completely
> hysterical. I should without question consider a person hysterical in whom
> an occasion for sexual excitement elicited feelings that were preponderantly
> or exclusively unpleasurable; and I should do so whether or not the person
> were capable of producing somatic symptoms.

Also, in Dora's feeling of disgust an obscure psychical mechanism called
the "reversal of affect" was brought into play; but so was another process,
and here Freud introduces—casually and almost as a throwaway—one more
of his grand theoretical-clinical formulations, namely the idea of the
"displacement of sensation," or as it has more commonly come to be
referred to, the "displacement upward." "Instead of the genital sensation
which would certainly have been felt by a healthy girl in such circumstances,
Dora was overcome by the unpleasurable feeling which is proper to the
tract of mucous membrane at the entrance to the alimentary canal—that
is by disgust." Although the disgust did not persist as a permanent symptom but remained behind residually and potentially in a general distaste
for food and poor appetite, a second displacement upward was the resultant
of this scene "in the shape of a sensory hallucination which occurred from
time to time and even made its appearance while she was telling me her
story. She declared that she could still feel upon the upper part of her body
the pressure of Herr K.'s embrace." Taking into account certain other of
Dora's "inexplicable"—and hitherto unmentioned—"peculiarities" (such
as her phobic reluctance to walk past any man she saw engaged in animated
conversation with a woman), Freud "formed in my own mind the following
reconstruction of the scene. I believe that during the man's passionate
embrace she felt not merely his kiss upon her lips but also his erect member
against her body. The perception was revolting to her; it was dismissed
from her memory, repressed, and replaced by the innocent sensation of
pressure upon her thorax, which in turn derived an excessive intensity
from its repressed source." This repressed source was located in the erotogenic oral zone, which in Dora's case had undergone a developmental
deformation from the period of infancy. And thus, Freud concludes, "the
pressure of the erect member probably led to an analogous change in the
corresponding female organ, the clitoris; and the excitation of this second
erotogenic zone was referred by a process of displacement to the simultaneous pressure against the thorax and became fixed there."

There is something questionable and askew in this passage of unques-
tionable genius. In it Freud is at once dogmatically certain and very uncertain. He is dogmatically certain of what the normative sexual response
in young and other females is, and asserts himself to that effect. At the same
time, he is, in my judgment, utterly uncertain about where Dora is, or was,
developmentally. At one moment in the passage he calls her a "girl," at

another a "child"—but in point of fact he treats her throughout as if this fourteen-, sixteen-, and eighteen-year-old adolescent had the capacities for sexual response of a grown woman—indeed at a later point he conjectures again that Dora either responded, or should have responded, to the embrace with specific genital heat and moisture. Too many determinations converge at this locus for us to do much more than single out a few of the more obvious influencing circumstances. In the first instance there was Freud's own state of knowledge about such matters at the time, which was better than anyone else's, but still relatively crude and undifferentiated. Second, we may be in the presence of what can only be accounted for by assuming that a genuine historical-cultural change has taken place between then and now. It may be that Freud was expressing a legitimate partial assumption of his time and culture when he ascribes to a fourteen-year-old adolescent—whom he calls a "child"—the normative responses that are ascribed today to a fully developed and mature woman. This supposition is borne out if we consider the matter from the other end, from the standpoint of what has happened to the conception of adolescence in our own time. It begins now in prepuberty and extends to—who knows when? Certainly its extensibility in our time has reached well beyond the age of thirty. Third, Freud is writing in this passage as an advocate of nature, sexuality, openness, and candor—and within such a context Dora cannot hope to look good. The very framing of the context in such a manner is itself slightly accusatory. In this connection we may note that Freud goes out of his way to tell us that he knew Herr K. personally and that "he was still quite young and of prepossessing appearance." If we let Nabokov back into the picture for a moment, we may observe that Dora is no Lolita, and go on to suggest that *Lolita* is an anti-*Dora*.

Yet we must also note that in this episode—the condensed and focusing scene of the entire case history—Freud is as much a novelist as he is an analyst. For the central moment of this central scene is a "reconstruction" that he "formed in [his] own mind." This pivotal construction becomes henceforth the principal "reality" of the case, and we must also observe that this reality remains Freud's more than Dora's, since he was never quite able to convince her of the plausibility of the construction, or, to regard it from the other pole of the dyad, she was never quite able to accept this version of reality, of what "really" happened. Freud was not at first unduly distressed by this resistance on her side, for part of his understanding of what he had undertaken to do in psychoanalysis was to instruct his patients —and his readers—in the nature of reality. This reality was the reality that modern readers of literature have also had to be educated in. It was conceived of as a *world of meanings.* As Freud put it in one of those stop-you-dead-in-your-tracks footnotes that he was so expert in using strategically, we must at almost every moment "be prepared to be met not by one but by several causes—by *overdetermination.*" Thus the world of meanings is a world of multiple and compacted causations; it is a world in which everything has a meaning, which means that everything has more than one meaning. Every symptom is a concrete universal in several senses. It not only embodies a network of significances but also "serves to represent several unconscious mental processes simultaneously." By the same token, since it is a world almost entirely brought into existence, maintained, and mediated through a series of linguistic transactions between patient and physician, it partakes in full measure of the virtually limitless complexity of language, in particular its capacities for producing statements characterized by multiplicity, duplicity, and ambiguity of significance. Freud lays particular stress on the ambiguity, is continually on the lookout for it, and brings his own formidable skills in this direction to bear most strikingly on the analyses of Dora's dreams. The first thing he picks up in the first of her dreams is in fact an ambiguous statement, with which he at once confronts her.

As if this were not sufficient, the actual case itself was full of such literary and novelistic devices or conventions as thematic analogies, double plots, reversals, inversions, variations, betrayals, etc.—full of what the "sharp-sighted" Dora as well as the sharp-sighted Freud thought of as "hidden connections"—though it is important to add that Dora and her physician mean different things by the same phrase. And as the case proceeds Freud continues to confront Dora with such connections and tries to enlist her assistance in their construction. For example, one of the least pleasant characteristics in Dora's nature was her habitual reproachfulness—it was directed mostly toward her father but radiated out in all directions. Freud regarded this behavior in his own characteristic manner: "A string of reproaches against other people," he comments, "leads one to suspect the existence of a string of self-reproaches with the same content." Freud accordingly followed the procedure of turning back "each simple reproach on the speaker herself." When Dora reproached her father with malingering in order to keep himself in the company of Frau K., Freud felt "obliged to point out to the patient that her present ill-health was just as much actuated by motives and was just as tendentious as had been Frau K.'s illness, which she had understood so well." At such moments Dora begins to mirror the other characters in the case, as they in differing degrees all mirror one another as well.

Part of that sense, we have come to understand, is that the writer is or ought to be conscious of the part that he—in whatever guise, voice, or persona he chooses—invariably and unavoidably plays in the world he represents. Oddly enough, although there is none of his writings in which Freud is more vigorously active than he is here, it is precisely this activity that he subjects to the least self-conscious scrutiny, that he almost appears to fend off. For example, I will now take my head in my hands and suggest that his extraordinary analysis of Dora's first dream is inadequate on just this count. He is only dimly and marginally aware of his central place in it (he is clearly incorporated into the figure of Dora's father), comments on it only as an addition to Dora's own addendum to the dream, and does nothing to exploit it. Instead of analyzing his own part in what he has done and what he is writing, Freud continues to behave like an unreliable narrator, treating the material about which he is writing as if it were literature but excluding himself from both that treatment and that material. At one moment he refers to himself as someone "who has learnt to appreciate the delicacy of the fabric of structures such as dreams," intimating what I surmise he incontestably believed, that dreams are natural works of art. And when, in the analysis of the second dream, we find ourselves back at the scene at the lake again; when Dora recalls that the only plea to her of Herr K. that she could remember is "You know I get nothing out of my wife"; when these were precisely the same words used by Dora's father in describing to Freud his relation to Dora's mother; and when Freud speculates that Dora may even "have heard her father make the same complaint ...just as I myself did from his own lips"—when a conjunction such as this occurs, then we know we are in a novel, probably by Proust. Time has recurred, the repressed has returned, plot, double plot, and counterplot have all intersected, and "reality" turns out to be something that for all practical purposes is indistinguishable from a systematic fictional creation.

Finally when at the very end Freud turns to deal—rudimentarily as it happens—with the decisive issue of the case, the transferences, everything is transformed into literature, into reading and writing. Transferences, he writes, "are new editions or facsimiles" of tendencies, fantasies, and relations in which "the person of the physician" replaces some earlier person. When the substitution is a simple one, the transferences may be said to be "merely new impressions or reprints": Freud is explicit about the metaphor he is using. Others "more ingeniously constructed...will no longer be new impressions, but revised editions." And he goes on, quite carried away by these figures, to institute a comparison between dealing with the transference and other analytic procedures. "It is easy to learn how to interpret dreams," he remarks, "to extract from the patient's associations his unconscious thoughts and memories, and to practise similar explanatory arts: for these the patient himself will always provide the text." The startling group of suppositions contained in this sentence should not distract us from noting the submerged ambiguity in it. The patient does not merely provide the text; he also *is* the text, the writing to be read, the language to be interpreted. With the transference, however, we move to a different degree of difficulty and onto a different level of explanation. It is only after the transference has been resolved, Freud concludes, "that a patient arrives at a sense of conviction of the validity of the connections which have been constructed during the analysis." I will refrain from entering the veritable series of Chinese boxes opened up by that last statement, and will content myself by proposing that in this passage as a whole Freud is using literature and writing not only creatively and heuristically — as he so often does — but defensively as well.

The writer or novelist is not the only partial role taken up unconsciously or semiconsciously by Freud in the course of this work. He also figures prominently in the text in his capacity as a nineteenth-century man of science and as a representative Victorian critic — employing the seriousness, energy, and commitment of the Victorian ethos to deliver itself from its own excesses. We have already seen him affirming the positive nature of female sexuality, "the genital sensation which would certainly have been felt by a healthy girl in such circumstances," but which Dora did not feel. He goes a good deal further than this. At a fairly early moment in the analysis he faces Dora with the fact that she has "an aim in view which she hoped to gain by her illness. That aim could be none other than to detach her father from Frau K." Her prayers and arguments had not worked; her suicide letter and fainting fits had done no better. Dora knew quite well how much her father loved her, and, Freud continues to address her:

> I felt quite convinced that she would recover at once if only her father were to tell her that he had sacrificed Frau K. for the sake of her health. But, I added, I hoped he would not let himself be persuaded to do this, for then she would have learned what a powerful weapon she had in her hands, and she would certainly not fail on every future occasion to make use once more of her liability to ill-health. Yet if her father refused to give way to her, I was quite sure she would not let herself be deprived of her illness so easily.

This is pretty strong stuff, considering both the age and her age. I think, moreover, that we are justified in reading an overdetermination out of this utterance of Freud's and in suggesting that he had motives additional to strictly therapeutic ones in saying what he did.

In a related sense Freud goes out of his way to affirm his entitlement to speak freely and openly about sex — he is, one keeps forgetting, the great liberator and therapist of speech. The passage is worth quoting at some length.

> It is possible for a man to talk to girls and women upon sexual matters of every kind without doing them harm and without bringing suspicion upon himself, so long as, in the first place, he adopts a particular way of doing it, and, in the second place, can make them feel convinced that it is unavoidable. ... The best way of speaking about such things is to be dry and direct; and that is at the same time the method furthest removed from the prurience with which the same subjects are handled in "society," and to which girls and women alike are so thoroughly accustomed. I call bodily organs and processes

by their technical names.... *J'appelle un chat un chat.* I have certainly heard of some people—doctors and laymen—who are scandalized by a therapeutic method in which conversations of this sort occur, and who appear to envy either me or my patients the titillation which, according to their notions, such a method must afford. But I am too well acquainted with the respectability of these gentry to excite myself over them.... The right attitude is: *"pour faire une omelette il faut casser des oeufs."*

I believe that Freud would have been the first to be amused by the observation that in this splendid extended declaration about plain speech (at this point he takes his place in a tradition coming directly down from Luther), he feels it necessary to disappear not once but twice into French. I think he would have said that such slips—and the revelation of their meanings—are the smallest price one has to pay for the courage to go on. And he goes on with a vengeance, immediately following this passage with another in which he aggressively refuses to moralize in any condemnatory sense about sexuality. As for the attitude that regards the perverse nature of his patient's fantasies as horrible:

I should like to say emphatically that a medical man has no business to indulge in such passionate condemnation. ... We are faced by a fact; and it is to be hoped that we shall grow accustomed to it, when we have learned to put our own tastes on one side. We must learn to speak without indignation of what we call the sexual perversions.... The uncertainty in regard to the boundaries of what is to be called normal sexual life, when we take different races and different epochs into account, should in itself be enough to cool the zealot's ardor. We surely ought not to forget that the perversion which is the most repellent to us, the sensual love of a man for a man, was not only tolerated by the people so far our superiors in cultivation as were the Greeks, but was actually entrusted by them with important social functions.

We can put this assertion into one of its appropriate contexts by recalling that the trial and imprisonment of Oscar Wilde had taken place only five years earlier. And the man who is speaking out here has to be regarded as the greatest of Victorian physicians, who in this passage is fearlessly revealing one of the inner and unacknowledged meanings of the famous "tyranny of Greece over Germany." And as we shall see he has by no means reached the limits beyond which he will not go.

How far he is willing to go begins to be visible as we observe him sliding almost imperceptibly from being the nineteenth-century man of science to being the remorseless "teller of truth," the character in a play by Ibsen who is not to be deterred from his "mission." In a historical sense the two roles are not adventitiously related, any more than it is adventitious that the "truth" that is told often has unforeseen and destructive consequences and that it can rebound upon the teller. But we see him most vividly at this implacable work in the two great dream interpretations, which are largely "photographic" reproductions of dramatic discourse and dialogue. Very early on in the analysis of the first dream, Freud takes up the dream element of the "jewel-case" and makes the unavoidable symbolic interpretation of it. He then proceeds to say the following to this Victorian maiden who has been in treatment with him for all of maybe six weeks.

> "So you are ready to give Herr K. what his wife withholds from him. That is the thought which has had to be repressed with so much energy, and which has made it necessary for every one of its elements to be turned into its opposite. The dream confirms once more what I had already told you before you dreamt it—that you are summoning up your old love for your father in order to protect yourself against your love for Herr K. But what do all these efforts show? Not only that you are afraid of Herr K., but that you are still more afraid of yourself, and of the temptation you feel to yield to him. In short, these efforts prove once more how deeply you love him."

He immediately adds that "naturally Dora would not follow me in this part of the interpretation," but this does not deter him for a moment from pressing on with further interpretations of the same order; and this entire transaction is in its character and quality prototypical for the case as a whole. The Freud we have here is not the sage of the Berggasse, not the master who delivered the incomparable *Introductory Lectures* of 1916-1917, not the tragic Solomon of *Civilization and Its Discontents*. This is an earlier Freud, the Freud of the Fliess letters, the Freud of the case of Dora as well. It is Freud the relentless investigator pushing on no matter what. The Freud that we meet with here is a demonic Freud, a Freud who is the servant of his *daimon*. That *daimon* in whose service Freud knows no limits is the spirit of science, the truth, or "reality"—it doesn't matter which; for him they are all the same. Yet it must be emphasized that the "reality" Freud insists upon is very different from the "reality" that Dora is claiming and clinging to. And it has to be admitted that not only does Freud overlook for the most part this critical difference; he also adopts no measures for dealing with it. The demon of interpretation has taken hold of him, and it is this power that presides over the case of Dora.

In fact as the case history advances it becomes increasingly clear to the careful reader that Freud and not Dora has become the central character in the action. Freud the narrator does in the writing what Freud the first psychoanalyst appears to have done in actuality. We begin to sense that it is his story that is being written and not hers that is being retold. Instead of letting Dora appropriate her own story, Freud became the appropriator of it. The case history belongs progressively less to her than it does to him. It may be that this was an inevitable development, that it is one of the typical outcomes of an analysis that fails, that Dora was under any circumstances unable to become the appropriator of her own history, the teller of her own story. Blame does not necessarily or automatically attach to

Freud. Nevertheless, by the time he gets to the second dream he is able to write, "I shall present the material produced during the analysis of this dream in the somewhat haphazard order in which it recurs to my mind." He makes such a presentation for several reasons, most of which are legitimate. But one reason almost certainly is that by this juncture it is his *own* mind that chiefly matters to him, and it is *his* associations to her dream that are of principal importance.

At the same time, as the account progresses, Freud has never been more inspired, more creative, more inventive; as the reader sees Dora gradually slipping further and further away from Freud, the power and complexity of the writing reach dizzying proportions. At times they pass over into something else. Due allowance has always to be made for the absolutizing tendency of genius, especially when as in the case of Dora the genius is writing with the license of a poet and the ambiguity of a seer. But Freud goes beyond this.

When Dora reports her second dream, Freud spends two hours of inspired insight in elucidating some of its meanings. "At the end of the second session," he writes, "I expressed my satisfaction at the results." The satisfaction in question is in large measure self-satisfaction, for Dora responded to Freud's expression of it with the following words uttered in "a depreciatory tone: 'Why, has anything so remarkable come out?'" That satisfaction was to be of short duration, for Dora opened the third session by telling Freud that this was the last time she would be there—it was December 31, 1900. Freud's remarks that "her breaking off so unexpectedly just when my hopes of a successful termination of the treatment were at their highest, and her thus bringing those hopes to nothing—this was an unmistakable act of vengeance on her part" are only partly warranted. There was, or should have been, nothing unexpected about Dora's decision to terminate; indeed Freud himself on the occasion of the first dream had already detected such a decision on Dora's part and had communicated this finding to her. Moreover, his "highest" hopes for a successful outcome of the treatment seem almost entirely without foundation. In such a context the hopes of success almost unavoidably become a matter of self-reference and point to the immense *intellectual* triumph that Freud was aware he was achieving with the material adduced by his patient. On the matter of "vengeance," however, Freud cannot be faulted; Dora was, among many other things, certainly getting her own back on Freud by refusing to allow him to bring her story to an end in the way he saw fit. And he in turn is quite candid about the injury he felt she had caused him. "No one who, like me," he writes, "conjures up the most evil of those half-tamed demons that inhabit the human breast, and seeks to wrestle with them, can expect to come through the struggle unscathed."

This admission of vulnerability, which Freud artfully manages to blend with the suggestion that he is a kind of modern combination of Jacob and Faust, is in keeping with the weirdness and wildness of the case as a whole and with this last hour. That hour recurs to the scene at the lake, two years before, and its aftermath. And Freud ends this final hour with the following final interpretation. He reminds Dora that she was in love with Herr K.; that she wanted him to divorce his wife; that even though she was quite young at the time she wanted "'to wait for him, and you took it that he was only waiting till you were grown up enough to be his wife. I imagine that this was a perfectly serious plan for the future in your eyes.'" But Freud does not say this in order to contradict it or categorize it as a fantasy of the adolescent girl's unconscious imagination. On the contrary, he has very different ideas in view, for he goes on to tell her,

> "You have not even got the right to assert that it was out of the question for Herr K. to have had any such intention; you have told me enough about him that points directly towards his having such an intention. Nor does his behavior at L———contradict this view. After all, you did not let him finish his speech and do not know what he meant to say to you."

He has not done with her yet, for he then goes on to bring in the other relevant parties and offers her the following conclusion:

> "Incidentally, the scheme would by no means have been so impracticable. Your father's relation with Frau K....made it certain that her consent to a divorce could be obtained; and you can get anything you like out of your father. Indeed, if your temptation at L ——— had had a different upshot, this would have been *the only possible solution for all the parties concerned*" [italics mine].

No one—at least no one in recent years—has accused Freud of being a swinger, but this is without question a swinging solution that is being offered. It is of course possible that he feels free to make such a proposal only because he knows that nothing in the way of action can come of it; but with him you never can tell—as I hope I have already demonstrated. One has only to imagine what in point of ego strength, balance, and self-acceptance would have been required of Dora alone in this arrangement of wife-and-daughter-swapping to recognize at once its extreme irresponsibility, to say the least. At the same time we must bear in mind that such a suggestion is not incongruent with the recently revealed circumstance that Freud analyzed his own daughter. Genius makes up its own rules as it goes along—and breaks them as well. This "only possible solution" was one of the endings that Freud wanted to write to Dora's story; he had others in mind besides, but none of them were to come about. Dora refused or was unable to let him do this; she refused to be a character in the story that Freud was composing for her, and wanted to finish it herself. As we now know, the ending she wrote was a very bad one indeed.

VI

In this extraordinary work Freud and Dora often appear as unconscious, parodic refractions of each other. Both of them insist with implacable will upon the primacy of "reality," although the realities each has in mind differ radically. Both of them use reality, "the truth," as a weapon. Freud does so by forcing interpretations upon Dora before she is ready for them or can accept them. And this aggressive truth bounds back upon the teller, for Dora leaves him. Dora in turn uses her version of reality—it is "outer" reality that she insists upon—aggressively as well. She has used it from the outset against her father, and five months after she left Freud she had the opportunity to use it against the K.'s. In May of 1901 one of the K.'s children dies. Dora took the occasion to pay them a visit of condolence—

> She took her revenge on them. ... To the wife she said: "I know you have an affair with my father"; and the other did not deny it. From the husband she drew an admission of the scene by the lake which he had disputed, and brought the news of her vindication home to her father.

She told this to Freud fifteen months after she had departed, when she returned one last time to visit him—to ask him, without sincerity, for further help, and "to finish her story." She finished her story, and as for the rest Freud remarks, "I do not know what kind of help she wanted from me, but I promised to forgive her for having deprived me of the satisfaction of affording her a far more radical cure for her troubles."

But the matter is not hopelessly obscure, as Freud himself has already confessed. What went wrong with the case, "its great defect, which led to its being broken off prematurely," was something that had to do with the transference; and Freud writes that "I did not succeed in mastering the transference in good time." He was in fact just beginning to learn about this therapeutic phenomenon, and the present passage is the first really important one about it to have been written. It is also in the nature of things heavily occluded. On Dora's side the transference went wrong in several senses. In the first place there was the failure on her part to establish an adequate positive transference to Freud. She was not free enough to respond to him erotically—in fantasy—or intellectually—by accepting his interpretations: both or either of these being prerequisites for the mysterious "talking cure" to begin to work. And in the second, halfway through the case a negative transference began to emerge, quite clearly in the first dream. Freud writes that he "was deaf to this first note of warning," and as a result this negative "transference took me unawares, and, because of the unknown quantity in me which reminded Dora of Herr K., she took her revenge on me as she wanted to take her revenge on him, and deserted me as she believed herself to have been deceived and deserted by him." This is, I believe, the first mention in print of the conception that is known as "acting out"—out of which, one may incidentally observe, considerable fortunes have been made.

We are, however, in a position to say something more than this. For there is a reciprocating process in the analyst known as the countertransference, and in the case of Dora this went wrong too. Although Freud describes Dora at the beginning of the account as being "in the first bloom of youth— a girl of intelligent and engaging looks," almost nothing attractive about her comes forth in the course of the writing. As it unwinds, and it becomes increasingly evident that Dora is not responding adequately to Freud, it also becomes clear that Freud is not responding favorably to this response, and that he doesn't in fact like Dora very much. He doesn't like her negative sexuality, her inability to surrender to her own erotic impulses. He doesn't like "her really remarkable achievements in the direction of intolerable behavior." He doesn't like her endless reproachfulness. Above all, he doesn't like her inability to surrender herself to him. For what Freud was as yet unprepared to face was not merely the transference, but the counter-transference as well—in the case of Dora it was largely a negative counter-transference—an unanalyzed part of himself. I should like to suggest that this cluster of unanalyzed impulses and ambivalences was in part respon-sible for Freud's writing of this great text immediately after Dora left him. It was his way—and one way—of dealing with, mastering, expressing, and neutralizing such material. Yet the neutralization was not complete; or we can put the matter in another way and state that Freud's creative honesty was such that it compelled him to write the case of Dora as he did, and that his writing has allowed us to make out in this remarkable fragment a still fuller picture. As I have said before, this fragment of Freud's is more complete and coherent than the fullest case studies of any-one else. Freud's case histories are a new form of literature—they are crea-tive narratives that include their own analysis and interpretation. Never-theless, like the living works of literature that they are, the material they contain is always richer than the original analysis and interpretation that accompany it; and this means that future generations will recur to these works and will find in them a language they are seeking and a story they need to be told.

Freud and the Poetic Sublime:
A Catastrophe Theory of Creativity

By Harold Bloom

Jacques Lacan argues that Freud "derived his inspiration, his ways of thinking and his technical weapons" from imaginative literature rather than from the sciences. On such a view, the precursors of Freud are not so much Charcot and Janet, Brücke and Helmholtz, Breuer and Fliess, but the rather more exalted company of Empedocles and Heraclitus, Plato and Goethe, Shakespeare and Schopenhauer. Lacan is the foremost advocate of a dialectical reading of Freud's text, a reading that takes into account those problematics of textual interpretation that stem from the philosophies of Hegel, Nietzsche and Heidegger, and from developments in differential linguistics. Such a reading, though it has attracted many intellectuals in English-speaking countries, is likely to remain rather alien to us, because of the strong empirical tradition in Anglo-American thought. Rather like Freud himself, whose distaste for and ignorance of the United States were quite invincible, Lacan and his followers distrust American pragmatism, which to them is merely irritability with theory. Attacks by French Freudians upon American psychoanalysis tend to stress issues of societal adjustment or else of a supposed American optimism concerning human nature. But I think that Lacan is wiser in his cultural vision of Freud than he is in his polemic against ego psychology, interpersonal psychoanalysis, or any other American school. Freud's power *as a writer* made him the contemporary not so much of his rivals and disciples as of the strongest literary minds of our century. We read Freud not as we read Jung or Rank, Abraham or Ferenczi, but as we read Proust or Joyce, Valéry or Rilke or Stevens. A writer who achieves what once was called the Sublime will be susceptible to explication either upon an empirical *or* dialectical basis.

The best brief account of Freud that I have read is *Sigmund Freud* by Richard Wollheim (1971), and Wollheim is an analytical philosopher, working in the tradition of Hume and of Wittgenstein. The Freud who emerges in Wollheim's pages bears very little resemblance to Lacan's Freud, yet I would hesitate to prefer either Wollheim's or Lacan's Freud, one to the other. There is no "true" or "correct" reading of Freud because Freud is so strong a writer that he *contains* every available mode of interpretation. In tribute to Lacan, I add that Lacan in particular has uncovered Freud as the greatest theorist we have of what I would call the necessity of misreading. Freud's text both exemplifies and explores certain limits of language, and therefore of literature, insofar as literature is a linguistic as well as a discursive mode. Freud is therefore as much the concern of literary criticism as he is of psychoanalysis. His intention was to found a science; instead he left as legacy a literary canon and a discipline of healing.

It remains one of the sorrows of both psychoanalysis and literary criticism that as modes of interpretation they continue to be antithetical to one another. The classical essay on this antithesis is still Lionel Trilling's "Freud and Literature," first published back in 1940 and subsequently revised in *The Liberal Imagination* (1950). Trilling demonstrated that neither Freud's notion of art's status nor Freud's use of analysis upon works-of-art was acceptable to a literary critic, but Trilling nevertheless praised the Freudian psychology as being truly parallel to the workings of poetry. The sentence of Trilling's eloquent essay that always has lingered in my memory is the one that presents Freud as a second Vico, as another great rhetorician of the psyche's twistings and turnings:

> In the eighteenth century Vico spoke of the metaphorical, imagistic language of the early stages of culture; it was left to Freud to discover how, in a scientific age, we still feel and think in figurative formations, and to create, what psychoanalysis is, a science of tropes, of metaphor and its variants, synecdoche and metonymy.

That psychoanalysis is a science of tropes is now an accepted commonplace in France, and even in America, but we do well to remember how prophetic Trilling was, since the *Discours de Rome* of Jacques Lacan dates from 1953. Current American thinkers in psychoanalysis like Marshall Edelson and Roy Schafer describe psychic defenses as fantasies, not mechanisms, and fantasies are always tropes, in which so-called "deep structures," like desires, become transformed into "surface structures," like symptoms. A fantasy of defense is thus, in language, the recursive process that traditional rhetoric named a trope or "turning," or even a "color," to use another old name for it. A psychoanalyst, interpreting a symptom, dream, or verbal slip, and a literary critic interpreting a poem, thus share the burden of having to become conceptual rhetoricians. But a common burden is proving to be no more of an authentic unifying link between psychoanalysts and critics than common burdens prove to be among common people, and the languages of psychoanalysis and of criticism continue to diverge and clash.

Partly this is due to a certain overconfidence on the part of writing psychoanalysts when they confront a literary text, as well as to a certain over-deference to psychoanalysis on the part of various critics. Psychoanalytic overconfidence, or courageous lack-of-wariness, is hardly untypical of the profession, as any critic can learn by conducting a seminar for any group of psychoanalysts. Since we can all agree that the interpretation of schizophrenia is a rather more desperately urgent matter than the interpretation of poetry, I am in no way inclined to sneer at psychoanalysts for their instinctive privileging of their own kinds of interpretation. A critical self-confidence, or what Nietzsche might have called a will-to-power over the text-of-life, is a working necessity for a psychoanalyst, who otherwise would cease to function. Like the shaman, the psychoanalyst cannot heal unless he himself is persuaded by his own rhetoric. But the writing psychoanalyst adopts, whether he knows it or not, a very different stance. As a writer he is neither more nor less privileged than any other writer. He cannot invoke the trope of the Unconscious as though he were doing more (or less) than the poet or critic does by invoking the trope of the Imagination, or than the theologian does by invoking the trope of the Divine. Most writing psychoanalysts privilege the realm of what Freud named as "the primary process." Since this privileging, or valorization, is at the center of any psychoanalytic account of creativity, I turn now to examine "primary process," which is Freud's most vital trope or fiction in his theory of the mind.

Freud formulated his distinction between the primary and secondary processes of the psyche in 1895, in his "Project for a Scientific Psychology," best available in English since 1964 in *The Origins of Psychoanalysis* (ed. Bonaparte, A. Freud, and Kris). In Freud's mapping of the mind, the primary process goes on in the system of the unconscious, while the secondary process characterizes the preconscious-conscious system. In the unconscious, energy is conceived as moving easily and without check from one idea to another, sometimes by displacement (dislocating) and sometimes by condensation (compression). This hypothesized energy of the psyche is supposed continually to reinvest all ideas associated with the fulfillment of unconscious desire, which is defined as a kind of primitive hallucination that totally satisfies, that gives a complete pleasure. Freud speaks of the primary process as being marked by a wandering-of-meaning, with meaning sometimes dislocated onto what ought to be an insignificant idea or image, and sometimes compressed upon a single idea or image at a crossing point between a number of ideas or images. In this

constant condition of wandering, meaning becomes multiformly determined, or even over-determined, interestingly explained by Lacan as
being like a palimpsest, with one meaning always written over another one.
Dreaming is of course the principal Freudian evidence for the primary
process, but wishing construed as a primitive phase of desiring may be
closer to the link between the primary process and what could be called
poetic thinking.

Wollheim calls the primary process "a primitive but perfectly coherent
form of mental functioning." Freud expounded a version of the primary
process in Chapter VII of his masterwork, *The Interpretation of Dreams*
(1900), but his classic account of it is in the essay of 1911, "Formulations on
the Two Principles of Mental Functioning." There the primary process is
spoken of as yielding to the secondary process when the person abandons
the pleasure principle and yields to the reality principle, a surrender that
postpones pleasure only in order to render its eventuality more certain.

The secondary process thus begins with a binding of psychic energy,
which subsequently moves in a more systematic fashion. Investments in
ideas and images are stabilized, with pleasure deferred, in order to make
possible trial runs of thought as so many path-breakings towards a more
constant pleasure. So described, the secondary process also has its links to
the cognitive workings of poetry, as to all other cognitions whatsoever.
The French Freudians, followers of Lacan, speak of the primary and
secondary processes as each having different laws of syntax, which is
another way of describing these processes as two kinds of poetry or figuration, or two ways of "creativity," if one would have it so.

Anthony Wilden observes in his *System and Structure* (1972): "The
concept of a primary process or system applies in both a synchronic and a
diachronic sense to all systemic or structural theories" (pp. 50-51). In
Freudian theory, the necessity of postulating a primary process precludes
any possibility of regarding the forms of that process as being other than
abnormal or unconscious phenomena. The Lacanian psychoanalyst O.
Mannoni concludes his study, *Freud* (English translation 1971), by emphasizing the ultimate gap between primary process and secondary process
as being the tragic, unalterable truth of the Freudian vision, since: "what
it reveals profoundly is a kind of original fracture in the way man is constituted, a split that opposes him to himself (and not to reality or society)
and exposes him to the attacks of his unconscious" (pp. 192-93).

In his book *On Art and the Mind* (1973), Wollheim usefully reminds us
that the higher reaches of art "did not for Freud connect up with that
other and far broader route by which wish and impulse assert themselves
in our lives: Neurosis" (p. 218). Wollheim goes on to say that, in Freudian
terms, we thus have no reason to think of art as showing any single or
unitary motivation. Freud first had developed the trope or conceptual

image of the unconscious in order to explain repression, but then had equated the unconscious with the primary process. In his final phase, Freud came to believe that the primary process played a positive role in the strengthening of the ego, by way of the fantasies or defenses of intro- jection and projection. Wollheim hints that Freud, if he had lived, might have investigated the role of art through such figures of identification, so as to equate art "with recovery or reparation or the path back to reality" (p. 219). Whether or not this surmise is correct, it is certainly very sug- gestive. We can join Wollheim's surmise to Jack Spector's careful conclusion in his *The Aesthetics of Freud* (1972) that Freud's contribution to the study of art is principally: "his dramatic view of the mind in which a war, not of good and evil, but of ego, super-ego, and id forces occurs as a secular *psychomachia.*" Identification, through art, is clearly a crucial weapon in such a civil war of the psyche.

Yet it remains true, as Philip Rieff once noted, that Freud suggests very little that is positive about creativity as an intellectual process, and there- fore explicit Freudian thought is necessarily antithetical to nearly any theory of the imagination. To quarry Freud for theories-of-creativity, we need to study Freud where he himself is most imaginative, as in his great phase that beings with *Beyond the Pleasure Principle* (1920), continues with the essay "Negation" (1925), and then with *Inhibitions, Symptoms, Anxiety* (1926, but called *The Problem of Anxiety* in its American edition), and that can be said to attain a climax in the essay "Analysis Terminable and Interminable" (1937). This is the Freud who establishes the priority of anxiety over its stimuli, and who both imagines the origins of conscious- ness as a catastrophe and then relates that catastrophe to repetition-com- pulsion, to the drive-towards-death, and to the defense of life as a drive towards agonistic achievement, an agon directed not only against death but against the achievements of anteriority, of others, and even of one's own earlier self.

Freud, as Rieff also has observed, held a catastrophe theory of the genealogy of drives, but *not* of the drive-towards-creativity. Nevertheless, the Freudian conceptual image of a catastrophe-creation of our instincts is perfectly applicable to our will-to-creativity, and both Otto Rank and more indirectly Sandor Ferenczi made many suggestions (largely unacceptable to Freud himself) that can help us to see what might serve as a Freudian theory of the imagination-as-catastrophe, and of art as an achieved anxiety in the agonistic struggle both to repeat and to defer the repetition of the catastrophe of creative origins.

Prior to any pleasure, including that of creativity, Freud posits the "narcissistic scar," accurately described by a British Freudian critic, Ann Wordsworth, as "the infant's tragic and inevitable first failure in sexual love." Parallel to this notion of the narcissistic scar is Freud's speculative discovery that there are early dreams whose purpose is not hallucinatory wish-fulfillment. Rather they are attempts to master a stimulus retroactively by first developing the anxiety. This is certainly a creation, though it is the *creation of an anxiety,* and so cannot be considered a sublimation of any kind. Freud's own circuitous path-breaking of thought connects this creation-of-an-anxiety to the function of repetition-compulsion, which turns out, in the boldest of all Freud's tropes, to be a regressive return to a death-instinct.

Freud would have rejected, I think, an attempt to relate this strain in his most speculative thinking to any theory of creativity, because for Freud a successful repression is a contradiction in terms. What I am suggesting is that any theory of artistic creation that wishes to use Freud must depart from the Freudian letter in order to develop the Freudian spirit, which in some sense is already the achievement of Lacan and his school, though they have had no conspicuous success in speculating upon art. What the Lacanians *have* seen is that Freud's system, like Heidegger's, is a science of anxiety, which is what I suspect the art of belatedness, of the last several centuries, mostly is also. Freud, unlike Nietzsche, shared in the Romantics' legacy of over-idealizing art, of accepting an ill-defined trope of "the Imagination" as a kind of mythology of creation. But Freud, as much as Nietzsche (or Vico before them both), provides the rational materials for demythologizing our pieties about artistic creation. Reading the later Freud teaches us that our instinctual life is agonistic and ultimately self-destructive and that our most authentic moments tend to be those of negation, contraction, and repression. Is it so unlikely that our creative drives are deeply contaminated by our instinctual origins?

Psychoanalytic explanations of "creativity" tend to discount or repress two particular aspects of the genealogy of aesthetics: first, that the creative or Sublime "moment" is a negative moment; second, that this moment tends to rise out of an encounter with someone else's prior moment of negation, which in turn goes back to an anterior moment, and so on. "Creativity" is thus always a mode of repetition *and* of memory and also of what Nietzsche called the will's revenge against time and against time's statement of: "It was." What links repetition and revenge is the psychic operation that Freud named "defense," and that he identified first with repression but later with a whole range of figurations, including identification. Freud's rhetoric of the psyche, as codified by Anna Freud in *The Ego and the Mechanisms of Defense* (1946), is as comprehensive a system of tropes as Western theory has devised. We can see now, because of Freud, that rhetoric always was more the art of defense than it was the art of persuasion, or rather that defense is always *prior* to persuasion. Trilling's pioneering observation that Freud's science shared with literature a reliance upon trope has proved to be wholly accurate. To clarify my argument, I need to return to Freud's trope of the unconscious and then to proceed from it to his concern with catastrophe as the origin of drive in his later works.

"Consciousness," as a word, goes back to a root meaning "to cut or split," and so to know something by separating out one thing from another. The unconscious (Freud's *das Unbewusste*) is a purely inferred division of the psyche, an inference necessarily based only upon the supposed effects that the unconscious has upon ways we think and act that can be *known*, that are available to consciousness. Because there are gaps or disjunctions to be accounted for in our thoughts and acts, various explanatory concepts of an unconscious have been available since ancient times, but the actual term first appears as the German *Unbewusste* in the later eighteenth century, to be popularized by Goethe and by Schelling. The English "unconscious" was popularized by Coleridge, whose theory of a poem as reconciling a natural outside with a human inside relied upon a formula that: "the consciousness is so impressed on the unconscious as to appear in it." Freud acknowledged often that the poets had been there before him, as discoverers of the unconscious, but asserted his own discovery as being the scientific *use* of a concept of the unconscious. What he did not assert was his intense narrowing-down of the traditional concept, for he separated out and away from it the attributes of creativity that poets and other speculators always had ascribed to it. Originality or invention are not mentioned by Freud as rising out of the unconscious.

There is no single concept of the unconscious in Freud, as any responsible reading of his work shows. This is because there are two Freudian topographies or maps of the mind, earlier and later (after 1920), and also because the unconscious is a dynamic concept. Freud distinguished his concept of the unconscious from that of his closest psychological precursor, Pierre Janet, by emphasizing his own vision of a civil war in the psyche, a dynamic conflict of opposing mental forces, conscious against unconscious. Not only the conflict was seen thus as being dynamic, but the unconscious peculiarly was characterized as dynamic in itself, requiring always a contending force to keep it from breaking through into consciousness.

In the first Freudian topography, the psyche is divided into Unconscious, Preconscious, and Conscious, while in the second the divisions are the rather different triad of id, ego, and super-ego. The Preconscious, descriptively considered, is unconscious, but can be made conscious, and so is severely divided from the Unconscious proper, in the perspective given either by a topographical or a dynamic view. But this earlier system proved simplistic to Freud himself, mostly because he came to believe that our lives began with all of the mind's contents in the unconscious. This finally eliminated Janet's conception that the unconscious was a wholly separate mode of consciousness, which was a survival of the ancient belief in a creative or inaugurating unconscious. Freud's new topology insisted upon the dynamics of relationship between an unknowable unconscious and consciousness by predicating three agencies or instances of personality: id, ego, super-ego. The effect of this new system was to devaluate the unconscious, or at least to demystify it still further.

In the second Freudian topography, "unconscious" tends to become merely a modifier, since all of the id and very significant parts of the ego and super-ego are viewed as being unconscious. Indeed, the second Freudian concept of the ego gives us an ego that is *mostly* unconscious, and so "behaves exactly like the repressed—that is, which produces powerful effects without itself being conscious and which requires special work before it can be made conscious," as Freud remarks in *The Ego and the Id*. Lacan has emphasized the unconscious element in the ego to such a degree that the Lacanian ego must be considered, despite its creator's protests, much more a revision of Freud than what ordinarily would be accounted an interpretation. With mordant eloquence, Lacan keeps assuring us that the ego, every ego, is essentially paranoid, which as Lacan knows *sounds* rather more like Pascal than it does like Freud. I think that this insistence is at once Lacan's strength and his weakness, for my knowledge of imaginative literature tells me that Lacan's conviction is certainly true if by the ego we mean the literary "I" as it appears in much of the most vital lyric poetry of the last three hundred years, and indeed in all literature that achieves the Sublime. But with the literary idea of "the Sublime" I come at last to the sequence of Freud's texts that I wish to examine, since the first of them is Freud's theory of the Sublime, his essay on "The 'Uncanny'" of 1919.

The text of "The 'Uncanny'" is the threshold to the major phase of Freud's canon, which begins the next year with *Beyond the Pleasure Principle*. But quite aside from its crucial place in Freud's writings, the essay is of enormous importance to literary criticism because it is the only major contribution that the twentieth century has made to the aesthetics of the Sublime. It may seem curious to regard Freud as the culmination of a literary and philosophical tradition that held no particular interest for him, but I would correct my own statement by the modification, no *conscious* interest for him. The Sublime, as I read Freud, is one of his major *repressed* concerns, and this literary repression on his part is a clue to what I take to be a gap in his theory of repression.

I come now, belatedly, to the definition of "the Sublime," before considering Freud as the last great theorist of that mode. As a literary idea, the Sublime originally meant a style of "loftiness," that is, of verbal power, of greatness or strength conceived agonistically, which is to say against all possible competition. But in the European Enlightenment, this literary idea was strangely transformed into a vision of the terror that could be perceived both in nature and in art, a terror uneasily allied with pleasurable sensations of augmented power, and even of narcissistic freedom, freedom in the shape of that wildness that Freud dubbed "the omnipotence of thought," the greatest of all narcissistic illusions.

Freud's essay begins with a curiously weak defensive attempt to separate his subject from the aesthetics of the Sublime, which he insists deals only "with feelings of a positive nature." This is so flatly untrue, and so blandly ignores the long philosophical tradition of the negative Sublime, that an alert reader ought to become very wary. A year later, in the opening paragraphs of *Beyond the Pleasure Principle,* Freud slyly assures his readers that: "Priority and originality are not among the aims that psycho-analytic work sets itself." One sentence later, he charmingly adds that he would be glad to accept any philosophical help he can get, but that none is available for a consideration of the meaning of pleasure and unpleasure. With evident generosity, he then acknowledges G. T. Fechner, and later makes a bow to the safely distant Plato as author of *The Symposium.* Very close to the end of *Beyond the Pleasure Principle,* there is a rather displaced reference to Schopenhauer when Freud remarks that "we have unwittingly steered our course into the harbor of Schopenhauer's philosophy." The apogee of this evasiveness in regard to precursors comes where it should, in the marvelous essay of 1937 "Analysis Terminable and Interminable," which we may learn to read as being Freud's elegiac *apologia* for his life's work. There the true precursor is unveiled as Empedocles, very safely remote at two and a half millennia. Perhaps psychoanalysis does not set priority and originality as aims in its *praxis,* but the first and most original of psychoanalysts certainly shared the influence-anxieties and defensive misprisions of all strong writers throughout history, but particularly in the last three centuries.

Anxieties when confronted with anterior powers are overtly the concerns of the essay on the "uncanny." E. T. A. Hoffmann's "The Sand-Man" provides Freud with his text, and for once Freud allows himself to be a very useful practical critic of an imaginative story. The repetition-compulsion, possibly imported backwards from *Beyond the Pleasure Principle* as work-in-progress, brilliantly is invoked to open up what is hidden in the story. Uncanniness is traced back to the narcissistic belief in "omnipotence of thoughts," which in aesthetic terms is necessarily the High Romantic faith in the power of the mind over the universe of the senses and of death. *Das Heimliche,* the homely or canny, is thus extended to its only apparent opposite, *das Unheimliche,* "for this uncanny is in reality nothing new or foreign, but something familiar and old-established in the mind that has been estranged only by the process of repression."

Freud weakens his extraordinary literary insight by the latter part of his essay, where he seeks to reduce the "uncanny" to either an infantile or a primitive survival in our psyche. His essay knows better, in its wonderful dialectical play on the *Unheimlich* as being subsumed by the larger or parental category of the *Heimlich*. Philip Rieff finely catches this interplay in his comment that the effect of Freud's writing is itself rather uncanny, and surely never more so than in this essay. Rieff sounds like Emerson or even like Longinus on the Sublime when he considers the condition of Freud's reader:

> The reader comes to a work with ambivalent motives, learning what he does not wish to know, or, what amounts to the same thing, believing he already knows and can accept as his own intellectual property what the author merely "articulates" or "expresses" for him. Of course, in this sense, everybody knows everything—or nobody could learn anything.

Longinus had said that reading a sublime poet "we come to believe we have created what we have only heard." Milton, strongest poet of the modern Sublime, stated this version of the reader's Sublime with an ultimate power, thus setting forth the principle upon which he himself read, in Book IV of his *Paradise Regained,* where his Christ tells Satan:

> ...who reads
> Incessantly, and to his reading brings not
> A spirit and judgment equal or superior
> (And what he brings, what needs he elsewhere seek?),
> Uncertain and unsettled still remains....

Pope followed Boileau in saying that Longinus "is himself the great Sublime he draws." Emerson, in his seminal essay "Self-Reliance," culminated this theme of the reader's Sublime when he asserted that: "In every work of genius we recognize our own rejected thoughts; they come back to us with a certain alienated majesty." That "majesty" is the true, high breaking light, aura or lustre, of the Sublime, and this realization is at the repressed center of Freud's essay on the "uncanny." What Freud declined to see, at that moment, was the mode of conversion that alienated the "canny" into the "uncanny." His next major text, *Beyond the Pleasure Principle,* clearly exposes that mode as being catastrophe.

Lacan and his followers have centered upon *Beyond the Pleasure Principle* because the book has not lost the force of its shock value, even to Freudian analysts. My contention would be that this shock is itself the stigma of the Sublime, stemming from Freud's literary achievement here. The text's origin is itself shock or trauma, the trauma that a neurotic's dreams attempt to master *after the event.* "Drive" or "instinct" is suddenly seen by Freud as being catastrophic in its origins, and as being aimed, not at satisfaction, but at death. For the first time in his writing, Freud overtly assigns priority to the psyche's fantasizings over mere biology, though this valorization makes Freud uneasy. The pleasure principle produces the biological principle of constancy, and then is converted, through this principle, into a drive back to the constancy of death. Drive or instinct thus becomes a kind of defense, all but identified with repression. This troping of biology is so extreme, really so literary, that I find it more instructive to seek the aid of commentary here from a Humean empiricist like Wollheim than from Continental dialecticians like Lacan and Laplanche. Wollheim imperturbably finds no violation of empiricism or biology in the death-drive. He even reads "beyond," *jenseits,* as meaning only "inconsistent with" the pleasure principle, which is to remove from the word the transcendental or Sublime emphasis that Freud's usage gave to it. For Wollheim, the book is nothing more than the working through of the full implication of the major essay of 1914, "On Narcissism: An Introduction." If we follow Wollheim's lead quite thoroughly here, we will emerge with conclusions that differ from his rather guarded remarks about the book in which Freud seems to have shocked himself rather more than he shocks Wollheim.

The greatest shock of *Beyond the Pleasure Principle* is that it assigns the origin of all human drives to a catastrophe theory of creation (to which I would add: "and of creativity"). This catastrophe theory is developed in *The Ego and the Id,* where the two major catastrophes, the drying-up of oceans that cast life onto land, and the Ice Age, are repeated psychosomatically in the way the latency period (roughly from the age of five until twelve) cuts a gap into sexual development. Rieff again is very useful when he says that the basis of catastrophe theory, whether in Freud or in Ferenczi's more drastic and even apocalyptic *Thalassa* (1921), "remains Freud's *Todestrieb,* the tendency of all organisms to strive toward a state of absence of irritability and finally 'the deathlike repose of the inorganic world.'" I find it fascinating from a literary critical standpoint to note what I think has not been noted, that the essay on narcissism turns upon catastrophe theory also. Freud turns to poetry, here to Heine, in order to illustrate the psychogenesis of eros, but the lines he quotes actually state a psychogenesis of creativity rather than of love:

...whence does that necessity arise that urges our mental life to pass on beyond the limits of narcissism and to attach the libido to objects? The answer which would follow from our line of thought would once more be that we are so impelled when the cathexis of the ego with libido exceeds a certain degree. A strong egoism is a protection against disease, but in the last resort we must begin to love in order that we may not fall ill, and must fall ill if, in consequence of frustration, we cannot love. Somewhat after this fashion does Heine conceive of the psychogenesis of the creation:

Krankheit ist wohl der letzte Grund
Des ganzen Schöpferdrangs gewesen;
Erschaffend konnte ich genesen,
Erschaffend wurde ich gesund.

To paraphrase Heine loosely, illness is the ultimate ground of the drive to create, and so while creating the poet sustains relief, and by creating the poet becomes healthy. Freud transposes from the catastrophe of creativity to the catastrophe of falling in love, a transposition to which I will return in the final pages of this essay.

Beyond the Pleasure Principle, like the essay on narcissism, is a discourse haunted by images (some of them repressed) of catastrophe. Indeed, what Freud verges upon showing is that to be human is a catastrophic condition. The coloring of this catastrophe, in Freud, is precisely Schopenhauerian rather than, say, Augustinian or Pascalian. It is as though, for Freud, the Creation and the Fall had been one and the same event. Freud holds back from this abyss of Gnosticism by reducing mythology to psychology, but since psychology and cosmology have been intimately related throughout human history, this reduction is not altogether persuasive. Though he wants to show us that the daemonic is "really" the compulsion to repeat, Freud tends rather to the "uncanny" demonstration that repetition-compulsion reveals many of us to be daemonic or else makes us daemonic. Again, Freud resorts to the poets for illustration, and again the example goes beyond the Freudian interpretation. Towards the close of section III of *Beyond the Pleasure Principle,* Freud looks for a supreme instance of "people all of whose human relationships have the same outcome" and he finds it in Tasso:

> The most moving poetic picture of a fate such as this is given by Tasso in his romantic epic *Gerusalemme Liberata.* Its hero, Tancred, unwittingly kills his beloved Clorinda in a duel while she is disguised in the armor of an enemy knight. After her burial he makes his way into a strange magic forest which strikes the Crusaders' army with terror. He slashes with his sword at a tall tree; but blood streams from the cut, and the voice of Clorinda, whose soul is imprisoned in the tree, is heard complaining that he has wounded his beloved once again.

Freud cites this episode as evidence to support his assumption "that there really does exist in the mind a compulsion to repeat which overrides the pleasure principle." But the repetition in Tasso is not just incremental, but rather is qualitative, in that the second wounding is "uncanny" or Sublime, and the first is merely accidental. Freud's citation is an allegory of Freud's own passage into the Sublime. When Freud writes (and the italics are his): *"It seems, then, that a drive is an urge inherent in organic life to restore an earlier state of things,"* then he slays his beloved trope of "drive" by disguising it in the armor of his enemy, mythology. But when he writes (and again the italics are his): *"the aim of all life is death,"* then he wounds his figuration of "drive" in a truly Sublime or "uncanny" fashion. In the qualitative leap from the drive to restore pure anteriority to the apothegm that life's purpose is death, Freud himself has abandoned the empirical for the daemonic. It is the literary authority of the daemonic rather than the analytical which makes plausible the further suggestion that:

> ...sadism is in fact a death instinct which, under the influence of the narcissistic libido, has been forced away from the ego....

This language is impressive, and it seems to me equally against literary tact to accept it or reject it on any supposed biological basis. Its true basis is that of an implicit catastrophe theory of meaning or interpretation, which is in no way weakened by being circular and therefore mythological. The repressed rhetorical formula of Freud's discourse in *Beyond the Pleasure Principle* can be stated thus: *Literal meaning equals anteriority equals an earlier state of meaning equals an earlier state of things equals death equals literal meaning.* Only one escape is possible from such a formula, and it is a simpler formula: *Eros equals figurative meaning.* This is the dialectic that informs the proudest and most moving passage in *Beyond the Pleasure Principle,* which comprises two triumphant sentences *contra* Jung that were added to the text in 1921, in a Sublime afterthought:

> Our views have from the very first been *dualistic,* and today they are even more definitely dualistic than before—now that we describe the opposition as being, not between ego-instincts and sexual instincts, but between life instincts and death instincts. Jung's libido theory is on the contrary *monistic;* the fact that he has called his one instinctual force "libido" is bound to cause confusion, but need not affect us otherwise.

I would suggest that we read *dualistic* here as a trope for "figurative" and *monistic* as a trope for "literal." The opposition between life drives and death drives is not just a dialectic (though it *is* that) but is a great writer's Sublime interplay between figurative and literal meanings, whereas Jung is exposed as being what he truly was, a mere literalizer of anterior mythologies. What Freud proclaims here, in the accents of sublimity, is the power of his own mind over language, which in this context *is* the power that Hegelians or Lacanians legitimately could term "negative thinking."

I am pursuing Freud as prose-poet of the Sublime, but I would not concede that I am losing sight of Freud as analytical theorist. Certainly the next strong Freudian text is the incomparable *Inhibitions, Symptoms, Anxiety* of 1926. But before considering that elegant and somber meditation, certainly the most illuminating analysis of anxiety our civilization has been offered, I turn briefly to Freud's essay on his dialectic, "Negation" (1925).

Freud's audacity here has been little noted, perhaps because he packs into fewer than five pages an idea that cuts a considerable gap into his theory of repression. The gap is wide enough so that such oxymorons as "a successful repression" and "an achieved anxiety," which are not possible in psychoanalysis, are made available to us as literary terms. Repressed images or thoughts, by Freudian definition, *cannot* make their way into consciousness, yet their content can, on condition that it is *denied*. Freud cheerfully splits head from heart in the apprehension of images:

> Negation is a way of taking account of what is repressed; indeed, it is actually a removal of the repression, though not, of course, an acceptance of what is repressed. It is to be seen how the intellectual function is here distinct from the affective process. Negation only assists in undoing *one* of the consequences of repression—namely, the fact that the subject-matter of the image in question is unable to enter consciousness. The result is a kind of intellectual acceptance of what is repressed, though in all essentials the repression persists.

I would venture one definition of the literary Sublime (which to me seems always a negative Sublime) as being that mode in which the poet, while expressing previously repressed thought, desire, or emotion, is able to continue to defend himself against his own created image by disowning it, a defense of *un-naming* it rather than *naming* it. Freud's word *"Verneinung"* means both a grammatical negation and a psychic disavowal or denial, and so the linguistic and the psychoanalytical have a common origin here, as Lacan and his school have insisted. The ego and the poet-in-his-poem both proceed by a kind of "misconstruction," a defensive process that Lacan calls *méconnaissance* in psychoanalysis, and that I have called "misprision" in the study of poetic influence (a notion formulated before I had read Lacan, but which I was delighted to find supported in him). In his essay "Aggressivity in Psychoanalysis" Lacan usefully connects Freud's notion of a "negative" libido to the idea of Discord in Heraclitus. Freud himself brings his essay on *"Verneinung"* to a fascinating double conclusion. First, the issue of truth or falsehood in language is directly related to the defenses of introjection and projection; a true image thus would be introjected and a false one projected. Second, the defense of introjection is aligned to the Eros-drive of affirmation, "while negation, the derivative of expulsion, belongs to the instinct of destruction," the drive to death beyond the pleasure principle. I submit that what Freud has done here should have freed literary discussion from its persistent over-literalization of his idea of repression. Freud joins himself to the tradition of the Sublime, that is, of the strongest Western poetry, by showing us that negation allows poetry to free itself from the aphasias and hysterias of repression, *without* however freeing the poets themselves from the unhappier human consequences of repression. Negation is of *no* therapeutic value for the individual, but it *can* liberate him into the linguistic freedoms of poetry and thought.

I think that of all Freud's books, none matches the work on inhibitions, symptoms, and anxiety in its potential importance for students of literature, for this is where the concept of defense is ultimately clarified. Wollheim says that Freud confused the issue of defense by the "overschematic" restriction of repression to a single species of defense, but this is one of the very rare instances where Wollheim seems to me misled or mistaken. Freud's revised account of anxiety *had* to distinguish between *relatively* non-repressive and the more severely repressive defenses, and I only wish that both Freud, and his daughter after him, had been more schematic in mapping out the defenses. We need a rhetoric of the psyche, and here the Lacanians have been a kind of disaster, with their simplistic over-reliance upon the metaphor/metonymy distinction. Freud's revised account of anxiety is precisely at one with the poetic Sublime, for anxiety is finally seen as a technique for mastering anteriority by *remembering* rather than *repeating* the past. By showing us that anxiety is a mode of expectation, closely resembling desire, Freud allows us to understand why poetry, which loves love, also seems to love anxiety. Literary and human romance both are exposed as being anxious quests that could not bear to be cured of their anxieties, even if such cures were possible. "An increase of excitation underlies anxiety," Freud tells us, and then he goes on to relate this increase to a repetition of the catastrophe of human birth, with its attendant trauma. Arguing against Otto Rank, who like Ferenczi had gone too far into the abysses of catastrophe theory, Freud enunciated a principle that can help explain why the terror of the literary Sublime must and can give pleasure:

> Anxiety is an affective state which can of course be experienced only by the ego. The id cannot be afraid, as the ego can; it is not an organization, and cannot estimate situations of danger. On the contrary, it is of extremely frequent occurrence that processes are initiated or executed in the id which give the ego occasion to develop anxiety; as a matter of fact, the repressions which are probably the earliest are motivated, like the majority of all later ones, by such fear on the part of the ego of this or that process in the id.

Freud's writing career was to conclude with the polemical assertion that "Mysticism is the obscure self-perception of the realm outside the ego, of the id," which is a splendid farewell thrust at Jung, as we can see by substituting "Jung" for "the id" at the close of the sentence. The id perceiving the id is a parody of the Sublime, whereas the ego's earliest defense, its primal repression, is the true origin of the Sublime. Freud knew that "primal repression" was a necessary fiction, because without some initial fixation his story of the psyche could not begin. Laplanche and Pontalis, writing under Lacan's influence in their *The Language of Psychoanalysis,* find the basis of fixation:

...in primal moments at which certain privileged ideas are indelibly inscribed in the unconscious, and at which the instinct itself becomes fixated to its psychical representative—perhaps by this very process constituting itself *qua* instinct.

If we withdrew that "perhaps," then we would return to the Freudian catastrophe theory of the genesis of all drives, with fixation now being regarded as another originating catastrophe. How much clearer these hypotheses become if we transpose them into the realm of poetry! If fixation becomes the inscription in the unconscious of the privileged idea of a Sublime poet, or strong precursor, then the drive towards poetic expression originates in an agonistic repression, where the agon or contest is set against the pattern of the precursor's initial fixation upon an anterior figure. Freud's mature account of anxiety thus concludes itself upon an allegory of origins, in which the creation of an unconscious implicitly models itself upon poetic origins. There was repression, Freud insists, before there was anything to be repressed. This insistence is neither rational nor irrational; it is a figuration that knows its own status as figuration, without embarrassment.

My final text in Freud is "Analysis Terminable and Interminable." The German title, *Die Endliche und die Unendliche Analyse,* might better be translated as "finite or indefinite analysis," which is Lacan's suggestion. Lacan amusingly violates the taboo of discussing how long the analytic session is to be, when he asks:

...how is this time to be measured? Is its measure to be that of what Alexander Koyré calls 'the universe of precision'? Obviously we live in this universe, but its advent for man is relatively recent, since it goes back precisely to Huyghens' clock—in other words, to 1659—and the *malaise* of modern man does not exactly indicate that this precision is in itself a liberating factor for him. Are we to say that this time, the time of the fall of heavy bodies, is in some way sacred in the sense that it corresponds to the time of the stars as they were fixed in eternity by God who, as Lichtenberg put it, winds up our sundials?

I reflect, as I read Lacan's remarks, that it was just after Huyghens' clock that Milton began to compose *Paradise Lost,* in the early 1660s, and that Milton's poem is *the* instance of the modern Sublime. It is in *Paradise Lost* that temporality fully becomes identified with anxiety, which makes Milton's epic the most Freudian text ever written, far closer to the universe of psychoanalysis than such more frequently cited works, in Freudian contexts, as *Oedipus Tyrannus* and *Hamlet.* We should remember that before Freud used a Virgilian tag as epigraph for *The Interpretation of Dreams* (1908), he had selected a great Satanic utterance for his motto:

Seest thou yon dreary plain, forlorn and wild,
The seat of desolation, void of light,
Save what the glimmering of these livid flames
Casts pale and dreadful? Thither let us tend
From off the tossing of these fiery waves,
There rest, if any rest can harbour there,
And reassembling our afflicted powers.
Consult how we may henceforth most offend
Our enemy, our own loss how repair,
How overcome this dire calamity,
What reinforcement we may gain from hope;
If not, what resolution from despair.

This Sublime passage provides a true motto for all psychoanalysis, since "afflicted powers" meant "cast down powers" or, as Freud would have said, "repressed drives." But it would be an even apter epigraph for the essay on finite and indefinite analysis than it could have been for the much more hopeful *The Interpretation of Dreams* thirty years before. Freud begins his somber and beautiful late essay by brooding sardonically on the heretic Otto Rank's scheme for speeding up analysis in America. But this high humor gives way to the melancholy of considering every patient's deepest resistance to the analyst's influence, that "negative transference" in which the subject's anxiety-of-influence seeks a bulwark. As he reviews the main outlines of his theory, Freud emphasizes its *economic* aspects rather than the dynamic and topographical points of view. The *economic* modifies any notion that drives have an energy that can be measured. To estimate the magnitude of such excitation is to ask the classical, agonistic question that *is* the Sublime, because the Sublime is always a comparison of two forces or beings, in which the agon turns on the answer to three queries: more? equal to? or less than? Satan confronting hell, the abyss, the new world, is still seeking to answer the questions that he set for himself in heaven, all of which turn upon comparing God's force and his own. Oedipus confronting the Sphinx, Hamlet facing the mystery of the dead father, and Freud meditating upon repression are all in the same economic stance. I would use this shared stance to redefine a question that psychoanalysis by its nature cannot answer. Since there is *no* biological warrant for the Freudian concept of libido, what is the energy that Freud invokes when he speaks from the economic point of view? Wollheim, always faithful to empiricism, has only one comment upon the economic theory of mind, and it is a very damaging observation:

> ...though an economic theory allows one to relate the damming up of energy or frustration at one place in the psychic apparatus with discharge at another, it does not commit one to the view that, given frustration, energy will seek

discharge along all possible channels indifferently. Indeed, if the system is of any complexity, an economic theory would be virtually un-informative unless some measure of selectivity in discharge was postulated....

But since Freud applied the economic stance to sexual drives almost entirely, no measure of selectivity *could* be postulated. This still leaves us with Freud's economic obsessions, and I suggest now that their true model was literary, and not sexual. This would mean that the "mechanisms of defense" are dependent for their formulaic coherence upon the traditions of rhetoric and not upon biology, which is almost too easily demonstrable. It is hardly accidental that Freud, in this late essay which is so much his *summa*, resorts to the textual analogue when he seeks to distinguish repression from the other defenses:

> Without pressing the analogy too closely we may say that repression is to the other methods of defense what the omission of words or passages is to the corruption of a text. ... For quite a long time flight and an avoidance of a dangerous situation serve as expedients. ... But one cannot flee from oneself and no flight avails against danger from within; hence the ego's defensive mechanisms are condemned to falsify the inner perception, so that it transmits to us only an imperfect and travestied picture of our id. In its relations with the id the ego is paralysed by its restrictions or blinded by its errors.

What is Freud's motive for this remarkably clear and eloquent recapitulation of his theory of repression and defense (which I take to be the center of his greatness)? The hidden figuration in his discourse here is his economics of the psyche, a trope which is allowed an overt exposure when he sadly observes that the energy necessary to keep such defenses going "proves a heavy burden on the psychical economy." If I were reading this essay on finite and indefinite analysis as I have learned to read Romantic poems, I would be on the watch for a blocking-agent in the poetic ego, a shadow that Blake called the Spectre and Shelley a daemon or *Alastor*. This shadow would be an anxiety narcissistically intoxicated with itself, an anxiety determined to go on being anxious, a drive towards destruction, in love with the image of self-destruction. Freud, like the great poets of quest, has given all the premonitory signs of this Sublime terror determined to maintain itself, and again like the poets he suddenly makes the pattern quite explicit:

> The crux of the matter is that the mechanisms of defense against former dangers recur in analysis in the shape of *resistances* to cure. It follows that the ego treats recovery itself as a new danger.

Faced by the patient's breaking of the psychoanalytic compact, Freud broods darkly on the war between his true Sublime and the patient's false Sublime:

Once more we realize the importance of the quantitative factor and once more we are reminded that analysis has only certain limited quantities of energy which it can employ to match against the hostile forces. And it does seem as if victory were really for the most part with the big battalions.

It is a true challenge to the interpreter of Freud's text to identify the economic stance here, for what is the source of *the energy of analysis,* however limited in quantity it may be? Empiricism, whether in Hume or in Wittgenstein, does not discourse in the measurement of its own libido. But if we take Freud as Sublime poet rather than empirical reasoner, if we see him as the peer of Milton rather than of Hume, of Proust rather than of the biologists, then we can speculate rather precisely about the origins of the psychoanalytical drive, about the nature of the powers made available by the discipline that one man was able to establish in so sublimely solitary a fashion. Vico teaches us that the Sublime or severe poet discovers the origin of his rhetorical drive, the catastrophe of his creative vocation, in *divination,* by which Vico meant both the process of foretelling dangers to the self's survival, and also the apotheosis of becoming a daemon or sort of god. What Vico calls "divination" is what Freud calls the primal instinct of Eros, or that "which strives to combine existing phenomena into ever greater unities." With moving simplicity, Freud then reduces this to the covenant between patient and analyst, which he calls "a love of truth." But, like all critical idealisms about poetry, this idealization of psychoanalysis is an error. No psychic economy (or indeed *any* economy) can be based upon "a love of truth." Drives depend upon fictions, because drives *are* fictions, and we want to know more about Freud's enabling fictions, which grant to him his Sublime "energy of analysis."

We can acquire this knowledge by a very close analysis of the final section of Freud's essay, a section not the less instructive for being so unacceptable to our particular moment in social and cultural history. The resistance to analytical cure, in both men and women, is identified by Freud with what he calls the "repudiation of feminity" *by both sexes,* the castration complex that informs the fantasy-life of everyone whatsoever: "in both cases it is the attitude belonging to the sex opposite to the subject's own which succumbs to repression." This is followed by Freud's prophetic lament, with its allusion to the burden of Hebraic prophecy. Freud too sees himself as the *nabi* who speaks to the winds, to the winds only, for only the winds will listen:

> At no point in one's analytic work does one suffer more from the oppressive feeling that all one's efforts have been in vain and from the suspicion that one is "talking to the winds" than when one is trying to persuade a female patient to abandon her wish for a penis on the ground of its being un-

realizable, or to convince a male patient that a passive attitude towards another man does not always signify castration and that in many relations in life it is indispensable. The rebellious over-compensation of the male produces one of the strongest transference-resistances. A man will not be subject to a father-substitute or owe him anything and he therefore refuses to accept his cure from the physician.

It is again one of Lacan's services to have shown us that this is figurative discourse, even if Lacan's own figurative discourse becomes too baroque a commentary upon Freud's wisdom here. Freud prophesies to the winds because men and women cannot surrender their primal fantasies, which are their poor but desperately prideful myths of their own origins. We cannot let go of our three fundamental fantasies: the primal scene, which accounts for our existence; the seduction fantasy, which justifies our narcissism; and the castration complex, which explains to us the mystery of sexual differentiation. What the three fantasy-scenes share is the fiction of an originating catastrophe, and so a very close relation to the necessity for defense. The final barrier to Freud's heroic labor of healing, in Freud's own judgment, is the human imagination. The original wound in man cannot be healed, as it is in Hegel, by the same force that makes the wound.

Freud became a strong poet of the Sublime because he made the solitary crossing from a realm where effect is always traced to a cause, to a mode of discourse which asked instead the economic and agonistic questions of comparison. The question of how an emptiness came about was replaced by the question that asks: more, less, or equal to?, which is the agonistic self-questioning of the Sublime. The attempt to give truer names to the rhetoric of human defense was replaced by the increasing refusal to name the vicissitudes of drive except by un-namings as old as those of Empedocles and Heraclitus. The ambition to make of psychoanalysis a wholly positive *praxis* yielded to a skeptical and ancient awareness of a rugged negativity that informed every individual fantasy.

Lacan and his school justly insist that psychoanalysis has contributed nothing to biology, despite Freud's wistful hopes that it could, and also that the life sciences inform psychoanalysis hardly at all, again in despite of Freud's eager scientism. Psychoanalysis is a varied therapeutic *praxis,* but it is a "science" only in the peculiar sense that literature, philosophy, and religion are also *sciences of anxiety.* But this means that no single rhetoric or poetic will suffice for the study of psychoanalysis, any more than a particular critical method will unveil all that needs to be seen in literature. The "French way" of reading Freud, in Lacan, Derrida, Laplanche, and others, is no more a "right" reading than the way of the ego-psychologists Hartmann, Kris, Erikson, and others, which Lacan and his followers wrongly keep insisting is the only "American reading." In this conflict of strong misreadings, partisans of both ways evidently need to keep forgetting what the French at least ought to remember: strong texts become strong by mistaking all texts anterior to them. Freud has more in common with Proust and Montaigne than with biological scientists, because his interpretations of life and death are mediated always by texts, first by the literary texts of others, and then by his own earlier texts, until at last the Sublime mediation of otherness begins to be performed by his text-in-process. In the *Essays* of Montaigne or Proust's vast novel, this ongoing mediation is clearer than it is in Freud's almost perpetual self-revision, because Freud wrote no definitive, single text, but the canon of Freud's writings shows an increasingly uneasy sense that he had become his own precursor, and that he had begun to defend himself against himself by deliberately audacious arrivals at final positions.

Chronology of Important Dates

1856	Freud born in Freiberg, Moravia (now Príbor, Czechoslovakia), on May 6.
1860	Freud family moves to Vienna.
1865	Enters Gymnasium.
1873	Enters University of Vienna as medical student.
1876-82	Works as assistant in Brücke's Institute of Physiology; meets Josef Breuer.
1877	First medical research articles published.
1880	Translates four essays by John Stuart Mill for a German edition of Mill's works.
1881	Takes medical degree.
1882	Engagement to Martha Bernays; begins work at Vienna General Hospital.
1885	Appointed *Privatdozent* (lecturer) in neuropathology at University of Vienna.
1885-86	Attends Charcot's lectures at the Salpêtrière in Paris, October to February.
1886	Marries Martha Bernays; begins private medical practice as specialist in nervous diseases.
1887	Meets Berlin physician and medical theorist Wilhelm Fliess; begins use of hypnotism in private practice.
1889	Visits Bernheim in Nancy for further researches into hypnosis.
1893	"Preliminary Communication" (with Breuer).
1894	"The Neuro-Psychoses of Defense."
1895	*Studies on Hysteria* (with Breuer, although cases and discussions written and signed separately); writes *Project for a Scientific Psychology* and mails it to Fliess (first published in 1950).

1896 Death of Freud's father, Jakob Freud; first use of term "psycho-analysis."

1897 Abandons seduction theory; begins self-analysis.

1899 "Screen Memories."

1900 *The Interpretation of Dreams* (published in December 1899, but postdated for the new century).

1901 *The Psychopathology of Everyday Life.*

1902 Appointed Professor Extraordinarius (associate professor) at University of Vienna; Wednesday evening meetings begin at Freud's house of the group that will become the Vienna Psychoanalytic Society; end of friendship with Fliess.

1905 *Three Essays on the Theory of Sexuality; Jokes and their Relation to the Unconscious;* Case of Dora ("Fragment of an Analysis of a Case of Hysteria").

1906 Jung makes contact with Freud.

1907 *Jensen's 'Gradiva.'*

1908 First international meeting of psychoanalysts at Salzburg; "Creative Writers and Day-Dreaming"; "'Civilized' Sexual Morality and Modern Nervous Illness."

1909 Visits America with Jung and Sandor Ferenczi; receives honorary degree from Clark University and delivers *Five Lectures on Psychoanalysis;* A. A. Brill's first English translations begin to appear; Case of Little Hans ("Analysis of a Phobia in a Five-Year-Old Boy"); Case of the Rat Man ("Notes upon a Case of Obsessional Neurosis").

1910 *Leonardo da Vinci and a Memory of his Childhood;* "'The Antithetical Sense of Primal Words.'"

1911 The Case of Schreber ("Psychoanalytic Notes on an Autobiographical Account of a Case of Paranoia").

1911-15 Papers on psychoanalytic technique.

1913 *Totem and Taboo;* association with Jung terminated; Jung secedes from International Psychoanalytic Association the following year.

1914 *The Moses of Michelangelo; On the History of the Psychoanalytic Movement;* "On Narcissism."

1915   Writes twelve papers on metapsychology, of which only five sur-
            vive ("Instincts and their Vicissitudes," "Repression," "The
            Unconscious," "A Metapsychological Supplement to the Theory
            of Dreams," "Mourning and Melancholia").

1915-17   Gives *Introductory Lectures* at University of Vienna.

1918   Case of the Wolf Man ("From the History of an Infantile
            Neurosis").

1919   "The 'Uncanny.'"

1920   *Beyond the Pleasure Principle.*

1921   *Group Psychology and the Analysis of the Ego.*

1923   *The Ego and the Id;* first of thirty-three operations for cancer of
            the jaw and palate.

1925   "A Note on the 'Mystic Writing-Pad'"; "Negation"; *An Auto-
            biographical Study.*

1926   *Inhibitions, Symptoms and Anxiety; The Question of Lay
            Analysis.*

1927   *The Future of an Illusion.*

1928   "Dostoyevsky and Parricide."

1930   Goethe Prize; *Civilization and its Discontents;* death of Freud's
            mother.

1933   Hitler comes to power; burning of Freud's books in Berlin; *New
            Introductory Lectures.*

1936   Eightieth birthday; formal celebrations; elected Corresponding
            Member of the Royal Society.

1937   "Analysis Terminable and Interminable."

1938   Nazis enter Austria; Freud leaves for England; *An Outline of
            Psychoanalysis* (published posthumously).

1939   *Moses and Monotheism;* dies on September 23 in Hampstead,
            London.

Notes on the Editor and Contributors

W. H. AUDEN (1907-73), poet, playwright, and essayist.

HAROLD BLOOM is DeVane Professor of Humanities at Yale. His works include *The Anxiety of Influence, Poetry and Repression, Wallace Stevens: The Poems of Our Climate,* and the novel *The Flight to Lucifer.*

KENNETH BURKE, American critic, poet, and theoretician. Among his principal works are *The Philosophy of Literary Form, A Grammar of Motives, A Rhetoric of Motives,* and *The Language of Symbolic Action.*

JACQUES DERRIDA teaches at the Ecole Normale Supérieure. Among his works available in English are *Of Grammatology, Writing and Difference,* and *Speech and Phenomena.*

STANLEY EDGAR HYMAN (1919-70), literary critic and historian, taught at Bennington. His books include *The Tangled Bank, The Armed Vision,* and studies of Flannery O'Connor and Nathanael West.

ALFRED KAZIN, American critic and essayist, is Distinguished Professor of English at the City University of New York. His many books include *On Native Grounds, Starting Out in the Thirties, A Walker in the City,* and *New York Jew.*

THOMAS MANN (1875-1955), German novelist, short-story writer, and essayist. He settled in the United States in 1938.

STEVEN MARCUS is George Delacorte Professor in the Humanities at Columbia. He is the author of *Dickens: From Pickwick to Dombey; Engels, Manchester and the Working Class; The Other Victorians;* and *Representations: Essays on Literature and Society.*

PERRY MEISEL, editor of this volume, teaches English at New York University, and is the author of *The Absent Father: Virginia Woolf and Walter Pater* and *Thomas Hardy: The Return of the Repressed.*

JOHN CROWE RANSOM (1888-1974), American poet, critic, and educator.

LIONEL TRILLING (1905-75), American critic, essayist, short-story writer, and novelist, taught at Columbia. His books are now being issued in a uniform edition under the general title *The Works of Lionel Trilling.*

Leonard Woolf (1880-1969), English writer, civil servant, editor, and publisher, founded the Hogarth Press with his wife Virginia in 1917. His many books include two novels, *The Wise Virgins* and *The Village in the Jungle,* as well as a five-volume autobiography.

Selected Bibliography

Works

The authoritative English translation of Freud is *The Standard Edition of the Complete Psychological Works of Sigmund Freud,* ed. James Strachey (London: The Hogarth Press and the Institute of Psycho-Analysis, 1953-74). The authoritative German edition is the *Gesammelte Werke,* eds. Anna Freud et. al. (Frankfurt am Main: S. Fischer Verlag, 1940-68). Selections from Freud's extant letters to Wilhelm Fliess (only extracts of which appear in the first volume of the *Standard Edition*) and an earlier translation of the *Project for a Scientific Psychology* are available in *The Origins of Psychoanalysis,* trans. Eric Mosbacher and James Strachey, eds. Marie Bonaparte, Anna Freud, and Ernst Kris (New York: Basic Books, 1954). In addition to the Fliess papers, Freud's published correspondence now runs to seven volumes, chief among them *The Letters of Sigmund Freud,* trans. Tania and James Stern, ed. Ernst L. Freud (New York: Basic Books, 1960), and *The Freud/Jung Letters,* trans. Ralph Mannheim and R.F.C. Hull, ed. William McGuire (Princeton, N.J.: Princeton University Press, 1974).

Life and Career

The principal biography of Freud is Ernest Jones's three-volume *The Life and Work of Sigmund Freud* (New York: Basic Books, 1953-57). Subsequent biographical accounts include the testament of Freud's physician, Max Schur, *Freud: Living and Dying* (New York: International Universities Press, 1972), and revisionist studies such as Paul Roazen's *Freud and His Followers* (New York: Alfred A. Knopf, 1975), and Frank Sulloway's *Freud: Biologist of the Mind* (New York: Basic Books, 1979). Much historical information is also available in Henri F. Ellenberger, *The Discovery of the Unconscious: The History and Evolution of Dynamic Psychiatry* (New York: Basic Books, 1970). Richard Wollheim's *Sigmund Freud* (New York: Viking, 1971) provides an excellent concise account of the development of Freud's ideas; Philip Rieff's *Freud: The Mind of the Moralist* (Chicago: University of Chicago Press, 1959; 3rd ed., 1979) remains a provocative and comprehensive introduction to the range and play of Freud's thought. For the best guide to Freudian terms, see Jean Laplanche and J.-B. Pontalis, *The Language of Psychoanalysis,* trans. Donald Nicholson-Smith (New York: Norton, 1973).

Selected Studies

Given the enormous scope of the literature on and about Freud, the following selected list of books and articles is limited to those studies that focus on the literary Freud. Of the increasingly large amount of material on the literary Freud available in French, selections have been made only from among those works translated into English.

Bersani, Leo. *Baudelaire and Freud.* Berkeley and Los Angeles: University of California Press, 1977.

Brooks, Peter. "Freud's Masterplot: Questions of Narrative." *Yale French Studies,* 55/56 (1977), 280-300.

Carroll, David. "Freud and the Myth of the Origin." *New Literary History,* 6 (1975), 513-28.

Cixous, Hélenè. "Fiction and Its Phantoms: A Reading of Freud's *'Das Unheimliche.'"New Literary History,* 7 (1976), 525-48.

Derrida, Jacques. "Coming into One's Own." Trans. James Hulbert. *Psychoanalysis and the Question of the Text: Selected Papers from the English Institute, 1976-77.* Ed. Geoffrey Hartman. Baltimore: Johns Hopkins University Press, 1978, pp. 114-48.

―――. "Fors." Trans. Barbara Johnson. *Georgia Review,* 31:1 (Spring 1977), 64-116.

―――. "The Purveyor of Truth." Trans. Hulbert, Domingo, et al. *Yale French Studies,* 49 (1975), 31-113.

―――. "Speculations—on Freud." Trans. Ian McLeod. *Oxford Literary Review,* 3:2 (1978), 78-97.

D[oolittle]., H[ilda]. *Tribute to Freud.* Rpt. New York: McGraw-Hill, 1975.

Etherington, Norman A. "Rider Haggard, Imperialism, and the Layered Personality." *Victorian Studies,* 22:1 (Autumn 1978), 71-87.

Fiedler, Leslie. "Master of Dreams." *Partisan Review,* 34 (1967), 339-56.

Galdston, Iago. "Freud and Romantic Medicine." *Bulletin of the History of Medicine,* 30:6 (November-December 1956), 489-507.

Heller, Erich. "Observations on Psychoanalysis and Modern Literature." *Psychiatry and the Humanities,* Vol. 1. Ed. Joseph H. Smith. New Haven, Conn.: Yale University Press, 1976, pp. 35-50.

Hertz, Neil. "Freud and the Sandman." *Textual Strategies.* Ed. Josué V. Harari. Ithaca, N.Y.: Cornell University Press, 1979, pp. 296-321.

Hesse, Hermann. "Artists and Psychoanalysis." *My Belief: Essays on Life and Art.* Ed. Theodore Ziolkowski, trans. David Lindley. New York: Farrar, Straus & Giroux, 1974, pp. 46-51.

Hyman, Stanley Edgar. "Psychoanalysis and the Climate of Tragedy." *Freud and the Twentieth Century.* Ed. Benjamin Nelson. New York: Meridian, 1957, pp. 167-85.

_____. *The Tangled Bank: Darwin, Marx, Frazer and Freud as Imaginative Writers.* New York: Atheneum, 1962.

Kazin, Alfred. "Freud and His Consequences." *Contemporaries.* Boston: Little, Brown, 1962, pp. 351-93.

_____. "The Freudian Revolution Analyzed." *Freud and the Twentieth Century.* Ed. Benjamin Nelson. New York: Meridian, 1957, pp. 13-21.

Laplanche, Jean. *Life and Death in Psychoanalysis.* Trans. Jeffrey Mehlman. Baltimore: Johns Hopkins University Press, 1976.

Mann, Thomas. "Freud's Position in the History of Modern Thought" (1929). *Past Masters and Other Papers.* Trans. H. T. Lowe-Porter. New York: Alfred A. Knopf, 1933, pp. 167-98.

Mehlman, Jeffrey. "How to Read Freud on Jokes: The Critic as *Schadchen.*" *New Literary History,* 6 (1975), 436-61.

_____. "Trimethylamin: Notes on Freud's Specimen Dream." *Diacritics,* 6:1 (Spring 1976), 42-45.

Rey, Jean-Michel. "Freud's Writing on Writing." Trans. Most and Hulbert. *Yale French Studies,* 55/56 (1977), 301-28.

Smith, Joseph H., ed. *The Literary Freud: Mechanisms of Defense and the Poetic Will,* Vol. 4, *Psychiatry and the Humanities.* New Haven, Conn.: Yale University Press, 1980.

Sollers, Philippe. "Freud's Hand." Trans. Barbara Johnson, *Yale French Studies,* 55/56 (1977), 329-37.

Trilling, Lionel. "Art and Neurosis." *The Liberal Imagination.* New York: Scribner's, 1950. Rpt. New York: Harcourt Brace Jovanovich, 1979.

_____. "Freud: Within and Beyond Culture." *Beyond Culture: The Works of Lional Trilling*. Rpt. New York: Harcourt Brace Jovanovich, 1978.

The Tropology of Freud. Diacritics, 9:1 (Spring 1979).

Weber, Samuel. "The Divaricator: Remarks on Freud's *Witz.*" *Glyph 1*. Baltimore: Johns Hopkins University Press, 1977, pp. 1-27.

_____. "The Sideshow, or: Remarks on a Canny Moment." *Modern Language Notes*, 88 (1973), 1102-33.